25ᵀᴴ ANNIVERSARY EDITION

MᶜCULLOCH'S WONDER

The Story of the Kettle Valley Railway

BARRIE SANFORD

whitecap

Edited by Marial Shea
Proofread by Alexandra Wilson
Cover design by Jacqui Thomas
Cover photograph courtesy of Canadian Pacific
Interior design by Warren Clark
Maps by Barrie Sanford

Printed and bound in Canada

National Library of Canada Cataloguing in Publication Data

Sanford, Barrie
   McCulloch's wonder

   Includes bibliographical references and index.
   ISBN 1-55285-402-7

   1. Kettle Valley Railway—History. 2. McCulloch, Andrew, 1864-1945.
3. Railroads—British Columbia—History. I. Title.
HE2810.K48S35 2002   385'.09711'62   C2002-910921-3

The publisher acknowledges the support of the Canada Council for the Arts and
the Cultural Services Branch of the Government of British Columbia for our
publishing program. We acknowledge the financial support of the Government
of Canada through the Book Publishing Industry Development Program for our
publishing activities.

To the navvies,

ultimate builders of the Kettle Valley Railway

Contents

ILLUSTRATIONS

Maps

Photographs

Foreword

by Randy Manuel
Director, Penticton Museum

Barrie Sanford's book *McCulloch's Wonder* is as remarkable as the Kettle Valley Railway itself. The continuing appeal of the book shows the passion Canadians have for railway history. The social and economic development of Western Canada is inexorably entwined with its railways, and Barrie has masterfully detailed one of the most fascinating chapters in that remarkable history. His story of the railway, named for the valley from where it commenced its western run, makes for some of the best reading on railway history anywhere.

The interest in the Kettle Valley Railway sparked by *McCulloch's Wonder* when it first rolled off the presses 25 years ago has spawned such a fascination with "The Kettle" that more than a dozen publications have hit the bookshelves since then. Those publications detail everything from anecdotal recollections to hiking and biking the entire length of its remaining railway roadbed. The railway has been the subject of several one-hour videos and two 30-minute clips shown across North America. One such video won a national award for its subject matter and presentation. "The Kettle" has even made it to the commercial scene, being featured in advertisements for White Spot Restaurants "Legends of B.C." A railway heritage group has preserved 16 kilometres of the railway in the Summerland area and operates a summer tourist steam train. Such is the legacy that has grown from *McCulloch's Wonder*.

Monumental projects like the building of the Kettle Valley Railway can be mind-boggling. The railway faced not only lofty mountains, roaring rivers and precipitous canyons, but also political and financial intrigue.

Barrie has skillfully crafted a complex story into an easy reading book. And in doing so, he has helped keep alive the excitement of the great era in southern British Columbia when gold, silver, copper and steam were supreme.

Today the sounds of blasting locomotive exhausts and steam whistles echoing across the canyons are gone, remembered only on film and in books. This is where it all started. Read and enjoy.

Introduction

Ninety miles east of Vancouver, in the quiet community of Hope, there was for many years a small wooden-frame railway station nestled amid a grove of fir trees at the north end of Third Avenue. It was hardly an unusual structure in outward appearance. Its architectural lines were pleasing, but nonetheless utilitarian and without embellishment. A pair of red mailboxes, one marked "East" and the other "West," hung by the doorway. Next to them a faded blackboard showed all trains to be "OT." A brace of train order hoops dangled from a wooden peg next to the station bay window, while overhead a pair of brightly painted red and white semaphore signals pointed skyward. It was, in every appearance, just another of the many small-town railway stations once scattered across this broad land. Even the tuscan red paint with which the station was chalked—well, who could say that paint has not been as much a part of the Canadian heritage as fearless Mounties and scarlet maple leaves?

Yet that modest little building in Hope was not just another small town railway station. It was the first station on the Kettle Valley Railway, and anyone asking why that fact should be of significance had only to look beyond the station platform to find the answer. There, directly to the east, a massive wall of mountains thrust upwards from the valley floor, an awesome and imposing monument of nature's power. Faced by this rugged mountain barrier, the earlier Canadian Pacific Railway, having followed the valley of the Fraser River from Vancouver, turned northward here at Hope and continued along that river's natural pathway to circuitously reach eastward. The Canadian National Railway and the Trans-Canada Highway, when they followed years later, did likewise. By going north before resuming the eastward journey, they all skirted this forbidding mountain barrier. However, the tracks leading away from that ordinary looking station in Hope did not go north. They went eastward, across the mountains the other two railways and the national highway had forsaken. It was destined, therefore, that this could be no ordinary railway.

Most significantly, the geographic challenge in building the railway was immense. The Kettle Valley Railway had to climb over the backbone of three major mountain ranges and pass through some of the most rugged river canyons on the face of the earth. Its construction was perhaps without parallel in Canadian railway history. But it was even more than an extraordinary railway. Although now virtually forgotten, its planning and construction was once the dominant issue of concern in British Columbia, and for a full quarter century news of the railway was rarely off the front pages of provincial newspapers. Forgotten too are the half dozen provincial governments that rose or fell largely on issues associated with this railway. Political conniving, personal rivalry and corporate greed combined to advance—or stymie—the railway's development in ways often too bizarre to be fiction.

The work of building this difficult railway was entrusted to its chief engineer, Andrew McCulloch. His mastery of the challenge resulted in the completed railway being dubbed "McCulloch's Wonder" by his astonished and admiring assistant engineers. Passengers also became admirers, perhaps less for McCulloch's engineering prowess than his civil gentility in naming stations along his railway after characters from the plays of Shakespeare. Romeo and Juliet, Othello, Lear and others became communities made alive by railway track workers, sectionmen, operating crews and their families, not simply names from English literature. However, McCulloch's Wonder proved to be as daunting to operate as it had been to build. Disruptions from avalanches and washouts were frequent. Rockslides knocked numerous trains into canyons, often with fatal results to train crews. Approximately 100 workers died during the railway's construction and operation. Remarkably, no passenger was ever killed throughout the line's entire history. Such was the compensation for the devotion and sacrifices of the railway employees in maintaining service on what came to be regarded as the most challenging railway to operate in all of Canada.

Not all agreed that the sacrifice in money and human lives was worth it. The Kettle Valley Railway generated controversy in its birth and throughout its existence, and continues to be a subject of debate among historians and scholars more than a decade after almost all the tracks have been removed. This book documents the essential history of the Kettle Valley Railway, placing it in context of its times and offering viewpoints on both the decisions made and some of the alternatives that might have been chosen.

While the wisdom or folly of constructing the Kettle Valley Railway is the debate of scholars, there can be no debate that the railway is indelibly etched into the heritage of British Columbia. The people who conceived, constructed and operated the Kettle Valley Railway bestowed upon those who followed a legacy of vision, daring and sacrifice. This is the story of that legacy.

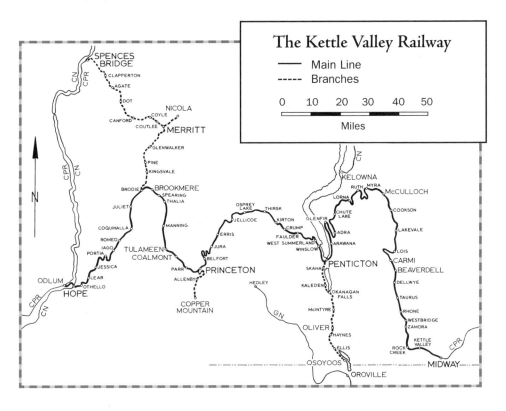

Corporate Abbreviations

(and Affiliations)

Nearly 50 corporations were involved in the Kettle Valley Railway story and many of those companies went through an evolution of ownership. This table of abbreviations and affiliations may prove a useful reference for readers.

Ind: means the company was independent of the Canadian Pacific Railway or Great Northern Railway when chartered. Where indicated, the company was sold or otherwise transferred to the CPR or GN. In some cases records of transfer no longer exist and can only be assumed on the basis of company activity or directorate.

(US): means charter issued in the United States of America

* Charter issued but no construction of consequence undertaken

Corporation	Abbreviation	Affiliation
British Columbia Southern Railway	BCS	Ind, CPR
Canadian Northern Pacific Railway	CNPR	Ind
Canadian Northern Railway	CNR	Ind
Coast-Kootenay Railway *	None	Ind
Columbia & Kootenay Railway & Navigation Company	C&K	CPR
Columbia & Kootenay Steam Navigation Company	CKSN	Ind, CPR
Columbia & Western Railway	C&W	Ind, CPR
Crow's Nest Southern Railway	CNS	GN
Grand Forks & Kettle River Railway	GF&KR	Ind
Great Northern Railway	GN	GN
Kaslo & Slocan Railway	K&S	GN
Kettle River Valley Railway (US) *	KRVR	Ind
Kettle River Valley Railway	KRVR	Ind, CPR

Corporation	Abbreviation	Affiliation
Kettle Valley Lines	KVL	Ind
Kettle Valley Railway	KVR	CPR
Midway & Vernon Railway	M&V	Ind
Nakusp & Slocan Railway	N&S	CPR
Nelson & Fort Sheppard Railway	N&FS	Ind, GN
New Westminster Southern Railway	NWS	GN
Nicola, Kamloops & Similkameen Coal & Railway Company	NK&S	Ind, CPR
Nicola Valley Railway *	NVR	Ind, CPR
Northern Pacific Railroad/Railway (US)	NP	Ind, GN
Penticton Railway *	None	GN
Republic & Kettle River Railway (US)	R&KR	Ind
Shuswap & Okanagan Railway	S&O	CPR
Spokane & British Columbia Railway (US)	S&BC	Ind
Spokane Falls & Northern Railway (US)	SF&N	Ind, GN
Spokane International Railway	SI	CPR
Vancouver & Coast-Kootenay Railway *	V&CK	Ind
Vancouver & Grand Forks Railway *	V&GF	CPR
Vancouver & Nicola Valley Railway *	V&NV	GN
Vancouver, Victoria & Eastern Railway & Navigation Company	VV&E	Ind, GN
Washington & Great Northern Railway	W&GN	GN

1: Coast-to-Kootenay: A Dream

Southern British Columbia 1846 to 1894

British Columbia is a land of mountain ranges. The Rockies. The Selkirks. The Monashees. The name of each range carries with it the colour and history of the province and each is as physically diverse as the people who inhabit Canada's westernmost province. Some of these ranges are comprised almost entirely of lofty and perpetually snow-covered peaks. Others are rolling hills and forested plateaus, scarcely worthy of being called mountain ranges alongside their more rugged neighbours. Without a single exception, however, every mountain range in British Columbia has one common characteristic: each lies with its axis parallel to the province's coastline.

This parallel alignment of mountain ranges has produced a predominance of rivers flowing in a northerly or southerly direction, with most rivers separated from adjacent watercourses by one or more of the mountain ranges. Only rarely have the transverse tributary streams been large enough to cut major valleys through the mountain ranges. This distinctive geographic feature has blessed the province with a wide variety of climates, and given it scenic wonders that rival any in the world. But it has also made travel in a northward or southward direction along the river valleys much easier than travel east or west across the mountains. This restriction in human mobility has been a dominant influence in the province's history. Indeed, it has been the greatest single factor shaping southern British Columbia's development.

Such would probably not have been the case had the continent's political divisions followed geographic logic, which would have suggested dividing western North America into regions whose political borders coincided with the mountain ridges. A division of this nature would have made the mountains serve as barriers against potentially hostile neigh-bours, while the broad river valleys of the interior would have provided the natural pathways of trade and commerce within each region.

However, geographic logic did not prevail. In 1846, the British and American governments decreed that a line extending westward along the 49th Parallel of North Latitude from near the Great Lakes to the Pacific Ocean would form the legal boundary between their territories. That their decision was profoundly in contradiction to the geographic reality of western North America seemed to matter little to either government. The leaders of both countries seemed far more concerned that they had reached a settlement of the touchy boundary matter without resorting to bloodshed.

Certainly the British seemed unconcerned. Aside from a few coastal fur trading posts, easily protected by the mighty Royal Navy, the land was deemed to have little potential for development. And all the evidence sup-ported that belief. In the next decade scarcely a murmur was heard from the vast wilderness stretching from the prairies to the Pacific Ocean. The quiet disregard on the part of Great Britain for its Pacific Coast colony came to an abrupt end in the late 1850s, when gold was discovered in British Columbia. Initially, gold was found on the bars of the Fraser River below its rugged canyon through the Coast Range. But soon other discov-eries were made. Two of the most significant were at Wild Horse Creek, near Cranbrook, and at Rock Creek, in the Boundary District.

What made these latter discoveries so significant was their location. Both gold centres were extremely close to the boundary with the United States—at Rock Creek the border was a scant mile away—and access from the south was virtually unimpeded. Thousands of Americans poured across the border from the American interior, many of them returning to the United States without paying the gold royalties assessed by Britain. The British colonial government did what it could to try and stop the free flow of gold across the border. However, it soon became obvious the geography of the Pacific colony acted greatly in favour of the Americans, who easily travelled along the broad river valleys of the southern interior leading to and from the United States, while the intervening mountains made a very effective barrier against British efforts to administer the colony from the coastal capital.

The colony's governor, James Douglas, concluded that the only way to successfully counter the American influence was to construct a pack trail across the interior near the southern boundary of British territory. Such a trail, envisioned Douglas, would allow the colony to secure control of the interior commerce away from the Americans. He promptly commissioned Edgar Dewdney to hack out the proposed trail from Hope, on the navigable waters of the Fraser River, eastward across the high mountain ridge formed by the Hope Range of the Coast Mountains and onward to the goldfields. This assignment Dewdney carried out with all the skill and care inherent to British tradition. However, the trail was completed only after the gold rush was essentially over, and the steep climb across the many mountain ranges of southern British Columbia rendered it ineffectual in competing with the easy water routes linking the southern interior with American centres. Even Douglas admitted the trail's shortcomings. Riding over the trail shortly after its completion, he said that his journey was ". . . compared to the passage of the Alps."[1] Others were even less generous in their assessment. One journalist noted that the trail served purely as "a monument to the good intentions of the British Columbia government."[2] In constructing the Dewdney Trail the colony's government had met its first encounter with both Americans and geography. Neither would ever be fully reconciled.

Not long after the gold rush, the British colonies in eastern North America confederated into a new country called Canada. An infant nation, young politically and weak economically, Canada was barely able to administer its own territory. Yet a few bold leaders argued that the fledgling nation could only survive by enlarging its boundaries to include all the territory west to the Pacific colony. Unless a union was formed—a Dominion from Sea to Sea they called it—British traditions would not long survive on a continent increasingly dominated by the United States. Daringly, Canada invited British Columbia to join the union, promising that, if it did, a railway would be built to span the continent. Such a railway would defeat the mountains that were a barrier to the colony's development and ensure that the Americans could never again dominate the commerce of British Columbia.

The Canadian offer was a tempting one for the young colony, but it was not easy to accept. Geographically, the western colony would always be a child of the United States. The wide, smooth river valleys of the interior acted like natural umbilical cords, binding it to the American republic. No one knew how well British Columbia could sever these cords and build new ties with an adopted mother who would always be across a mountain barrier. British Columbia hesitated, and then accepted the offer. Joining Confederation was a giant step for the young province.

As a dozen history books have recorded, the eastern politicians kept their promise, and on a cold and misty November morning in 1885, steel banged upon steel at Craigellachie in Eagle Pass to bind the troth. Of the many books about the Canadian Pacific Railway, none mentions that not every Canadian believed the railway assured British Columbia's future. While no one seemed to deny the importance of this new connection with eastern Canada, there were those who voiced criticisms. The most serious criticism against the Canadian Pacific Railway came from a small handful of men, who were mindful of the American invasion of the southern interior a quarter century earlier. These men voiced the opinion that the CPR route—entering the province through Kicking Horse Pass and crossing the central interior—was too far north of the international boundary line to keep the Americans from dominating the commerce of the southern interior. Only the final 90 miles of the railway, from Hope west to tidewater, was within reasonable proximity of the border. A more satisfactory route, the critics argued, would have been along the Dewdney Trail, where any potential American influence could be effectively countered. They warned that the chosen route was an invitation to future disaster.

The federal government, under the leadership of Prime Minister John A. Macdonald was quick to offer a defense for the railway. Macdonald asserted the CPR route had been chosen only after intensive consideration and detailed surveys spanning more than a decade. He admitted that these surveys did not include the Dewdney Trail route suggested by the railway's critics, but he emphasized that preliminary surveys of the route had shown it presented even more formidable challenges than the route through Kicking Horse Pass and the Fraser Canyon, which had nearly bankrupted the CPR. British Columbians, opined Macdonald, should be grateful for the railway, not critical of it. After all, this was British Columbia's railway—all 3,000 miles of it—built because the province was important enough to be part of Canada. British Columbians should appreciate Ottawa's generosity in grubstaking a pioneer railway many had said would never earn its axle grease. As for the Americans, they would stay on their own side of the border; the new railway would see to that. Few doubted Macdonald's words.

As it turned out, Macdonald was right. Right, that is, until one warm spring day in 1887 when two bearded and mud-caked brothers by the names of Osmer and Winslow Hall trudged into the smelter city of Butte, Montana and dropped upon an assayer's desk a sackful of silver ore so rich it transformed the history of the British Columbia interior in a single afternoon. The Halls had discovered the ore during the previous winter on their Silver King claim, near what is now the Kootenay District community of Nelson. The location was all the information people needed. Within days the first American had crossed the boundary into Canada to stake his silver fortunes in the Kootenays. A thousand more were on his heels. Aided by the natural geography of the southern interior and the close proximity to the border of the recently completed American railway line, the Northern Pacific Railroad, it took only a few weeks for the horde of incoming Americans to secure control of the Kootenays as effectively—and almost as dramatically—as if invading by military force.

Not that the Americans were conquest minded. On the contrary, they were generally obedient to Canadian laws and respectful of residents. However, their numbers, coupled with the ease with which silver ore could flow across the border into the United States and American goods could flow in from the Northern Pacific, effectively turned the territory around Nelson into a commercial annex of the United States. Trade with Canadian centres was all but non-existent. Even the few Canadians who joined in the Kootenay silver stampede traded with the Americans. It was far cheaper, they quickly discovered, to receive their goods via the Northern Pacific, just an easy boat ride across the border, than to have them brought over the crude pack trails from Canadian centres.

Quite understandably, this abrupt American takeover of the Kootenays alarmed British Columbia's political leaders as much as the American takeover of a quarter century earlier, but there really wasn't very much they could do. Geography all but gave the Americans legal title to the Kootenays. And the Canadian Pacific Railway, just as the critics had warned, was too far north of the international boundary to offer any effective challenge to American domination. As a consequence, federal leaders quickly found themselves under severe criticism for having allowed the CPR route decision of only a few years earlier to be made with such apparent indifference to the needs of southern British Columbia. Indeed, resentment towards the railway and federal government became intense as Vancouverites watched the rich Asian imports being carried east by the CPR and the mineral wealth of the province's interior being carted south by the Americans. The celebrated trans-continental railway suddenly appeared to have been built, not to secure Canadian unity, but to fill the pocketbooks of eastern merchants and the coffers of the CPR. British Columbia seemed little more than a barren rock pile through which the railway, much to the regret of eastern Canadians, had to pass on the way to the treasurehouse of the Orient.

The perceived insensitivity of the federal government and the CPR to the American occupation of the Kootenays generated an intense feeling of alienation in many British Columbians. However, it also generated a fierce determination win back the Kootenays from American control. And if the federal government and the CPR would not do it, then British Columbians resolved to do it themselves. To do so would require a second railway across the province; one built along the border route of the Dewdney Trail rejected by the CPR and far-away federal government, a railway that could challenge the American domination of the southern interior and bring the wealth of the Kootenays to British Columbia's seaports. Only when such a railway—the Coast-to-Kootenay railway, as some forgotten sage coined its name—was complete would British Columbia gain political and economic unity.

British Columbians could not likely have foreseen that three decades of tumultuous struggle would pass before they would see their railway complete. Nor could they have known that the corporation of which they were being much critical, the Canadian Pacific Railway, would play a commanding role in that railway's construction through its subsidiary Kettle Valley Railway. What British Columbians did know was that their province needed this railway. Out of disillusionment and disappointment they had forged a destiny; in alienation and frustration they had found their dream.

Although British Columbians enthusiastically seized upon the idea of connecting coastal British Columbia with the Kootenays directly by rail, it was obvious from the start that the proposed railway faced serious, perhaps insurmountable, difficulties. First, provincial geography was daunting. In traversing the southern interior the railway would have to cross a dozen mountain ranges and river valleys, a fact CPR management had not overlooked in its decision to choose a more northerly route for the transcontinental rail line. The difficult geography meant high construction costs. It would also require long sections of severely adverse grades, which would dictate against the movement of heavy freight trains. This restriction would, in turn, challenge the economic wisdom of large construction expenditures.

The second difficulty was the question of money. A project of such magnitude as the Coast-to-Kootenay railway would require a great deal of money, perhaps more than British Columbia could generate alone. Who, then, would provide it? Not likely the CPR. That corporation, although reaping sizable operating profits from the Asian trade just as British Columbians suspected, had large debts to repay for the building of the transcontinental railway. Thus its disinterest in the early proposals to build the Coast-to-Kootenay railway was not without justification. Similarly, the federal government had poured millions of dollars into the construction of the Canadian Pacific Railway, which had been of more obvious benefit to the west than the east. Macdonald no doubt believed it politically unwise to suggest further allocation of massive funds for western railway construction at a time when many other worthy causes were being championed.

The third difficulty in building a Coast-to-Kootenay railway (or line) was the matter of the Americans. They were strong in the Kootenays, and growing more powerful each day. Indeed, it was an American who would build the first railway connecting the Kootenays with the outside world.

That man was Daniel Chase Corbin, an American of bountiful resourcefulness and talent. Following the Northern Pacific Railroad west in the early 1880s, Corbin quickly established his reputation as a skillful entrepreneur by building a profitable railway and boat system in the Coeur d'Alene Lake district east of Spokane Falls, the fledgling city that would soon be renamed Spokane and become the most important centre in the interior Northwest. The news reports of the rich silver strikes of the Kootenays attracted Corbin's attention and in April 1888 he chartered his own corporation, the Spokane Falls & Northern Railway, with the objective of building a railway to Nelson. After a brief delay in organizing the affairs of his company, Corbin soon had his tracks pushing northward from Spokane Falls towards Canada. By late 1889, the railway was all but complete to the Little Dalles, the lower limits of navigable waters on the Columbia River stretching across the international boundary only a few miles to the north.

Reaching the Little Dalles had been no serious problem for Corbin. However, to continue onward to Nelson, the centre of the Kootenay mining bonanza and his obvious goal, Corbin had to secure a railway charter from Canadian authorities. Therefore, in December 1889 Corbin petitioned the British Columbia government for a charter to construct a rail line from the international boundary to Nelson. Corbin also submitted a second petition, requesting an additional charter for a rail line branching off the SF&N line at Marcus, below the Little Dalles, and following the Kettle River westward, ultimately terminating in Vancouver. In the words of his attorney, the two rail lines: ". . . would form one continuous line of railway from the south end of Kootenay Lake to the Coast, with a short detour into American territory, rendered necessary by the difficulties of penetrating the chain of mountains on the west bank of the Columbia River."[3]

Nelson residents, then mostly Americans, naturally supported Corbin's proposal with great enthusiasm. At first, people in the coastal cities also rallied quick support because of Corbin's promise to contruct the dreamed-of Coast-to-Kootenay railway. Soon though, their support for him faded. Many British Columbians came to suspect that Corbin had proposed the railway to the coast only as a means of ensuring passage of his charter request to reach Nelson. They feared that, once the easy line to Nelson had been built and the Kootenay ore flowing over it to Spokane, Corbin would abandon any attempt to build the more costly line to the coast.

In his quest for support, Corbin formed a short-lived alliance with James Baker, a member of the provincial Legislative Assembly in Victoria. Baker had earlier proposed his own railway line across the southern interior—appropriately called the British Columbia Southern Railway—but he had been unable to raise capital for its construction.[4] He hoped to solve his capital shortage by associating with Corbin, to whom he offered liberal promises of political assistance. Corbin accepted Baker's proposal for an alliance and on February 27, 1890 Baker introduced their proposed scheme to the Legislature. The provincial government was understandably favourable to both Baker and his plans for the Coast-to-Kootenay railway, but when Corbin saw the draft charter request Baker had submitted to the Legislature, he concluded Baker was setting things up too much in his own favour and Corbin withdrew his promised support for the Coast-to-Kootenay line. As a result, the first serious proposal for a railway across southern British Columbia died a sudden death.

As for Corbin's own petition for a railway from the border to Nelson, Premier John Robson, who had an abiding fear of anything American, turned thumbs down on the proposal. His members, following their leader's example, soundly rejected the petition. Having met with failure in his attempt to secure a charter from the British Columbia government, Corbin packed his bags for Ottawa, where he hoped to present his case more successfully.

On March 4, 1890 Corbin's petition for a federal railway charter was placed before Parliament. Premier Robson, who had already done his best to keep Corbin out of British Columbia, moderated his position in a telegram he sent to Ottawa as the debate opened. His original scorching opposition to Corbin was considerably toned down because he had an intense desire to see the Coast-to-Kootenay railway built and, for the moment at least, Corbin appeared to be the only one with the resources to construct such a line. But Robson, like many other British Columbians, still feared that Corbin's dual railway proposal was merely a ruse to secure charter for the more profitable connection with Spokane. As a compromise, Robson agreed to support Corbin if the railway charters contained clauses guaranteeing the simultaneous construction of both lines.

Others expressed more virulent doubts. The City of Vancouver shared none of Robson's optimism that Corbin harboured even the remotest notion of building a railway to the coast, and voiced its complete opposition in a statement of policy to the Ottawa MPs. The president of the CPR, William Van Horne, also sent a letter stating his corporation, like the City of Vancouver, was unconditionally opposed to Corbin. He promised if Parliament refused Corbin's charter request, the CPR would undertake an immediate construction program to put Canadian rails into the Kootenays. The Macdonald government, which regarded the CPR as its personal pet, was strongly impressed by Van Horne's promise. Several government members openly confessed they had supported Corbin only in an attempt to pressure the CPR into building a Kootenay railway. When John Mara, an MP from British Columbia who was promoting his own transportation system in the Kootenays, was given the opportunity to speak, Corbin was doomed. The votes were counted. Only three members supported Corbin; everyone else was opposed.

Naturally, Corbin was disappointed by his defeat. But he was not alone in his disappointment. Nelson residents, annoyed by Vancouver's opposition to Corbin's plan to connect Nelson with the outside world by rail, refused to stock any Vancouver goods no matter how meagre the existing volume. Others, too, felt Corbin had been harshly treated. Ironically, Corbin's most enthusiastic ally became John Mara, the MP who had assisted so eloquently in the defeat of Corbin's petition in Ottawa.

Mara, along with two other British Columbians, had just formed the Columbia & Kootenay Steam Navigation Company, a steamboat operation soon commonly known by its abbreviations CKSN. With Corbin legally barred from crossing the international boundary with a railway, the CKSN found itself having all the business it could handle carrying the ore from the Kootenay mines down the Columbia River to Corbin's railhead at the Little Dalles. Thus, under the convincing influence of business prosperity, Mara quickly forgot both the Ottawa incident and the desire of his fellow British Columbians to halt the flow of Kootenay ore to the United States. Corbin was equally willing to forget the past. With the CKSN assisting him, he overnight became the most influential force in the Kootenays. Border or not, charter or not, Corbin commanded southern British Columbia.

The alarming ease with which Daniel Corbin secured control of the Kootenays without so much as having his railway cross the international boundary made the disparities of interior geography all the more distressing to British Columbians. CPR president Van Horne was also worried. After all, he had promised Parliament his corporation would take steps to counter the American influence in the Kootenays if Parliament refused Corbin's charter, which it had done. Moreover, nationalism aside, the silver mines of the Kootenays were revealing themselves to be among the richest in the world, far too profitable to be overlooked by an institution with such free-enterprise spirit as the Canadian Pacific Railway.

In formulating a strategy to oust Corbin from the Kootenays, Van Horne decided the first step should be to build a "portage railway" along the unnavigable section of the Kootenay River between Robson and Nelson, a distance of about 25 miles. Such a rail line would connect the silver mines of Nelson with the Columbia River at Robson, from which point steam vessels could operate, during season, over the long route up the Arrow Lakes and Columbia River to the CPR mainline at Revelstoke. Rather than engage in the lengthy and complex procedure of amending the CPR charter to secure authorization to build the proposed rail line, Van Horne had one of the CPR's senior officers, Harry Abbott, petition the provincial government for a charter incorporating the Columbia & Kootenay Railway & Navigation Company.[5] This was done with dispatch. Effective August 20, 1890, Abbott leased the charter to the CPR for 999 years, and by the following spring the railway was complete and in operation.

The CPR's Columbia & Kootenay Railway, like the Dewdney Trail before it, was more symbolic than strategic. A smelter built at Revelstoke in the hope of securing Kootenay ore over the new railway soon closed down, largely for want of ore. Not that the Kootenay mines were failing to produce ore. But the water haul upstream to Revelstoke from the loading wharf at Robson was much longer than the easy haul downstream to Corbin's railway at the Little Dalles, and the CPR route was regularly disrupted by ice in winter and low water in summer, so the C&K was ineffectual in reversing more than a token volume of Kootenay traffic. Even Van Horne, upon inspecting the spidery tracks of the hastily built C&K, disparagingly termed it ". . . a railroad from nowhere to nowhere."[6]

Nevertheless, it was a beginning. Canadian rails were now in the Kootenays, and Van Horne, obviously impressed by his visit to the region despite the lack of immediate success of the Columbia & Kootenay Railway, stated shortly afterwards that this fledgling rail line would eventually form part of a through CPR line across southern British Columbia. In so saying, Van Horne was admitting the early critics of the CPR mainline route had been correct that the CPR mainline was too far north to preserve Canadian control of the southern interior. However well the mainline might serve as the link between eastern and western Canada, Van Horne knew it had to be supplemented by a second railway across the province, south of the original mainline. So convinced of this did Van Horne become that, shortly after his return to Montreal, he personally assigned engineer J.A. Coryell to survey a railway route west from the C&K at Robson to the Fraser River and the CPR mainline at Hope, 90 miles east of Vancouver.[7] Like the British Columbians who dreamed of a Coast-to-Kootenay railway, Van Horne did not foresee the years of struggle that would ensue before the railway would be completed. But from that misty morning when Coryell and his assistants stepped onto the boat landing at West Robson to begin their arduous trek across the wilderness of southern British Columbia, Van Horne had made his commitment.

The entrance of the CPR into the Kootenays intensified Daniel Corbin's desire to complete his own rail line into Nelson, and with the experience gained by his defeats in Victoria and Ottawa, Corbin felt confident he could yet win a battle in the political arena north of the 49th Parallel. Corbin considered that the most valuable lesson he had learned from his unsuccessful charter attempts in 1890 was an appreciation of the abiding fear Canadian politicians had of Americans. His success in achieving through Mara and the CKSN what he had not been able to achieve himself reinforced that belief. Therefore when Corbin resubmitted his Nelson railway proposal to the British Columbia Legislature, he was wily enough to have it presented by five well-known and respected British Columbia businessmen. They asked for a charter to be granted for the Nelson & Fort Sheppard Railway, named for its terminal points, Nelson and Fort Sheppard, the latter an abandoned Hudson Bay Company post on the international boundary, within hailing distance of the end of Corbin's Spokane Falls & Northern Railway.

A second petition was also submitted to the Legislature, this one by Corbin himself. Like his petition in 1890, this one requested approval to build a railway along the Kettle River westward to the coast. Many people questioned why Corbin chose to submit this petition himself. The answer became clear soon enough: the provincial politicians were so preoccupied with rejecting Corbin's petition—because he was an American—that the Nelson & Fort Sheppard charter slipped through with barely a note of opposition. The message to Corbin from Victoria was clear: British Columbians could do no wrong, and Americans could do no right. Corbin merely smiled.

Having duped the British Columbia government into granting a charter to reach Nelson, Corbin set to work building his railway as quickly as he could. However, the CPR was not about to allow Corbin to expand his grip on the Kootenays without a determined fight. Just as Corbin's railway nudged through the bush back of Nelson, a CPR land agent appeared on the spot bearing a letter, signed by Premier Robson, granting the CPR an exclusive reserve on all the foreshore land on Kootenay Lake adjacent to the City of Nelson. The grant effectively killed Corbin's chances of reaching Nelson proper, but it failed to deter him. A wharf was quickly built at Five Mile Point, east of Nelson and outside the CPR reserve, to act as a connection with the boats on Kootenay Lake, and in December 1893 Corbin's rail line opened. It was not a high quality railway by any means, but for the first time an all-rail route into the Kootenays existed. With the Columbia River frozen solid from Arrowhead to Revelstoke, the CPR passed the winter with its Kootenay link effectively severed, while Corbin's trains carried away the Kootenay ore. Obstructed at Ottawa, nudged out of Nelson, Corbin remained in command.

Discouraging as this situation was for those hoping to establish Canadian control in the Kootenays, it became even more dismal in 1893

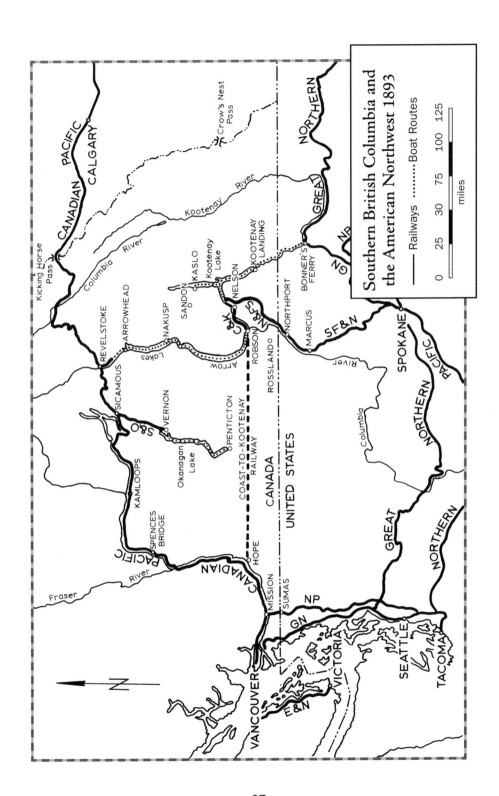

Southern British Columbia and the American Northwest 1893

Railways ——— Boat Routes ....

miles

0   25   30   75   100   125

when yet another American entered the complex drama of southern British Columbia railroading. In that year, the second major rail line in the American northwest, the Great Northern Railway, was completed. This new rail line represented a far more serious threat to the cause of economic unity in British Columbia than either Corbin or the earlier Northern Pacific. First of all, the Great Northern was even closer to the international boundary than the Northern Pacific. And second, but no less important, the Great Northern's president, James Jerome Hill, had locked horns with the CPR—in particular, with Van Horne—in the past, and this would lead to fierce conflict and competition.

Hill was a Canadian by birth, an irony considering his many contributions to railway development in the United States. At one time Hill had also been a director in the CPR until he and William Van Horne—an American who had come to Canada to join the CPR at Hill's invitation—disputed bitterly over the choice of the CPR route east of Winnipeg. Hill had wanted to run the railway through the United States, via Chicago and a connection with the existing Grand Trunk Railway; not only would this avoid the costly construction along the rocky and largely barren northern shore of Lake Superior, it would bring traffic to Hill's own rail lines in the American Midwest. Van Horne disagreed. He insisted Canadian Pacific had to be true to its name, Canadian as well as Pacific. Of course, compromise on such an issue was impossible, and when the majority of CPR directors supported the northern route, Hill left the CPR, swearing revenge against Van Horne: "I'll get even with him if I have to go to hell for it and shovel coal!"[8] Hill promptly began aggressive railway expansion in the American northwest that would earn him the majestic title "The Empire Builder" and make his railway system a formidable rival of the CPR.

At the time of this split, Van Horne had given little consideration to Hill's threat. Preoccupied with the Herculean task of constructing a transcontinental railway across 3,000 miles of Canadian wilderness, while simultaneously forced to endure the wrath of several million disbelieving Canadians who were convinced he would give away the Canadian west to his Yankee brothers, Van Horne had no time to worry about Hill. However, when Hill tried to gain control of the Duluth & Winnipeg Railway and the Soo Line in 1888, thereby extending American rails into Manitoba, Van Horne skillfully outmanoeuvered him and secured both lines for Canadian Pacific. This was a clear indication to Hill that Van Horne was ready to fight any war Hill wanted to start.

In retaliation Hill began driving a rail line northward from Seattle to Vancouver, with the objective of siphoning off the CPR's lucrative Asian trade. However, this rail line—the Canadian section was called the New Westminster Southern Railway—was not a major success for Hill. With his Great Northern mainline still under construction, Hill could not muster the capital to build the costly bridge needed to cross the half-mile wide Fraser River south of Vancouver, so his rail line was 15 miles short of inflicting any serious wounds upon the CPR. However, Van Horne knew Hill too well to believe the war was over with so few skirmishes. When Hill completed his mainline, he would possess the rail line that could command all of southern British Columbia. Van Horne knew Hill would be back, scrapping for a fight.

Van Horne's premonition—later proved to be correct—that Hill would be the greatest obstacle to the establishing Canadian control in the Kootenays reinforced his opinion that a second CPR rail line across British Columbia was needed. In his own picturesque words, Van Horne wanted the CPR to be ". . . strong enough to mop the floor with the Northern Pacific, or any other American company extending its lines into the Northwest."[9] However, others in CPR management did not support building the Coast-to-Kootenay railway. Coryell's survey had revealed that such a line would be frightfully expensive, both to construct and to operate. Except for British Columbians, only two men would champion this cause: Van Horne and the young man he had brought with him from the United States, who would succeed him as CPR president, Thomas Shaughnessy.

These ongoing problems of difficult geography, competition and lack of support from CPR management were shortly to be compounded. Early in 1893, business conditions began to slump badly, pinching off the sources of capital for potential railway construction. As the year progressed, matters grew worse. In June, the New York stock market crashed, precipitating a rash of business failures. Stores and real estate offices closed. Banks folded. Railways shuddered. Because of the collapsing business conditions nearly every North American railway reduced or suspended dividend payments. Expansion projects had to be abandoned in the middle of construction. In August, the giant Northern Pacific Railroad went bankrupt, throwing many Northwest communities into chaos. Then in November, the United States government repealed its silver purchase act, cutting off the principal market for the Kootenay mines.

Financial disaster was then followed by calamities of nature. After a perilously distressing winter, British Columbia experienced record flooding during the spring of 1894. The CPR mainline in the Fraser Valley was washed out, severing connections between Vancouver and the east for 41 days, the longest closure of the CPR mainline in history, before or since. In the Kootenays, large sections of both Corbin's N&FS and the CPR's C&K were also destroyed by flooding and washouts. The nationalistic rivalry between the two railways all but vanished in a singular, desperate struggle for survival.

Under the conditions prevailing in 1894, the prospect for the early completion of the Coast-to-Kootenay railway could not have seemed more remote. Indeed, there appeared to be no need for the railway because the Kootenay mining communities had turned into virtual ghost towns. But Van Horne knew the depression would not last forever. The Kootenay mines would one day reawaken and when they did, it would be the Americans who would be in control unless a Canadian railway spanned southern British Columbia. Thus Van Horne kept alive the Coast-to-Kootenay railway dream. To him is due that credit. All around him during those gloomy days of 1894 were men who were convinced the dreamed-of Coast-to-Kootenay railway would never be anything more than just that—a dream.

2: Empire Building

Southern British Columbia 1895 to 1899

The financial depression that began in 1893 proved hard on southern British Columbia. Railroad building came to a complete halt. Mining development all but ceased. Even train service on the N&FS and C&K was curtailed drastically. The succeeding year offered no improvement. However, the rich mineral wealth of the Kootenays proved to be a strong economic foundation on which to build. Early in 1895, as business conditions improved, the Kootenay mines began reawakening, inspiring in turn a revival of the dreams of Kootenay railways.

The pessimistic years of the depression had not destroyed William Van Horne's faith in the great potential of the Kootenays, nor his conviction that constructing a Canadian railway across southern British Columbia was essential to returning control of the Kootenays to Canada. Equally resolute in that conviction were most British Columbians, although many of them did not want the Canadian Pacific Railway to build this railway out of fears the CPR could expand its monopoly in western Canada. But the monopoly held by the CPR in other parts of the west did not extend to the Kootenays. Indeed, by far the greater portion of Kootenay trade fell into American hands, and as the depression ended there were strong indications to Van Horne that the CPR would have a major fight to maintain even the token influence it had established in the Kootenays. In almost every part of that region the Americans were pushing in rail lines with more aggressive enterprise than ever.

By far the most dramatic entry of an American into the Kootenays was that of the intrepid James J. Hill. Just as the return of prosperity had spurred Van Horne's hope for expansion into southern British Columbia, it had also caused Hill to focus his covetous eyes on the rich Kootenay mines along the northern edge of his Great Northern Railway mainline. At the time, Hill had no legal authority to enter the Kootenays directly with a railway. However, this obstacle was quickly bypassed by an alliance with John Hendry, one of the province's most influential businessmen. Back before the depression, Hendry had chartered the Kaslo & Slocan Railway, with authority to build a rail line from Kaslo—a community on Kootenay Lake just a half-day boat ride from the GN at Bonner's Ferry, Idaho—to Sandon, the mining centre of the Slocan Valley, where silver ore had been discovered not long after the 1887 strike at Nelson. Because of the depression, Hendry had been unable to raise capital for construction. Hill willingly furnished the financial support Hendry needed, and in April 1895 work began in pushing the three-foot gauge K&S over the mountains to Sandon.

For Van Horne, the news of Hill's rush upon Sandon could hardly have been more disturbing. Van Horne had long feared Hill would use his easy access to Kootenay Lake as a means of attempting to control trade of that region. But Hill's thrust at the Slocan was totally unexpected. It was all the more disturbing because the Slocan was one of the few areas of the Kootenays in which the CPR had been able to muster strong competition to the Americans, thanks to a string of rails of its own called the Nakusp & Slocan Railway. The CPR had started building this rail line from Nakusp, on the boat run to Revelstoke, towards the Slocan, prior to the depression forcing a halt in construction. For two years the CPR had relied on packhorses to bring a limited amount of Slocan ore to railhead on its partly completed railway. Van Horne knew this method of transportation would collapse once Hill's railway was complete. For Van Horne there could be only one answer: work was immediately begun in spiking down CPR steel for Sandon, the capital of the Slocan.

Seemingly enjoying the reaction he had evoked from Van Horne, Hill worked his men night and day to construct the Kaslo & Slocan Railway. By late October of 1895, he had completed his line to Sandon, comfortably ahead of his hated rival. Despite its tardiness, the CPR was not about to give up the race. A handsome station and freight shed were erected within the Sandon townsite even before the arrival of its tracks, as evidence that the CPR would give Hill's K&S a genuine fight. As of December 15, 1895, when the CPR's Nakusp & Slocan Railway was completed, the fight—quite literally—began.

The two companies had already been disputing for several weeks over the location of the N&S station and freight shed. Hill alleged they were located on K&S land and, by some talented legal footwork on his part, he had been able to persuade the local magistrate to grant an injunction preventing the N&S from using its facilities. The CPR considered Hill's actions purely obstructive, for it had a bulging dossier of legal documents to counter Hill's claim. When this evidence was presented to the courts on December 14, the day before the N&S was due to open, the attending judge issued a counter order dissolving the earlier injunction and granting the CPR full authority to use the disputed station and freight shed. The CPR quickly moved in, scorning Hill in the process.

James J. Hill was known to possess a personality intolerant of disrespect. Perhaps no one suspected what his response to the CPR's actions would be. Shortly after dark the next evening, just as the residents of Sandon began celebrating the completion of the N&S, some 70 K&S employees were loaded onto a train at Kaslo. As soon as the train left, the crews were informed of the purpose of their mysterious journey into the night. The train was to run directly to Sandon and, upon its anticipated arrival at three o'clock in the morning, the crews were to demolish the offending station and freight shed claimed by the CPR. The matter was that simple. The detailed assignment of special groups to specific tasks, such as cutting the CPR telegraph wires, left little doubt in the minds of the K&S crewmen that the whole scheme had been masterminded by someone intent upon revenge on the CPR. Suspicion was quickly replaced by enthusiasm. Never in the history of southern British Columbia had anything quite so daring been undertaken.

Once into Sandon during the black hours of early morning on December 16, 1895, it did not take the Kaslo & Slocan "raiders" long to secure complete control of the town. Within minutes, the CPR telegraph lines had been cut, thereby denying the N&S men any chance of securing reinforcements, most of the N&S men were rounded up as "prisoners of war" captured as they stumbled, dazed and bewildered, out of the bush-entangled gully where the bunk cars in which they had been sleeping crashed after being pushed off the tracks by the K&S crews. Another few minutes were all that was needed to destroy a CPR trestle west of town. By sunup, the freight shed had been levelled and the station gutted. To finish off, a cable was tied from the station chimney to the drawbar of a nearby locomotive and, in a twinkling, the last of the CPR's new station crashed into a heap of broken timber. Roaring with laughter, the K&S men boarded their train for home, leaving only one prominent K&S official who, as the *Nelson Miner* reported, ". . . could not see what right the N&S could possibly have to the property."[1]

Not surprisingly, Hill denied any responsibility for the destruction of the CPR property at Sandon, but as time went on it became obvious that if Hill had not actually planned and ordered the attack, he had at least sanctioned it. Nor would this be Hill's last physical attack on the CPR. He had just begun to demonstrate the tactics he would employ again and again in his war of rivalry and vengeance against his former employer. Indeed, it was Hill's personal desire for vengeance against the CPR—first displayed at Sandon—that strongly influenced Great Northern policy in southern British Columbia, often beyond the point of economic logic. As George Stephen, the CPR's first president, said of Hill, he ". . . will never like the CPR or be able to forgive that it did not burst, as he thinks it ought to have done."[2]

While Hill had dramatically ejected the CPR from Sandon and Corbin had secured direct entry into Nelson, these men were not the only Americans challenging the CPR in southern British Columbia. Glib 26-year old Frederick Augustus Heinze was another railway builder who came north to seek his fortune in the Kootenays.

"Fritz" Heinze, dubbed the "Boy Wonder of Mining," was an American of considerable talent and accomplishment. A self-made millionaire before the age of 23, Heinze had built a smelter at Butte, Montana, and turned it into a thriving enterprise easily able to provide him with the money needed to support the flashy life style he had come to love. In July of 1895, on the advice of one of his agents, Heinze visited Rossland, a rising mining camp above the Columbia River, a stone's throw north of the international boundary. Rossland was rapidly becoming the principal mining town of the Kootenays owing to the rich gold and copper claims on nearby Red Mountain, and Heinze was impressed with what he saw. He immediately started construction of a smelter at Trail Creek on the Columbia River, seven miles below Rossland. To supply his smelter with ore, he also began construction of a 13-mile long narrow gauge railway using switchbacks to cover the steep descent from Red Mountain to Trail Creek. Soon the railway was completed and the smelter turning out money faster than the Dominion Mint. However, Heinze was aware both Corbin and the CPR would try to break his lucrative Rossland monopoly. Ultimately, survival, Heinze knew, depended upon his ability to secure an independent connection with the outside world. Instinctively, his thoughts turned westward.

In January 1896, Heinze announced he would petition the British Columbia government for a charter for a railway from the Columbia River westward to Penticton, appropriately called the Columbia & Western Railway. To Heinze, the petition must have represented something of a compromise. Reaching Penticton would free him from dependence on either the CKSN or Corbin and would access many potentially rich mines en route as sources of supply for his smelter. But at Penticton he would still be dependent upon the CPR, via its Okanagan Lake boat connection, to reach the coast. Perhaps Heinze believed if he could build a line from Trail to Penticton first, he might secure additional provincial help to complete the line to the coast in light of the government's strong desire for a railway across southern British Columbia. In any case, Heinze boldly ignored Corbin's hard-earned lessons about Americans and went to Victoria to lobby for his charter and subsidy. His appearance obviously had more impact than Corbin's because Heinze's charter bill was given almost unanimous passage in the Legislature. As Heinze had also anticipated, a subsidy of 20,000 acres of public land for each mile of standard gauge railway he built was included.

Unfortunately for Heinze, the general public in British Columbia did not share the opinion of the members of the Legislature. The fact Heinze was an American was bad enough in the eyes of most British Columbians, but as well Heinze had thrown one of the most elaborate parties in Victoria's history for the members of the Legislature and their wives just before the vote on the charter and subsidy bills. This chicanery aroused loud accusations of political bribery. *The Province*, one of British Columbia's leading newspapers, bitterly denounced the charter: "One must sit with folded hands while gross acts of robbery of public property are being perpetrated."[3] Heinze, however, considered himself not a robber, but a shrewd businessman. After the voting had taken place, he confided to his companions that the members of the British Columbia Legislature were the most unspoiled and unsophisticated of any politicians with whom he had ever dealt. "I went down there prepared to spend $50,000 among them," he chortled, "and all it cost me to get my bill through was $240 for a good dinner at the Driard."[4] Corruptive influence or not, Heinze left Victoria openly bragging he would have rails into Penticton by the year's end.

Heinze's arrival in the Kootenays, along with the tightening grip of Hill and Corbin, reinforced in Van Horne's mind the immediate need for the CPR to push a rail line across southern British Columbia. However, money was a serious problem for the CPR. Unlike Hill and Corbin, who had geography in their favour, the CPR would face a very costly undertaking in building across the difficult terrain of southern British Columbia. Having only just struggled to its feet financially after the near-bankruptcy days of construction, the CPR had been dealt a severe blow by the depression of the early 1890s, which had stripped its coffers to the Mother Hubbard level they had been a decade earlier. Van Horne did not believe the CPR could undertake construction of a line into southern British Columbia without assistance. Instinctively, he thought of the federal government, whose cash subsidies had helped construct the mainline a decade earlier. Perhaps, he reasoned, it would provide financing for this project as well.

Taking this approach, Van Horne instructed the CPR vice-president, Thomas Shaughnessy, to write to Prime Minister Charles Tupper on April 15, 1896. The letter stated: "The most important work of any kind now requiring the attention of the government is the construction of a railway from Lethbridge or Fort Macleod through Crow's Nest Pass, East Kootenay and a part of West Kootenay to Nelson, B.C."[5] A similar letter was sent to the British Columbia government, although in the letter to the province, Shaughnessy promised the rail line would be constructed west of Nelson through to Hope after the eastern portion of the railway had been completed. To indicate his sincerity, Shaughnessy promised that until the through railway was completed, freight rates would be reduced on all coastal goods shipped to the Kootenays via Revelstoke.

The CPR's letter to the federal government was strategically timed two months before the summer federal election, no doubt in the hope the Conservative government would offer aid to the CPR for a second railway across British Columbia. The Conservatives seemed quite agreeable to the suggestion, in part because of the comfortable relationship established with the CPR when their combined forces threw 3,000 miles of railway track across the continent. But by 1896 the Conservatives had stagnated after 17 continuous years in office, and as the election approached it became obvious the new Liberal leader, Wilfrid Laurier, was going to win by a landslide. Mindful of the major role he and his corporate cohorts had played in the defeat of the Liberals in the 1892 election, Van Horne could only grit his teeth. He felt certain Laurier would not entertain any sympathy for the CPR. True to predictions, the Liberals won the election by a huge majority.

Despite what must have seemed a severe setback to his cause, Van Horne remained convinced Canadian Pacific had to strengthen its position in southern British Columbia, limited though its resources were. Van Horne was particularly concerned about the CPR's boat connection between the mainline at Revelstoke and its two Kootenay rail lines. Up to that time, the CPR had relied entirely on the CKSN to provide the connection, not a very satisfactory arrangement in Van Horne's mind. Not that CKSN service was bad; quite the contrary, its service was superb. But service, Van Horne knew, was only part of the reason for the success of the CKSN. From its inception, the CKSN had maintained defiant neutrality in the corporate and nationalistic railway wars of the Kootenays, providing service to anyone paying the bill, be it Hill, Corbin, Heinze or the CPR. Because of this neutrality, the major powers in the Kootenays seemed to have overlooked the strategic position the CKSN held.

Van Horne was quick to change that. Late in 1896, he announced the CPR was about to build a fleet of boats powerful enough to drive the CKSN off the lakes. Having thus established a good bargaining position, Van Horne promptly sat down with Mara and his partners to negotiate a sale, and in December 1896 the CPR purchased all the assets of the CKSN for $280,000. What followed was as predictable as the next day's sunrise. Boat service to the GN at Bonner's Ferry and the N&FS at Five Mile Point was immediately discontinued, leaving Hill and Corbin high and dry, their accustomed connections with the Kootenay Lake mining communities unceremoniously and ungraciously severed.

The CPR's move in securing the CKSN was obviously unexpected by both Hill and Corbin. However, Hill immediately responded by purchasing several independent boats on Kootenay Lake, quickly restoring his lost connections. He also announced his intention to build a rail line from Bonner's Ferry north into the Kootenay Lake country. Hill made it clear he would fight for the Kootenays.

For Van Horne, the situation had suddenly become critical. The purchase of the CKSN, instead of strengthening the CPR's position in southern British Columbia, had prompted a reaction from Hill that could only serve to weaken it. If Hill was to be fenced off at the border, not a moment could be lost in starting construction of the planned CPR line across southern British Columbia. Van Horne was convinced Prime Minister Laurier had no love for the CPR because of its long ties with the Conservative Party, but he wondered if the new Liberal government might be persuaded to provide financial assistance to build the proposed railway out of national, if not CPR, interest. A feeler to the government was extended through Clifford Sifton, Laurier's Minister of the Interior, with whom both Van Horne and Shaughnessy had already worked on colonization programs.

Sifton, it turned out, was receptive to Van Horne's suggestion. Laurier too was positive, stating his government was not averse to assisting the CPR to build a rail line into southern British Columbia. Van Horne and Shaughnessy could hardly believe their ears. They jumped on Laurier's offer. A public announcement was immediately made that the CPR and federal government were formally negotiating terms of a subsidy agreement to aid the CPR in building a rail line into the Kootenays.

James Baker, still in possession of his British Columbia Southern Railway charter, saw in the announcement a golden opportunity. He offered to turn his charter over to the CPR, saving it any delay in securing a charter of its own, provided he was given a portion of the provincial land grant promised the railway upon successful completion. Van Horne initially spurned the offer, saying of Baker: "Five minutes talk with him will satisfy you that he is a drowning man in search of a straw!"[6] But speed was vital in the race against Hill so the CPR accepted Baker's offer anyway. Surveys were immediately started and construction crews readied to follow on the heels of the surveyors.

Throughout the winter of 1896-97, as the surveyors dragged their tapes and rods through the snow of Crows Nest Pass and as stockpiles of construction supplies mounted in the foothills of the Rockies, negotiations between the CPR and the federal government continued, but Van Horne was not happy with their progress. Once winter was over, construction would have to begin as early as possible if the railway was not to be delayed. Unfortunately the wheels of the Ottawa political machinery were moving much too slowly and it became increasingly obvious to Van Horne that the subsidy agreement would not likely be concluded by the time the winter snow had gone. Bills also had to be paid. Solely on the strength of the government's promise of financial assistance, Van Horne had already ordered the rails needed to reach Kootenay Lake.

What Van Horne needed was oil to lubricate the political wheels. In his search for such a lubricant, the CPR president casually hinted that the CPR might consider a rate reduction throughout the entire west if a substantial cash grant were immediately forthcoming. That proved to be the secret formula—CPR freight rates were a universal sore point in the west—and Ottawa's rusty political machine surged forward with unaccustomed speed. A government bill was quickly drawn up giving the CPR a cash grant of $11,000 per mile, up to a total of $3,630,000, in return for the CPR agreeing to reduce rates on a number of key commodities shipped in western Canada, most notably grain. The CPR also agreed to grant the federal government control of rates on the new railway. Finally, the CPR agreed to give the federal government 50,000 acres of coal land coming to it via the provincial government's British Columbia Southern Railway grant, thereby ensuring the CPR could not monopolize the coal supply of western Canada. Popularly known as the "Crows Nest Agreement," the bill had the distinction of being the only occasion in North American history when, rather than receive a land grant from a government, a railway gave a land grant to a government. As any scholar of Canadian history knows, the bill later earned the distinction of being the most controversial piece of railway legislation in the dominion's history.

News of the agreement was first greeted with caution in the east. But when reports filtered through of the value of Kootenay trade being lost to the United States, eastern support became widespread. Eastern journalists praised the brilliant efforts of Van Horne and Sifton in securing new markets for eastern manufacturers. Construction of the railway was started in earnest.

Starkly contrasting its reception in eastern Canada, news of the Crows Nest Agreement met with bitter outcry in coastal British Columbia. Angry assertions came from Vancouver citizens that the federal government and the CPR had betrayed them by secretly arranging to build only the eastern half of this railway they had envisioned crossing the whole of southern British Columbia. Half a railway, they argued, was useless. Eastern Canadian cities were much too far away to compete with Spokane. Only a line to the coast could bring the Kootenays close enough to a Canadian centre of sufficient economic stature to restore Canadian control. British Columbians further despaired that, even if the Crows Nest railway did succeed in securing the Kootenays away from the Americans, it would turn control of the trade over to eastern Canadian cities, not coastal British Columbia. Rather than being the financial answer British Columbians had hoped for, the Crows Nest Agreement was interpreted as just another example of exploitation by the east. Indeed, the rate reductions specified in the agreement did not apply to goods shipped from manufacturers and suppliers within British Columbia; only goods coming from eastern Canada were assigned preferential rates.[7]

William Templeton, the mayor of the City of Vancouver, was one of the loudest critics of the Crows Nest Agreement, and he did not stop with mere criticism. He stated that, since the federal government and CPR would build only half the railway across southern British Columbia, he would personally charter his own corporation to build the second half. He said he and his fellow citizens were sick of watching the eastern cities and the CPR grow fat on the rich Asian trade passing through Vancouver, and he would not stand idly by while the CPR and greedy eastern merchants carved up the Kootenays, with the blessing of Ottawa. Of course Templeton had conveniently forgotten that, whatever benefit it had been to eastern cities, Oriental trade was responsible for Vancouver's own remarkable growth. But there was no question Templeton had the support of coastal British Columbians. The editor of *The Province* newspaper acridly echoed him: "We want no Van Horne fingers in our railway pie. Sir William has shown himself a hopeless incompetent in the way he has let his own countrymen, the Yankees, get their railways into our territories and steal his own railway's trade under his very nose."[8]

Templeton's defiant declaration that he would build a railway to the Kootenays was followed shortly afterwards by his formal request to the provincial Legislature for a railway charter. Joining him in the request were the three McLean brothers, Lachlan, Hugh and Norman, of Vancouver, who owned and managed a large engineering and construction company, and Dr. George Milne, a leading citizen of Victoria. With the addition of Milne, the proposal was expanded to include a rail line and ferry connection between the mainland and Victoria, an attempt to secure strong support from the capital. Their proposed railway and ferry system was called the Vancouver, Victoria & Eastern Railway & Navigation Company, a name the press and public quickly shortened to its initials VV&E, by which title the company was almost exclusively thereafter known.

The City of Vancouver, under Templeton's direction, passed a resolution in support of the company even before it had been incorporated into legal existence. Shortly afterwards, the VV&E chief engineer reported he had found a suitable route through the rugged Hope Mountains at the head of the Fraser Valley.[9] With Vancouver already building a smelter in readiness for the Kootenay ore, optimism ran high. Indeed, on December 24 Vancouver got a most welcome Christmas present when the VV&E promoters announced that all financial arrangements to build the railway had been completed and work would begin in the spring. Premier John Turner added that his government would grant cash aid to the project. In response, Vancouver's relations with the dominion government and the CPR hit rock bottom.[10]

In the Kootenays, most people were happy with the VV&E's success. Not "Fritz" Heinze. His public support in the province had never been strong, but with the arrival of the VV&E, sponsored by British Columbians and promising a railway from the Kootenays through to the coast, not merely Penticton, Heinze found himself with little support. To make matters worse, financiers in London were likewise unenthusiastic about his railway proposal. Despite these problems, Heinze pushed ahead with his usual boldness. In December 1896 he announced that his rail line to Penticton would proceed, and he awarded a contract for the construction of its first 21 miles. Heinze also announced he would visit Ottawa to seek aid from the Dominion government.

When Heinze reached Ottawa, he discovered the VV&E had also submitted a request for aid, and he was required to appear before Parliament's Railway Committee on June 8, 1897, the same day Dr. Milne appeared for the VV&E. Railway Committee members heard each presentation, but when the day had ended, it was obvious they had not been greatly impressed by either one. A polite suggestion was tendered that the two parties return with an amalgamated proposal. Milne and Heinze heeded the suggestion and on June 16 it was reported that Heinze had agreed to allow the VV&E a free hand in building the railway in return for a portion of the anticipated subsidy.

When the two men appeared before the committee the following day an argument developed, and the committee members abandoned the meeting in disgust and left on their overdue summer vacation.

Government rejection could hardly have come at a worse time for Heinze. By now, Corbin had a competing railway into Rossland and Heinze had been forced to mortgage his Montana smelter to obtain funds to cover the cost of the start of his railway westward. Despite his youthful years, the strain of the episode was showing on his face when he returned from Ottawa. Heinze tried to solve his problems in his usual glib manner, in this case by offering a CPR official a poker hand to settle a price for the CPR to purchase the Columbia & Western Railway. The official declined the invitation to cards but did accept Heinze's suggestion of a possible purchase, as this would allow the CPR access to Rossland. In February 1898, a formal agreement was signed transferring to the CPR all of Heinze's Kootenay assets except for a half interest in the unearned C&W land grant. The CPR, it was said, balked at Heinze's stubborn insistence the Trail smelter be included in the sale, an irony considering the smelter would later become a far more profitable asset to the company than the railway. It was further said that an unwritten part of the agreement, insisted upon by the CPR, was Heinze must never again show his face in British Columbia. This was also an irony because Heinze later returned to win a bitterly contested court case brought against him by the CPR. Heinze's role as a dynamic force in the development of the province had ended.

While the sale of Heinze's assets to the CPR directed public attention to Rossland, there were already signs that Rossland, like Nelson and the Slocan before it, was being nudged out as the principal mineral-producing area of southern British Columbia. With the CPR showing strong interest in quickly constructing its recently purchased Columbia & Western Railway westward to the Boundary District, the low-grade copper camps of that region sprang to prominence. Of course, low-grade ore required cheap transportation to be profitably exploited. In that respect, the Boundary District was soon to become yet another area of contest between Canadian and American railway interests.

It was Daniel Corbin who had first eyed the Boundary District. His proposal to build a railway along the Kettle River through the Boundary District and west to the coast had been suggested as far back as 1889, and his many failures to secure a charter had not caused Corbin to lose sight of his dream. In fact, during the summer and fall of 1897, Corbin's survey crews had been busy laying out a railway route from his SF&N through the Boundary Country. Corbin knew the CPR was every bit as disapproving of his presence in the Boundary as it had been in the Kootenays. But whatever victories the CPR had gained over him in Ottawa, Corbin still led in the competitive business of moving boxcars. With the CPR using all its constructive resources to push rails through Crows Nest Pass, Corbin concluded the time was right for a strike on the Boundary.

On March 19, 1898, Daniel Corbin incorporated the Kettle River Valley Railway Company in the State of Washington as the American portion of the rail line he proposed to build westward from the SF&N at Marcus. Simultaneously, he pressed Ottawa for a Canadian charter of the identical name covering the section of railway projected into southern British Columbia. The CPR's stand on Corbin's application for a charter need not be stated. But the citizens of Greenwood and Grand Forks piled lengthy petitions upon the Railway Committee's desks as evidence of their support of the American.

Corbin's personal appearance and the supporting petitions obviously made a favourable impression on the committee, as did the assurance by one of its members that any telegrams allegedly from British Columbians opposing the application were merely fakes produced by the CPR's telegraph department, which controlled the principal communication system in the country. After considerable debate, the committee approved the charter request on March 31 by a narrow vote of 54 to 48, and submitted the bill to Parliament for ratification. Parliamentary support for Corbin seemed in line with that of the Railway Committee. When the bill approached debate in the House of Commons on April 15 a telegram arrived from the British Columbia government stating: "Such a surrender of British Columbia's interests as is contemplated in the Kettle River Valley Railway charter, it is felt, should meet with the most vigorous opposition of all genuine Canadians."[11] The telegram tipped the scales of the narrow Parliamentary vote and the KRVR bill was defeated. Once more Corbin had been barred from Canada.

Corbin's defeat aroused furious controversy in British Columbia, especially when the eastern press reported the CPR had run special trains to carry MPs back to Ottawa from their Easter vacation if they promised to vote against Corbin's charter bill. Corbin's comments to the press following his defeat bore more resolute determination than bitterness. "I have had one satisfaction," he said, "in knowing that I gave Canadian Pacific the hardest fight it ever had, and I am not through with it yet."[12]

Shortly after his Ottawa defeat, as he readied for yet another attempt to secure entry into the Boundary District, Corbin made the distressing discovery that Spokane Falls & Northern Railway stock was being purchased in large blocks by an undisclosed buyer in New York. Corbin instinctively feared the CPR was secretly acquiring stock in his railway to elbow him out of the Kootenays and thrust the dagger of CPR competition into the American Northwest. Corbin quickly solicited prominent New York financier J.P. Morgan to buy all the SF&N stock he could in an effort to keep the CPR out of Spokane. This Morgan did, at least until it was revealed it was J.J. Hill, not the CPR, behind the secret move to buy out the SF&N. Morgan, more anxious to placate Hill than Corbin, turned over all the stock he had purchased to Hill at cost. The amount of stock thus acquired by Hill was enough to give him controlling interest in the SF&N and its subsidiaries, and on July 1, 1898 the Great Northern Railway formally took over possession of all Corbin's lines in British Columbia and Washington State. Hill lost little time in giving Corbin the boot.

As much as it had surprised Daniel Corbin, Hill's sudden purchase of Corbin's railways was no surprise to William Van Horne. Hill's bold move in securing control of the Northern Pacific following its bankruptcy reorganization five years earlier had made it clear to Van Horne that Hill was out to corner the transportation market of the entire northwest. Given this objective, Corbin's railways, reaching across the border to the lucrative mines of the Kootenays, could scarcely be expected to escape Hill's grasp. But Van Horne astutely knew the Kootenays were only part of the reason for Hill's acquisition of Corbin's lines. Hill could easily command Nelson, Kaslo, the Slocan and all of Kootenay Lake with the line he was building north from Bonners Ferry and an upgraded boat fleet on Kootenay Lake. The purchase of the SF&N was unnecessary to establish control of Kootenay Lake. Even Hill called the steeply graded, tightly twisting railway to Nelson "a sloppy line."[13] Van Horne knew that Hill's objective in the purchase was access to the territory west of the Kootenays. Indeed, as Van Horne watched the final spike being driven on the CPR's Crows Nest line at Kootenay Landing on October 15, 1898, he knew the astounding, almost unbelievable record of the Crows Nest railway's construction—some 300 miles of mostly mountainous rail line built in just over a year—would have to be equalled with a railway westward.[14] Hill, by his action, not his words, had made clear his challenge: this was a war for all of southern British Columbia.

Caught in the middle of the collision course the two railway giants had set for themselves was the one remaining independent force in southern British Columbia, the VV&E. Of course, the VV&E promoters had suffered a severe setback by their defeat in Ottawa, but Milne and his associates were not disheartened. They still possessed a provincial charter for their railway and an assurance of aid from the provincial government, both valuable considerations. They also held one trick in their hand that was to catch both Hill and the CPR off guard. That trick was their trump card, Mackenzie and Mann.

William Mackenzie and Donald Mann—names to become inseparable in Canadian history as a result of their later Canadian Northern Railway—were just beginning their career together when, during the summer of 1897, the VV&E promoters approached them for financing. Impressed by the potential of southern British Columbia, Mackenzie and Mann signed an agreement with the VV&E syndicate on September 23, 1897 acquiring the controlling interest in the VV&E for an amount the press reported to be $75,000. Vancouver news editors, temporarily glancing up from their desks covered with news of the Yukon gold rush, reported they were happy to see the VV&E in the hands of two such competent men. In reality, the transfer had no immediate effect, since Mackenzie and Mann were preoccupied with a Yukon railway scheme. However, as the winter dragged on, and the original glamour and excitement of the Yukon faded, the attention of both the public and Mackenzie and Mann once more returned to southern British Columbia. Confirmed reports that Mackenzie and Mann were buying heavily into several Boundary District mines were taken as sure signs this rising syndicate from eastern Canada was about to begin construction of the hoped-for railway to the Kootenays.

Amid all the optimism of early 1898, Mackenzie and Mann had one disconcerting report for the provincial government. The Coast-to-Kootenay railway, the pair asserted, would be extremely costly to build. In order to be assured of a reasonable dividend on their heavy capital investment, the pair insisted that the rich Boundary District copper traffic must be exclusively theirs; if Corbin—who at that time had not yet been elbowed out by Hill—or the CPR gained entry into the Boundary, not one inch of the VV&E would be built. The provincial government knew if Corbin entered the Boundary District, the CPR would almost certainly build. However, the government members believed neither Corbin nor the CPR would build through to the coast. The choice, as the provincial government saw it, was to support Corbin and get two railways into the Boundary District or take the offer by Mackenzie and Mann of a railway through to the coast. The provincial government decided to back Mackenzie and Mann, dispatching to Ottawa the aforementioned telegram resulting in the defeat of Daniel Corbin's Kettle River Valley Railway charter in April of 1898.

Facing an election in July of 1898, the provincial premier, John Turner, was in the market for something showy to present the electorate. He knew nothing could be as impressive to the voters of 1898 as a railway to the Kootenays, but in the event any voters felt left out, he decided his platform would also include a railway to the Yukon. He promptly set out to amend the Loan Act of 1897 to permit his government to borrow $2.5 million, principally to aid his two proposed railways, and on May 19, 1898 he dissolved the Legislative Assembly and announced proudly: "I have very great pleasure in stating the railway from Rossland to the Coast will be commenced immediately, and that the line from Teslin Lake to the Coast of the Province will also be under construction within the next few weeks."[15]

Having presented this attractive plum to the voters, Turner had just over one month to fulfill his proposed railway promises. Unquestionably, Turner had been counting on Mackenzie and Mann to build both railways, especially after he had aided the pair in keeping Corbin out of the Boundary District. Instead of the anticipated reciprocation, Turner received an extremely distressing reply from Donald Mann. Mann stated that the defeat of Daniel Corbin would probably have been enough to keep the CPR out of the Boundary District, but Hill's surprise purchase of Corbin's railway system had changed the situation completely. Even as he spoke, Mann warned, the CPR was mobilizing its forces for a rush into the Boundary District. With Hill and the CPR tearing apart the trade of that region, there would be precious little left over for Mackenzie and Mann. As far as Mann was concerned the VV&E was dead.

Needless to say, Turner was mortified. Fortunately for Turner, CPR vice-president Thomas Shaughnessy was in the west on an inspection tour and Mann was already in Vancouver. He wired both, requesting a meeting in Victoria in an effort to reach a settlement of sufficient strength to hold up his tottering election platform. Both men agreed, and during the second week of June all three men met in the premier's office.

Mann opened the meeting by repeating that he and his partner were unwilling to build the VV&E now that the CPR had made definite steps to build west from Robson to Penticton. Shaughnessy equally firmly asserted that under no circumstances would the CPR delay or forgo construction of its projected line west from Robson because of its commitment to save the valuable trade of the Boundary District for the people of Canada—and of course for the CPR. Clearly there was a stalemate.

Clutching for straws, Turner suggested a compromise, mentioning a town whose name echoed compromise: Midway. Turner's idea was for the CPR to construct its projected railway west from Robson but only as far as Midway, meeting its demand for a line into the Boundary. Mackenzie and Mann would build from the coast to Midway, where their rail line could accept traffic from the CPR for the coast. The potential for the VV&E to easily extend a railway from Midway down the gentle valley of the Kettle River to a connection with Hill's Kootenay railways would serve as an inducement for the CPR not to attempt short-changing the VV&E on coast-bound traffic. The compromise seemed acceptable to everyone and the three men shook hands in a gentlemen's agreement.

Despite the fact that Turner had achieved a rather important understanding with two of the most important railwaymen in Canada, he felt the need for something showier for the public and he pressed Mann to stay in Victoria to formalize the verbal agreement. On June 15, 1898, three contracts were signed between Mann and the Turner government. The first contract was for the construction of a railway from Penticton to the Boundary District at or near Midway; the government agreed to grant Mackenzie and Mann $4,000 per mile of completed railway, provided work began at Penticton by August 8, 1898. The second contract was for Mackenzie and Mann to build from the coast to Penticton; the same rate of subsidy was to apply on this section but work was not required to begin before May 8, 1899. The third contract concerned the proposed Yukon railway.

Pressed by Turner to get work on the first contract underway before the election, Mackenzie and Mann prepared to construct the railway, and on June 27, 1898 the first contingent of their work force, comprised of nine men and a team of horses, arrived at Penticton. They promptly set to work grading a railway roadbed from the government wharf on Okanagan Lake through town towards Midway. Simultaneously, engineering surveys were begun near Chilliwack. The *Vancouver News-Advertiser*, which had no sympathies for the Turner government, reported that this small amount of work was obviously just an election ruse staged by "a mule and a bale of hay outfit."[16] Turner countered that, despite its meagre beginnings, the VV&E would soon increase its work force and the whistle of trains from the Boundary would soon be heard in the City of Vancouver. On July 9, 1898, the unimpressed electorate ungratefully voted Turner out of office.

Turner's successor, Charles Semlin, firmly believed no railway could be of value to the province unless it was the result of his own administration's forethought. On October 19, 1899, the government wrote Mackenzie and Mann cancelling the Coast-Penticton and Yukon railway contracts. A few months later it repealed the Loan Act of 1987 and its amendments of 1898, thereby withdrawing aid for the Penticton-Midway section. A week later, on February 27, 1899, a bill was passed granting a new subsidy under virtually identical terms as Turner had except for one subtle clause Semlin inserted in the act effectively prohibiting Mackenzie and Mann from being the ones to collect the grant. Obviously no legislation was to be any good if it was not of Semlin's own making.

The repeal of provincial aid for their railway caused Mackenzie and Mann to lose heart in the VV&E and orders were issued to disband the construction force at Penticton. It is almost certain Mackenzie and Mann had kept the small crew working at Penticton solely to comply with the terms of their original agreement with Turner to undertake continuous construction while they sought to add a federal subsidy. Whether or not they would have then built the railway is now conjecture. During the half-year in which the small force of men was at work at Penticton, nearly four miles of roadbed was completed between Okanagan Lake and Skaha Lake. Several roads in the Penticton area owe their existence to this early construction attempt by the VV&E.[17]

Unlike the fate of Turner, whose political career had been terminated by the VV&E, the death knell of the VV&E only signified to Mackenzie and Mann that it was time to pack their bags and set off for the next town and their next railway. Like Heinze and Corbin before them, Mackenzie and Mann had built themselves a "railroad" and had passed into history. Later they would return. However, the VV&E's role as an independent force in the shaping of southern British Columbia's history had effectively ended.

Despite the termination of construction on the VV&E, the dream of a Coast-to-Kootenay railway was not dead. Hill's surprise purchase of Corbin's railway lines had convinced Van Horne and Thomas Shaughnessy, who in June of 1899 succeeded Van Horne as president of the Canadian Pacific Railway, the CPR must push westward from its established railway at Robson. Through the winter of 1898-99, the Columbia & Western Railway was rushed as fast as human labour—and it was predominantly human labour in those days—could do the job. Even as heavy snows mounted and temperatures dropped far below freezing, the pace of construction was not relaxed. Van Horne and Shaughnessy were not to be disappointed by their construction forces either. Notwithstanding the difficult nature of the work, grading the railway roadbed was completed barely a year after it had been started, and on September 18, 1899 the first official train rolled into Grand Forks. Shaughnessy had planned to be aboard the first train and missed the occasion only because of pressing business commitments. He rode over the line a few weeks afterwards and expressed pleasure in the line's fine construction and rapid completion.

In fact, Shaughnessy's statement was not entirely correct. At the time of his trip, the line west of Grand Forks did not yet have track on it owing to a shortage of rails. But by early 1900, CPR trains were running into Midway and on a branch line from Eholt to the mountaintop copper camp of Phoenix. Shaughnessy also announced during his trip over the line that, in keeping with his agreement with the former premier, John Turner, the CPR would not extend west of Midway, at least not immediately. "We are something like a tired horse after climbing a long hill," he said, reminding British Columbians of the tremendous investment the CPR had made in building a rail line that now stretched halfway across the province's rugged southern interior. "We want to rest a little before going on further."[18]

Having reached the Boundary District, the CPR had obviously scored a major victory in the struggle to re-establish Canadian control in southern British Columbia. In fact, much of the heavy volume of traffic the CPR found coming over its new railway was destined to the American communities along the Kettle River and tributary valleys well south of the international boundary line, as the CPR line made it easier for these American communities to ship goods from Canada than use the long and rough wagon roads leading to Hill's system. Thus, for once the geography of the interior was working to the advantage of Canadians. For once, too, the CPR was gaining the upper hand.

Still Shaughnessy did not relax. If the CPR was turning the tide in southern British Columbia, Shaughnessy recognized it was as much the result of default on the part of J.J. Hill as it was the result of the CPR's efforts. While the CPR pushed rails into the Boundary, Hill had done nothing. Mysteriously, he had not made even a single move to utilize the strategic advantage that both geography and the surprise purchase of Corbin's railways had given him. Hill's line at Marcus was a scant 30 miles from the Boundary District, every inch of it along the easy valley of the Kettle River, a marked contrast to the 70 miles of stiff grade CPR trains had to surmount to reach Grand Forks from the Columbia River Valley. Hill had not even attempted to counter the CPR's growing trade with the American communities south of the Boundary District. Indeed, in a public statement strongly akin to the fable about the fox and the sour grapes, Hill publicly announced late in 1899 that at no time had he considered constructing a railway along the Kettle River into Canada, nor could he see why the CPR was so anxious to push its tracks into such barren territory as the Boundary District.

To Shaughnessy, Hill's statements were nothing more than a ruse. The Boundary District was far from barren. In truth, during the first year of the Columbia & Western Railway's operation, the CPR was plagued with problems keeping up with the demand for rail service. Shaughnessy also knew Hill had surveyors in Crows Nest Pass and the Boundary District, even west into the Okanagan Valley, for good reason. If Shaughnessy was mystified over the Great Northern president's statements or his failure to counter Canadian Pacific's growing strength in southern British Columbia, he was mystified only by Hill's sense of timing, not by his ultimate motives. Whatever Hill said to the public, Shaughnessy believed he wanted control of southern British Columbia. Hill would not be content to continue domination of the trade of Nelson, Rossland and Kootenay Lake alone. He would expand east into Crows Nest Pass and west into the Boundary District, reaching out to snatch away the valuable trade of those two regions that the CPR, through great effort and tremendous investment, had been able to secure for itself. When he did, Shaughnessy knew, the CPR's existing link with eastern Canada through Crows Nest Pass could not stop him. It was too long and geographically adverse to compete. Without direct connections with the coast, the CPR could not survive an attack by Hill.

Perhaps that is why, late one afternoon in January 1900, a gang of browbeaten and half-frozen surveyors struggled into the tiny village of Hope, 90 miles east of Vancouver, after having staked a survey line all the way west from the end of the CPR trackage at Midway down the tortuous canyon of the Coquihalla River to Hope. Shaughnessy, in directing the survey work, seemed to be echoing what Van Horne had said of southern British Columbia a decade before: "The Canadian Pacific Railway cannot and will not surrender that region to any other company."[19]

In Vancouver, astonished citizens turned their heads in disbelief. Was the survey really ordered by the man who, only a few months before, had said the CPR would not extend its railway west of Midway for some time to come? Was it really the CPR that was laying out a rail line across the vast sea of mountains between Hope and the mines of the Kootenays? To many it seemed unlikely. But who else would do it? Not Heinze or Corbin, as they were both gone. Not Mackenzie and Mann with their VV&E; they were gone too. Not J.J. Hill, for he seemingly had lost all interest in British Columbia. Even if he had not lost interest, why would he, an American, undertake the construction of such a difficult and expensive railway when the mineral treasurehouse of southern British Columbia lay so ready to be tapped by cheaply constructed feeder lines thrown across the border from his Great Northern Railway in the United States? Yes, it had to be the CPR. That same resourceful, oft-maligned, always unappreciated Canadian Pacific Railway—the company that had amazed the world in building the Canadian transcontinental railway in half the time the most optimistic believers had said it would take—was the corporation behind the railway surveys.

The CPR's years of public criticism in British Columbia were forgotten in an instant. Overnight, a generation of complaints were cast aside. On the streets of Vancouver, praise for the CPR was heard for the first time in more than a decade. Even the Vancouver newspaper editor who had previously damned the CPR for everything from freight-rate piracy to causing the flood of 1894 was impressed enough to stoically remark: "It seems almost too good to be true!"[20]

3: Mountains, Men and Paper Railroads

Southern British Columbia 1900 to 1903

The twentieth century dawned upon British Columbia with new hope kindled in the hearts of its people that the cherished dream of a Coast-to-Kootenay railway would soon materialize. The Canadian Pacific Railway had reached Midway with a rail line from the east, covering half the distance across southern British Columbia with trackage, and the company was carrying out extensive surveys on the remaining section from Midway to the coast. Moreover, the map tucked into the back of the CPR Annual Report of 1900 showed a dotted line from Midway to Hope labelled "Projected Trackage". To most British Columbians these were certain signs the railway would soon be built. However, in a brief announcement shortly after the survey work was completed, Thomas Shaughnessy announced the CPR would not consider construction of the railway in the immediate future owing to the high projected cost of construction.[1]

Shaughnessy's announcement quickly ended the CPR's brief reign of public acclaim in Vancouver. If British Columbians were critical of the CPR for its reluctance to commit itself to the construction of a direct rail line to the Kootenays, they were to find their own government in Victoria no better. The Semlin administration had not come through with its election promise of a grand, sweeping railway policy. Except for the cancellation and week-later reinstatement of the act offering aid for a railway between Penticton and Midway, the Semlin government had done nothing in regards to the Coast-to-Kootenay railway.

In truth, Semlin was not solely to blame for his administration's lack of accomplishment. The defeat of Turner's administration during the July 1898 election had been far from decisive, and Semlin had been left to limp along with a majority so precariously slim that during the Speech from the

Throne at the opening session of 1900, the acceptance vote was split dead even between the government and the opposition. Had the Speaker of the House not stepped in to support him, Semlin and his administration might have collapsed right there. The reprieve was brief. Less than a month later the government was defeated on a redistribution bill and power passed to Joseph Martin, who lasted a mere 106 days. In the face of this unstable political situation, the Lieutenant Governor asked James Dunsmuir, the coal baron of Vancouver Island and a member of the House, to form a new administration. On June 16, 1900 Dunsmuir became premier.

Dunsmuir's ascension marked the fourth government administration to assume power in British Columbia in two years; none of these administrations attempted to tackle the principal problem facing the government, that of mounting provincial debt. Despite the gravity of the situation—the province was tottering on the verge of official bankruptcy—Dunsmuir, like all his unsuccessful predecessors, immediately launched a program of comprehensive railway development fostered by promises of generous grants from the public coffers.

Dunsmuir's offers of aid drew no response from the CPR. During a visit to Vancouver on October 2, 1900, Thomas Shaughnessy repeated his earlier statements about his company's reluctance to complete a line to the coast until economic conditions were more favourable. However, two weeks later William Mackenzie showed up in Vancouver and announced that he and his partner were ready to go back to work on the VV&E if the provincial and federal governments would pass legislation to back up the frequent promise of financial aid. With this newly resurrected hope for a railway to the Kootenays, Vancouver papers instantly added the two governments to their list of institutions upon which to heap vehement damnation. The government bungling, said the papers, was all that was delaying the VV&E from going to work.

The reawakening of the VV&E after two years of hibernation caused suspicions that new blood had been transfused into its veins. Mere promises of government aid could not account for its resurrection because, as generous as the government grants may have seemed, they represented only about 15% of construction costs. A few daring individuals speculated the most likely person to be pumping new blood into the VV&E was the American, Jim Hill. The growing mining camps of the Boundary District made the VV&E an obviously tempting prize for Hill because it was virtually the only railway charter still on the books in southern British Columbia that neither he nor the CPR had not already absorbed. If he secured control of the VV&E, Hill would have all the legal authority he needed to enter Canada without having to go through the political gymnastics his predecessor, Daniel Corbin, had faced. Hill initially denied any involvement, but on December 13, 1900 a VV&E representative stated that an agreement had just been negotiated with "a corporation who have been successful in all their great enterprises in Canada."[2] It was also announced the VV&E would be started immediately, not only connecting Vancouver and Victoria with the Kootenays, but forming part of a new transcontinental railway connecting with the Grand Trunk Railway at Chicago. Most people believed it could only be Hill.

Just minutes after the VV&E announced it had procured outside backing, the CPR released its own announcement—strategically timed to be published in the same newspaper editions as the VV&E press release— that an application for a provincial charter for a railway from the coast to Grand Forks had just been made. All the petitioners were prominent Canadian Pacific officials and the proposed line, called the Vancouver & Grand Forks Railway, was designated to follow the exact route surveyed by the CPR crews a year earlier. Hill would not be alone if he tried to build the VV&E to the Kootenays from Vancouver. A battle was brewing hot enough to make the Kettle boil!

Ironically, the CPR's announcement did more to boost Hill's image than its own. People didn't actually hold Hill in high regard over the CPR. Public distrust of all railroad barons was simply too widespread for that. But the Sandon war and other Kootenay battles had shown that where one railway was allowed to build the other was quick to follow. If, by supporting Hill, the public could pressure the CPR into building, there was the likelihood the coast would enjoy not one, but two, rail lines to the Kootenays, both built in record time. Competition was the watchword of the age. The news the CPR was rising to accept Hill's challenge sparked excitement in the heart of British Columbians. One Vancouver newspaper said that with Hill and the CPR racing to build, "the grader's pick will soon be busy solving the remainder of the problems."[3]

Sensing a surge of public sympathy for Hill, Dunsmuir announced, on the day before Christmas in 1900, that the $4,000 per mile subsidy originally granted the VV&E and later cancelled by the Semlin government would be reinstated at the next sitting of the Legislative Assembly. The opening of the Assembly passed without the promised legislation, and on March 6, 1901, a large public meeting was held in Vancouver where it was voted to send a delegation to Victoria to press for the promised subsidy. Many people at the meeting voiced the opinion that the province would benefit more by aiding the VV&E from the public purse than by allowing the CPR, even without a subsidy, to expand in British Columbia.[4] One newspaper editor wrote: "Only those who are blinded by selfish and servile interests oppose the construction of the Coast-Kootenay line by a company independent of the CPR. The people of British Columbia have groaned long enough under the burdens of monopoly."[5]

On March 19, 1901 a second major public meeting was held, this time in Victoria. At the meeting, lawyer E.V. Bodwell, acting on behalf of the VV&E, did a thorough job of rousing public emotion in favour of the VV&E. It was important, he said, to keep the CPR from gaining a monopoly on any more of the province. In his own words, he "did not think Providence had created this province for the C.P.R."[6] The *Victoria Times* echoed his condemnation of the CPR: "When it suits their purpose, as in the present instance, they hoist the old flag over their works and patriotically direct attention to the stars on Jim Hill's hat and the stripes on his trousers."[7]

Bodwell further blamed the CPR for the delay in the reinstatement of aid to the VV&E. He said the CPR was putting pressure on Dunsmuir, who personally held a valuable contract with the CPR for the supply of locomotive coal from his mines on Vancouver Island. Two days later public attention was diverted away from this issue by a telegram Bodwell released to the press: "New York. March 21. If you think advisable you may announce that Great Northern Railway and Mackenzie & Mann & Co. are equally interested in Victoria, Vancouver & Eastern railway stock. Signed James J. Hill and Wm. Mackenzie."[8]

The air was cleared considerably by the official announcement that Hill was indeed a partner in the VV&E. Dunsmuir proceeded to clear the air further the next day by declaring that any aid offered by the government would be in the form of a competitive prize awarded to the company offering the best terms for the concession of building and operating the railway. "The government is going to make the best possible bargain for the country," Dunsmuir asserted, "It doesn't matter a button whether it is the VV&E, the CPR, or any other company."[9] The province reacted with shocked silence.

A week later, on March 28, Dunsmuir stated the terms of his railway aid plan. A cash subsidy of $4,000 per mile would be awarded to a company of the government's choice if that company constructed the projected railway from Midway to the coast, with a ferry connection to Vancouver Island. Included was the proviso the railway must allow the government "absolute control" of the freight rates and return 4% of the annual gross earnings from the railway's operation to the government. Dunsmuir's unprecedented suggestion won strong support from the editor of the *Vancouver Province*, who stated: "It is a gratifying sign of the times to find the principle asserted and maintained that the public chest is entitled to some return for the charters and assistance given railroad companies."[10]

Bodwell rejected the terms, saying the investors in any enterprise were traditionally entitled to the first dividend. Victoria residents felt snubbed because their city had not been specifically named as the Vancouver Island ferry terminal. Indeed, as the weeks passed, the debate seemed to centre more on which of the two coastal cities would be the terminal of the railway than on any furtherance that might actually get the railway built.

On April 24, 1901 James Dunsmuir put his verbal promises on paper and presented them to the Legislative Assembly as a new government railway bill. The bill called for aid of $500,000 to construct a combined railway and general traffic bridge across the Fraser River at New Westminster to form part of the new line to the Kootenays. Of more immediate consequence, although Dunsmuir did not mention it, the bridge would allow Hill's line from Seattle access into Vancouver. The bill also promised aid for a railway from English Bluff, near the present community of Tsawwassen, to Midway, with connections from English Bluff to Victoria via a ferry system. Four other railways were to be aided. Dunsmuir requested that any company interested in securing the subsidies submit a letter to the government outlining the conditions under which it would build the railway. In regard to the railway between the coast and Midway, three letters were forthcoming.

The first letter came from E.V. Bodwell. Despite his earlier rejection of Dunsmuir's plan, Bodwell was willing to compromise: if the government would lower its tax on gross earnings from 4% to 2%, the VV&E would begin work at once and complete 30 miles of track in the Vancouver area and 30 miles in the interior by the end of summer. Bodwell emphasized that Hill and Mackenzie and Mann were planning to commence work on several large projects and if the government did not accept his offer immediately, no men and equipment would be available for the VV&E until the following year.

A second letter came from the law partnership of Hunter & Oliver. They stated that one of their clients had applied for a provincial charter, to be called the Coast-Kootenay Railway, and were prepared to build if the federal government also gave aid and the provincial government would accept the 4% levy on gross earnings in lieu of all other taxation.[11]

The Canadian Pacific Railway also responded, offering to build a railway from a point on its Mission-Huntingdon branch, near Abbotsford, to Chilliwack during 1901, extending it through to Midway when conditions warranted. The CPR asked for a subsidy only for the difficult mountainous section east of Hope and, as an additional plum, suggested willingness to discuss the touchy issue of freight rates.

With at least three tangible offers before him, Dunsmuir perhaps believed he would have little difficulty in getting the railway built, but the CPR had refused to commit itself to a definite schedule of construction, and no one had ever heard of the newcomer, the Coast-Kootenay Railway. That left the VV&E as the only corporation with the known capabilities to undertake early construction. But even the VV&E was in trouble, and as spring dragged on it became increasingly obvious it was unlikely to start work that year. The VV&E's problem was that its act of incorporation in 1897 had divided its proposed route into a number of sections that had to be completed within stipulated time periods. This it had failed to do. Now that Hill was behind the VV&E, the question of the legal validity of its charter was being raised by the eager young lawyers the CPR seemed to keep to "accidentally" dig up such questions when they would be most damaging to the opposition. And to add to the VV&E's woes, Prime Minister Laurier asserted that no federal money would be forthcoming for a Coast-to-Kootenay railway that year.

The CPR remained firm on its original offer and the citizens of Vancouver and Victoria returned to their usual jealous debate over which city should be the railway terminal on the yet-to-be-built railway. On May 11, 1901, the Dunsmuir government moved to grant charters to both the Vancouver & Grand Forks Railway and the Coast-Kootenay Railway. Otherwise nothing was done.

The people of British Columbia were naturally disappointed the provincial government had been unable to offer more positive results in respect to the Coast-to-Kootenay railway. But those who hoped for early construction could gain some consolation from the fact that Jim Hill, subsidy or not, was actively interested in seeing at least part of the VV&E built that year. In June 1901, it was announced that Hill had purchased Mackenzie and Mann's interest in the VV&E and now held almost exclusive control.[12] On June 23, 1901, a week after this announcement, the Great Northern's chief engineer, John F. Stevens, stepped off the train at Marcus carrying a freshly inked charter just issued by American authorities for yet another Hill subsidiary, the Washington & Great Northern Railway. Within two weeks, Stevens had a large force of men grading the W&GN northward up the Kettle River towards Canada. Simultaneously, a rail line was started north from the Great Northern mainline at Rexford, Montana, thrusting into the CPR's great coal stronghold of Crows Nest Pass.

The conservative *Victoria Colonist* termed Hill's aggressive thrust upon southern British Columbia "an invasion."[13] It warned of the dire consequences that would follow once Hill had made the Boundary District and Crows Nest Pass yet two more satellites of Spokane and accused Hill of using the VV&E charter illegally. This was no concern to Hill. For him, railroad building consisted solely of laying track—a task at which he was incredibly accomplished—and British Columbians were stunned when, only two weeks after work had begun at Marcus, Hill's construction crews roared across the border into Canada slashing out the VV&E right-of-way, oblivious to any concerns regarding the legality of their actions. Less than a week later, the cleared right-of-way was being graded in preparation for tracklaying. Surveyors were also swarming over the hills west from the Boundary heading full speed for the coast. All the while Hill remained silent about his intentions.

Premier Dunsmuir, to his distress, was really as much in the dark as the general public. Nevertheless, he thought he could at least garner some favourable press from all the publicity Hill's railway construction work was generating. One major question that remained unanswered was the choice of the coastal terminal. Dunsmuir no doubt deemed it would be political suicide to choose sides on that touchy issue. Another question— that of a railway route through the rugged Hope Mountains—also remained unanswered. This was a subject Dunsmuir believed would be safe to address. It was known that the CPR, the VV&E and several others had done surveys in the Hope Mountains, but the comprehensiveness of those surveys or their findings had never been released to the public.

Dunsmuir therefore suggested that the mystery of the Hope Mountains could be cleared up once and for all if a government survey were undertaken. In publicizing his idea, Dunsmuir stated that the information from such a survey would be made available to the CPR, the VV&E or anyone else desiring to build the railway, and it would give the government an accurate estimate of the cost of construction should it later decide to build the railway as a public undertaking. Dunsmuir reasoned that this approach would appeal to everyone. Besides, it was an inexpensive way for the government to look busy until better times came along. In July of 1901, Edgar Dewdney was commissioned to take charge of the government survey.

The government could hardly have picked an older man for the task than Edgar Dewdney, as more than 40 years had passed since he had blazed his famous trail across the Hope Mountains. But Dewdney's long experience more than compensated for his lack of youthful agility. He accepted the assignment with vigour and promptly hired two of the most competent engineers in the country to assist him, Henry Carry and Frank Moberly, the latter being the son of Walter Moberly who had been instrumental in the surveying of the CPR mainline.[14] On August 1, 1901, the complete party of some 30 men departed from Victoria by steamer for Hope. Although their survey work was completed before winter, Dewdney declined to discuss his findings until a formal report had been submitted to the government.

While Dewdney and his assistants laboured in the Hope Mountains, Hill continued to push his railway expansion in southern British Columbia. By summer's end the W&GN line from Marcus to the border was essentially complete. Construction of the connecting VV&E line through Canada and the remainder of the W&GN line south along the Kettle River and Curlew Creek to Republic also continued, although the rapid pace with which Hill had begun was severely set back because of litigation over the acquisition of certain right-of-way lands. Frank Bernard, one of those promoting the rival Coast-Kootenay Railway, called Hill's push into the Boundary District "the most unrighteous hold-up people ever witnessed."[15] Bernard did not evoke much public sympathy; most people knew the provincial treasury was empty, and whatever other faults Hill may have had he at least was laying track with his own money. Not surprisingly, the winter of 1901-02 passed with Hill as busy as ever and everyone else merely observing.

Early in 1902, Dunsmuir suggested the provincial and federal government jointly build the Coast-to-Kootenay railway as a public enterprise over which trackage rights would be sold to the CPR and GN to help repay the cost of construction. This novel idea was no doubt an attempt to get the federal government to share financing, but the words of Conservative Dunsmuir fell on deaf ears in Liberal Ottawa. Even so, the proposal had its merits. Such an arrangement would have prevented either the CPR or the GN from monopolizing the trade of the southern interior without the uneconomic duplication of trackage so often accompanying unrestricted competition. Ironically, after another decade and a half of bitter conflict between the two rival corporations, that suggestion would be adopted in only slightly modified form.

On March 31, 1902, after it had become obvious Ottawa was ignoring his suggestions, Dunsmuir announced an agreement was being negotiated with the three McLean brothers, who had reappeared with another railway proposal to build to the Kootenays. The amount of aid was to be $4,800 per mile for the mountainous section of the route, plus a land grant of a million acres. Dunsmuir also used the occasion to announce that a contract had just been let for the construction of the New Westminster Bridge, the first link in the line to the Kootenays.

Reaction to Dunsmuir's announcements did not meet his hopes. The idea of further alienation of public lands for railway construction was distinctly unpopular. Nor were many people happy that public funds were being offered the McLean brothers, who had already received one charter—for the original VV&E—and allegedly sold it for a handsome profit. The *Vancouver Province* correctly summed up general public feelings when it said the agreement was merely something "for promoters to play political and financial poker with."[16] Adding fuel to the already roaring fire, Edgar Dewdney unsuspectingly chose the same week to present his long-awaited report to the Legislature, a report offering little encouragement to Dunsmuir's plan for a rail line to the Kootenays.

Dewdney reported establishing three possible routes for a railway between Hope and Princeton.[17] He emphasized all three routes involved very heavy construction and long stretches of severely adverse grades. He added: "The result of the survey shows that the Hope Mountains cannot be crossed without encountering serious engineering difficulties which necessitate a very large expenditure of money, and I know of nothing so pressing, either in the way of development or along any line which might

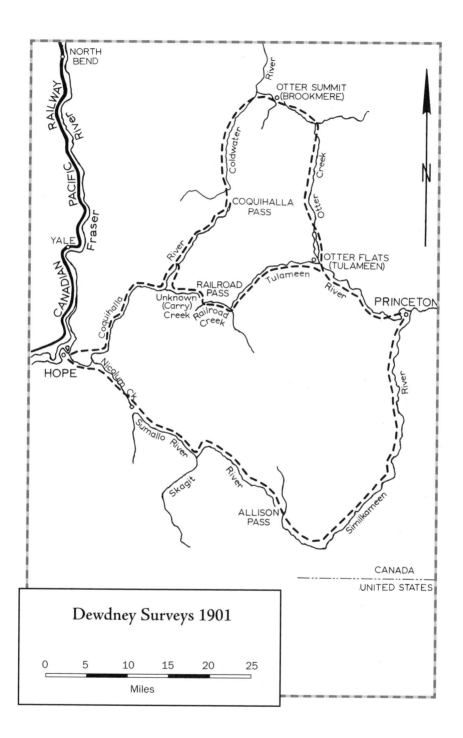

NORTH
BEND

RAILWAY

PACIFIC

CANADIAN

Fraser River

YALE

River

OTTER SUMMIT
(BROOKMERE)

Coldwater

Otter Creek

COQUIHALLA
PASS

N

OTTER FLATS
(TULAMEEN)

River

RAILROAD
PASS

Tulameen River

PRINCETON

Coquihalla

Unknown
(Carry)
Creek

Railroad
Creek

HOPE

Nicolum Ck.

Sumallo River

Skagit

River

ALLISON
PASS

Similkameen

River

CANADA
UNITED STATES

Dewdney Surveys 1901

0   5   10   15   20   25

Miles

be determined on to warrant its construction. Outside of a few prospects that have been brought in by miners, there is nothing at present to give encouragement for this expenditure, except the existence of some very fine timber on the west slope."[18]

Despite this setback, Dunsmuir asserted that his railway program would go ahead.[19] On May 5, 1902 he introduced his railway package to the Legislature. A key component was titled "The Coast-Kootenay Railway Aid Act—1902." This act incorporated the Vancouver & Coast-Kootenay Railway Company, without naming an interim directorate as was customarily done. The reason for this open structuring, said Dunsmuir, was so that any syndicate chosen by the government could immediately proceed to build the railway without legal complications. But most people believed Dunsmuir had done this purely to ensure a charter was ready for the McLean brothers, who did not already have one.

The public and legislative opposition to Dunsmuir was substantial. In fact, only by abandoning one major railway proposal, eliminating the million-acre land grant from the Coast-Kootenay Railway Aid Bill and reducing the aid from $4,800 per mile to $4,500 per mile was Dunsmuir able to salvage enough support in the Legislature to stay in power. On June 21, 1902, after an exhaustive legislative marathon, the amended act was passed.[20] True to expectation, Dunsmuir immediately signed an agreement giving the aid to the McLean brothers. Norman McLean left for Ottawa a week later to seek financing and federal government assistance.

McLean soon wired from Ottawa that he had found a group of investors willing to finance the Vancouver & Coast-Kootenay Railway. He promised work would begin as soon as the federal government granted "a reasonable subsidy which will satisfy the Eastern capitalists."[21] No doubt McLean thought the news would be of great interest to Dunsmuir. However, when McLean arrived back in Victoria, he discovered Dunsmuir was gone and a new premier, Edward Prior, was in command. Prior, like all those before him, wanted to build his own railway empire. He informed McLean that all Dunsmuir legislation would be cancelled and land grants would be offered in place of cash to help alleviate the government's tight financial situation. This was no help to the McLean brothers; they needed cash, not land. With the September 1, 1903 deadline for the commencement of construction specified in the provincial agreement fast approaching, some hasty action was required to keep the subsidy alive. Late in August, a party of surveyors started laying out the Vancouver &

Coast-Kootenay Railway route from Vancouver to New Westminster. There is evidence some token construction work was also performed. On September 21, 1903, the Vancouver papers headlined the proud announcement that full construction of the Vancouver & Coast-Kootenay Railway would be underway within two weeks.

This was followed two weeks later by another major announcement, but not by the Vancouver & Coast-Kootenay Railway. This time it was the federal government, stating it had decided to concentrate its financial backing on the Grand Trunk Pacific Railway and would contribute no money to a railway to the Kootenays. With that announcement the end came swiftly and unmercifully; no further work was ever done on the Vancouver & Coast-Kootenay Railway.

The collapse of the Vancouver & Coast-Kootenay Railway was the climax to four years of intense frustration for British Columbians. Ever since early in 1900, when the CPR announced it would not commit itself to early completion of a rail line between Midway and the coast, British Columbians had been looking to their legislative representatives to provide the stimulation to build the Coast-to-Kootenay railway first dreamed of a decade and a half earlier. But such leadership had not been forthcoming, with five government administrations in as many years accomplishing nothing in regards to a Coast-to-Kootenay railway.

Indeed, political impotence was compounded by corruption. British Columbians had always been suspicious of James Dunmuir's relationship with the CPR. This distrust was followed shortly afterwards by allegations that Dunmuir's chief commissioner of lands and works, W.C. Wells, had attempted to bribe several CPR officials to gain special favours from the railway. A government official was also found to have in his personal possession the deeds to several large and valuable tracts of land in Crows Nest Pass, deeds rightfully belonging to the CPR. The rumours of corruption within the Dunsmuir cabinet were so widespread that one of Prior's first actions as premier was to order the formation of a special committee to investigate the allegations. The committee quickly found many irregularities, and by the time it had heard testimony from its subpoenaed witnesses—and sifted through 12 years of government papers—the investigative committee's report had swelled to more than a thousand pages.

Prior was one of the few government members to escape being soiled by the investigation. But at the moment of the greatest public tumult over the committee's findings, Prior was caught with his own fingers in the till;

it was learned that he had awarded a major government contract to his own construction firm after reviewing the bids submitted by competing firms before his own firm had submitted its bid. The province exploded. On June 1, 1903, just four days after the report dealing with the activities of the Dunsmuir government had been released to the public, the lieutenant governor dismissed Prior from office. The embittered editor of the *Kaslo Kootenaian* wrote: "British Columbia has been in her political life cursed with a horde of hobos who are utterly inconsistent and apparently without the remotest sense of responsibility."[22] Few in the province were ready to disagree with that statement.

The lieutenant governor called upon 33-year old Richard McBride to salvage the pieces of the shattered political scene and form a new government. It was a challenge of the highest order for the province's youngest and first native-born premier. A decade of appalling legislation would have to be corrected and the deep pit of financial ruin filled. Above all, the tragic gap between the people of British Columbia and their elected representatives would have to be closed. McBride resolved to achieve these goals. He decided his first step in building a solid house would be the removal of all rotten wood. Thus he called an election.

In his election campaign, McBride made no deals. He made it clear the province was on the verge of bankruptcy, and only by long years of hard work, heavy taxation and unpleasant belt tightening could affairs be put in order. Public expenses would have to be husbanded to the bone. In particular, no money would be forthcoming in aid of railway construction. For some time to come, the many dreams of railway expansion within the province would have to remain as dreams, and the most cherished of them all, that of a Coast-to-Kootenay railway, would have to join the list of cancelled projects. For British Columbians, that very special dream, which had once seemed so near to reality, now seemed further away than ever.

Hope station on the Kettle Valley Railway, looking eastward towards Coquihalla Pass. This is the scene described in the Introduction. When this photo was taken in 1967 the tracks ended a few hundred feet beyond the station and were virtually unused. The station was moved shortly afterwards and later demolished.
PHOTO BY BARRIE SANFORD

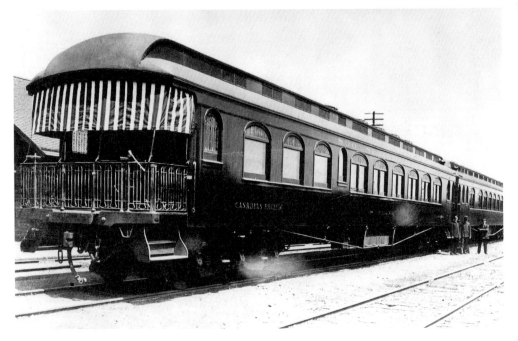

The luxury equipment of the CPR's Spokane Flyer exemplified the intense competition between the Canadian Pacific Railway and the Great Northern Railway in the border country of the Pacific Northwest that culminated in the construction of the Kettle Valley Railway. CANADIAN PACIFIC RAILWAY

Railroad rivalry in southern British Columbia frequently manifested itself in physical confrontation. At Grand Forks the Kettle River Valley Railway responded to the Great Northern's surprise crossing of its rail line in November 1902 by blocking the offending crossing with one of its locomotives.

This forgotten cut in the hillside above Kalamalka Lake south of Vernon was one man's contribution to railway history. Here the Midway & Vernon Railway employed a single worker to dig out the railway roadbed in keeping with the company's charter requirement to undertake "continuous construction" until the railway was completed. PHOTO BY BARRIE SANFORD

This poor quality but rare photograph shows the Midway & Vernon Railway grade west of Midway just prior to being taken over by the Kettle Valley Railway for use on its line from Midway to Penticton. The Kettle River appears on the right. PHOTO COURTESY ANDREW MCCULLOCH FOUNDATION

Engineman Teddy Hosker and fireman Harry Ades pose in the cab of CPR 4-4-0 25 near Clapperton Tunnel during construction of the CPR Nicola Branch in 1906, later part of the Kettle Valley Railway. The locomotive was built by Dubs & Company of Glasgow in 1882 and scrapped in 1931. Harry Ades was the son of Albert Ades, for whom Ades station on the CPR mainline near North Bend was named.
PHOTO FROM THE COLLECTION OF BARRIE SANFORD

When the CPR's Nicola Branch was completed in 1907 a simple boxcar served as the station at Merritt until a more permanent structure could be erected. PHOTO FROM THE COLLECTION OF BARRIE SANFORD

Middlesboro Collieries, Merritt. This was the largest coal mine in the Nicola Valley and a major traffic generator for the CPR and KVR. PHOTO FROM THE COLLECTION OF BARRIE SANFORD

This alternate view of Middlesboro Collieries was taken from the hillside southwest of the mine. The extensive mine railway yard is visible on the right, with the town of Middlesboro in the distance. The CPR spur to mine tipple is visible on the extreme left. The town of Merritt is off the photo to the left.
PHOTO FROM THE COLLECTION OF BARRIE SANFORD

Sir Thomas George Shaughnessy, president of the Canadian Pacific Railway from 1899 to 1918. The construction of the Kettle Valley Railway was largely due to this man's conviction of the need to connect coastal British Columbia with the Kootenays. PHOTO COURTESY PUBLIC ARCHIVES OF CANADA

Andrew McCulloch, the brilliant engineer who directed the construction of the Kettle Valley Railway and who was involved with its operation for nearly two decades after the railway's completion.
PHOTO COURTESY ANDREW MCCULLOCH FOUNDATION

Pile driving at Coldwater River Bridge 5 between Kingsvale and Brodie, 1911. This location ultimately became mile 113.4 Princeton Subdivision. PHOTO COURTESY ANDREW MCCULLOCH FOUNDATION

Construction labourers pose in a shallow rock cut, probably on the railway grade above Naramata. The rock would be initially fractured with explosives, but the "spoil" had to be removed by human and animal muscle. Most of the Kettle Valley Railway was constructed in a similar manner.

PHOTO COURTESY PENTICTON MUSEUM, KATHLEEN DEWDNEY COLLECTION

Penticton reeve E. Foley-Bennett addresses Penticton citizens prior to turning the first sod on Kettle Valley Railway construction at Penticton on July 1, 1911. PHOTO COURTESY PENTICTON MUSEUM

KVR wharf and station at Penticton under construction, 1912. PHOTO COURTESY PENTICTON MUSEUM

Myra Canyon, showing five of the 18 trestles originally constructed through the canyon. The railway roadbed through the canyon is now a popular hiking trail. PHOTO COURTESY ANDREW MCCULLOCH FOUNDATION

West Fork Canyon Creek trestle in Myra Canyon under construction, 1914. The cable across the chasm was for transporting trestle timbers into position. PHOTO COURTESY PENTICTON MUSEUM

Kettle Valley Railway locomotive 1 positions cars for a steam shovel loading gravel ballast at Winslow, January 1913. Ballasting was one of the few phases of the KVR's construction that could be undertaken predominantly by machine power rather than muscle power. PHOTO COURTESY PROVINCIAL ARCHIVES OF BRITISH COLUMBIA

Trout Creek Bridge near Summerland under construction in the spring of 1913. The crane appears to be placing the first piece of steel on the 250-foot long centre deck truss span, which may have been why the photograph was taken. At 241 feet from rail to creek level, Trout Creek Bridge was the highest bridge on the KVR and third highest railway bridge in British Columbia. PHOTO COURTESY PENTICTON MUSEUM

Completed track ready for ballasting between Glenfir and Adra in the spring of 1914. The roadbed above "Big Tunnel" closer to Chute Lake is visible above the foreground track. PHOTO COURTESY PENTICTON MUSEUM

KVR locomotive 1 provides the motive power for three carloads of excursionists stopped for a view at "Little Tunnel" east of Penticton in August 1914. It would be another two months before track from Penticton was connected with track from Midway. PHOTO COURTESY PENTICTON MUSEUM

Even before formal completion of the Kettle Valley Railway the company was enjoying a thriving log hauling business in the Coldwater Valley. In this 1913 photograph CPR 2-6-0 3000, on lease to the KVR, prepares to leave Glen Walker with a string of log cars destined to the mill at Canford.
PHOTO FROM THE COLLECTION OF BARRIE SANFORD

Work begins on the construction of the combined road-rail bridge across the Fraser River at Hope in December 1913. The completed bridge is still in use, but only for highway traffic. PHOTO FROM THE COLLECTION OF BARRIE SANFORD

The difficulties faced by surveyors and construction workers is amply illustrated by this photo of four surveyors posing on a crude trail cut from the rocks at the Quintette Tunnels. This site is now easily reached by a walking trail in Coquihalla Canyon Provincial Park. PHOTO COURTESY ANDREW MCCULLOCH FOUNDATION

This photo shows the completed railway grade in Coquihalla Pass ready for bridge construction and tracklaying, viewed from high above Boston Bar Creek. Just off the right edge of the photo is Portia, one of the stations named by Andrew McCulloch after characters from the plays of Shakespeare. Today this location is an interchange on the Coquihalla Highway. PHOTO COURTESY ANDREW MCCULLOCH FOUNDATION

Tracklaying just east of Princeton, April 1915. Wooden crossties were pushed forward on the right side of the tracklaying machine, while rails were pushed through on the left. Crews would generally lay about half a mile of track per day. PHOTO COURTESY PROVINCIAL ARCHIVES OF BRITISH COLUMBIA

Driving the last spike on the Midway-Merritt section of Kettle Valley Railway at Princeton on April 23, 1915. Mrs. G.D. Griffiths, wife of the local Anglican minister, appears to have her husband's approval to make the final hammer tap on the spike. PHOTO COURTESY PRINCETON MUSEUM

Kettle Valley Railway locomotive 4 arrives at Penticton's lakeshore station with the first passenger train into that community following the official opening of the KVR on May 31, 1915. PHOTO COURTESY PENTICTON MUSEUM

4: The Race for Republic

The Kettle Valley Railway is born

The opening years of the twentieth century had not produced a political atmosphere conducive to major railway expansion in British Columbia. However, the entry of the CPR into the Boundary District late in 1899 sparked a period of intensive railway development within the region that was to continue well into the new century. What had attracted the CPR was the Boundary District's rich endowment of low-grade copper ore. Since cheap transportation was the catalyst necessary for the profitable exploitation of this resource, it did not take long for the new railway to prove its value. In May 1900, the Granby Consolidated Mining & Smelting Company opened its first mine at Phoenix and began shipping ore to the Trail smelter. Three months later, on August 21, 1900, the company fired up the first furnace of its own smelter at Grand Forks. Other companies quickly opened mines at Deadwood Camp and Boundary Creek to the west, and shortly afterwards came smelters at Greenwood and Boundary Falls. In fact, within a year of the railway's completion, the Boundary District had become the principal mineral producing area of the province and one of the most prominent mining regions in North America.

The rapid rise of the Boundary District was one of the main reasons for the advancement of so many grandiose schemes for a direct rail connection between the coast and the southern interior during the stagnant political years following the turn of the century. It was ironic that amid all this elaborate scheming an unassuming man named Tracy Holland was quietly working on a modest dream of his own that would one day influence in bringing to reality the much larger dream of a Coast-to-Kootenay railway.

A native of Ontario, Tracy Holland came west as the provincial manager of the Dominion Permanent Loan Company. He acquired his interest in railways early in 1900 when he was in Grand Forks handling business matters relating to the Grand Forks Townsite Company. With fascination, Holland had watched the steady progress being made in the erection of the Granby smelter just north of town. As carloads of Phoenix ore rumbled into Grand Forks, his enterprising mind wondered how a businessman of modest means, such as himself, could profit from the lucrative mining and transportation trade of the region. Holland knew the CPR had the rail market of the Boundary District well fortified against competitive inroads and he would have no chance of breaking this monopoly with his limited resources. However, he astutely recognized that a significant part of the CPR's business was coming from the American community of Republic, 35 miles south of Grand Forks. This community, despite the sizable market it represented and its known reserves of copper ore, was without rail connections. Geography denied it easy access to the GN or NP, and the CPR, because of a management policy at the time that opposed construction of company rail lines into the United States, had declined to provide Republic with a branch line connection.

For Holland, such a deficiency presented a personal opportunity. The thought of connecting Grand Forks and Republic by railway was made more appealing by the easy construction represented by the 35 miles along the Kettle River and Curlew Creek separating the two communities. With the Phoenix mines pouring out more ore than the CPR could handle, Holland had no difficulty envisioning his own railway soon overflowing with Republic ore destined for the rising smelter at Grand Forks.

Tracy Holland communicated his ideas to his brother, Frederick Holland, who was also in the management of the Dominion Permanent Loan Company. Favourably impressed, Frederick secured the backing of three others: James Stratton, provincial secretary for Ontario; Thomas Coffee, manager of the Trusts & Guarantee Company in Toronto; and George H. Cowan, a Vancouver lawyer and Member of Parliament. The five men promptly petitioned the British Columbia government for a charter authorizing them to build a railway from Grand Forks over the three miles to the international boundary at Carson, a railway they proposed to name the Grand Forks & Kettle River Railway. They sought a similar charter from American authorities for the longer portion of the line in the United States.

At first, members of the provincial Legislative Assembly did not embrace Holland's proposal with much enthusiasm. Many of them were mindful of the earlier episodes with Daniel Corbin and harboured fears that any railway along the Kettle River would be detrimental to Canadian interests. Only after considerable alteration to the wording of the charter bill was it passed, and even then by only two votes at four thirty-five in the morning on August 31, 1900, the last day of one of the longest legislative sessions in provincial history. Moreover, the passage of the charter did not exempt Holland from other difficulties. Canada's constitution at the time did not permit provincially chartered railways to cross provincial boundaries.[1] That restriction meant Holland had to await the opening of Parliament in January 1901 to obtain federal sanction for his enterprise. Holland also found the citizens of Washington State as enthusiastic about a Canadian railway hauling their ore to a Canadian smelter as British Columbians had been about the American railways that had aggressively tried to capture the Kootenay ore market a few years earlier. Only after a long and difficult struggle was the charter for the American portion of Holland's proposed rail line—legally titled the Republic & Kettle River Railway—granted.

In the matter of securing federal authority to cross the international boundary line, Holland and his colleagues presented a petition to the Ottawa government on March 8, 1901. The petition was almost identical to the GF&KR but asked for additional authority to build three branch lines: a 50-mile line from Grand Forks up the North Fork of the Kettle River (also known as the Granby River) to Franklin Camp; a line from Grand Forks west to Midway; and a line from Grand Forks east to Cascade City. The proposed line to Cascade City followed the Kettle River downstream to the international boundary, the same route Corbin had been refused only two years previously. Adding insult to injury on Corbin's failure, Holland titled his proposed railway the Kettle River Valley Railway.

The CPR was favourable to Holland's plan to construct a rail line to Republic, as it seemed likely to serve as a feeder line to the CPR system. It was much less enthusiastic about Holland's request for a line to Cascade City. At Cascade City the KRVR would be only 35 miles from the SF&N at Marcus, an inclusion that would make the charter a tempting prize to sell to Hill and thus bring the American competitor into the profitable Boundary copper trade. Without the line to Cascade City, the CPR argued, Holland's railway would only serve to encourage trade into Canada.

The Parliamentarians acknowledged the CPR's reservations but accepted Holland's assurance the line to Cascade City had been requested only because a smelter had been proposed for that location. On May 23, 1901 the charter act of the Kettle River Valley Railway was officially assented to by the Government of Canada, thus formally opening the pages of history on one of Canada's most colourful railways.

Although Holland returned from Ottawa with his charter, the people of the Grand Forks area were more concerned about the long delay since he first put forth his railway proposal than they were about his success in Ottawa. Because of the delay, Holland's railway had been dubbed the "Hot Air Line," a title that, despite Holland's best efforts to discourage, stuck with his corporation for the rest of its days.[2] Moreover, the citizens of Grand Forks did not accept Holland's name for the American portion of the railway, since it failed to even mention their city. They much preferred, in verbal conversation and editorial print, to refer to the line as the Grand Forks & Republic Railway. For some reason, the Americans followed suit and dubbed the American portion of the line the Republic & Grand Forks Railway. Neither name was legally correct. Thus, with three official and three unofficial names for his not-yet-built railway, Holland awarded a contract for construction on August 31, 1901. Work began immediately.

On October 28, 1901, the KRVR-R&KR accepted delivery of its first locomotive, a well-used, second-hand 4-4-0 of decidedly limited tractive effort that soon inherited the local name "The Tin Whistle."[3] Naturally, such an occasion was deemed a suitable cause for celebration by the Grand Forks citizenry, and that afternoon virtually the entire population followed the town band across the Kettle River to watch John Manly, one of the town's leading citizens, pound down the first spike on the railway at the junction point with the CPR, a spot soon named Cuprum in recognition that copper was expected to be the lifeblood of the railway. Manly's wife added formal flair by breaking a bottle of imported champagne across the first rail. Completing the homespun celebration for the homespun railway a horse-drawn wagon, bearing a large blacksmith bellows on which some imaginative sage had hung a sign "Hot Air," pulled up beside the track and the newly delivered locomotive. Hot air or not, the railway to Republic had been started and more than one Grand Forks citizen that day must have been eagerly awaiting the wealth of business expected to pour down from Republic.

Although the occasion was festive, Holland and his associates were distinctly less joyous than they would have liked. While construction of their railway had started, so had construction of Jim Hill's railway from Marcus to the Boundary District, and with Hill openly promising that his railway, once into Canada, would loop south to Republic, the easy little moneymaking railway scheme dreamed up by Holland had suddenly turned into a nightmare battle with Hill's giant empire. Any ordinary mortal would have quit right then and there. Not Holland. With strong support in the Grand Forks area, Holland encountered no difficulty enlisting the sympathy of local landowners to refuse Hill's VV&E a right-of-way into Grand Forks or across the grasslands south of town. The VV&E possessed the legal power of expropriation, so Holland knew his tactic could not stop Hill; however, expropriation procedures would take time and perhaps this would tangle up Hill long enough that, with a little luck, the fledgling KRVR-R&KR could be the first to reach Republic.

Holland pushed construction of his railway, but by January 2, 1902, the original expected completion date, the line had only reached Curlew, half way to Republic, and Hill was catching up rapidly. Searching for ways to derail "Empire Builder" Jim Hill, Holland secured an injunction prohibiting the VV&E from crossing the KRVR tracks, which Hill would almost certainly have to do to reach Grand Forks. Holland also entered another injunction, this one prohibiting the VV&E from trespassing on the extensive land holdings of the Yale Hotel, owned by KRVR supporters. He further filed a court affidavit alleging that the VV&E charter had expired and, in case it hadn't, alleging that Hill was using it as an obvious front for the Great Northern Railway to build lines not authorized by its own act of incorporation or the original VV&E charter. A court order was granted prohibiting Hill from continuing work until the legal questions were settled and, in anticipation of the court ruling on the VV&E's charter validity, the Railway Committee in Ottawa postponed approval of Hill's request for lines to Grand Forks and Phoenix.

Hill promptly retaliated by securing his own injunction prohibiting the R&KR from crossing the right-of-way staked out by Hill's subsidiary Washington & Great Northern Railway near Curlew, where the R&KR had been building a wooden bridge to cross a section of right-of-way previously surveyed by Hill. The injunction, Hill believed, was certain to delay the R&KR as much as its injunctions were delaying him in Canada. However, Holland's scrappy little company took one look at the injunction paper, thumbed its nose and kept right on building. Hill's injunction had

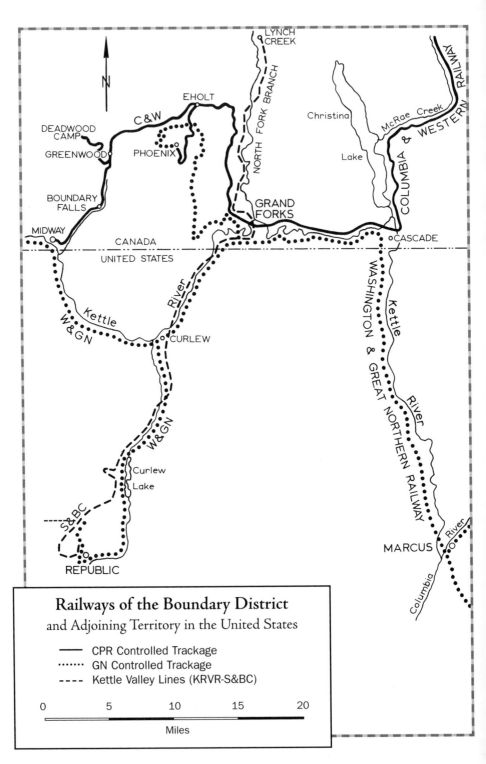

LYNCH
CREEK

EHOLT

C & W

DEADWOOD
CAMP

GREENWOOD

PHOENIX

NORTH FORK BRANCH

Christina

McRae Creek

COLUMBIA & WESTERN RAILWAY

Lake

BOUNDARY
FALLS

GRAND
FORKS

MIDWAY

CASCADE

CANADA

UNITED STATES

Kettle

River

W&GN

CURLEW

WASHINGTON & GREAT NORTHERN RAILWAY

Kettle

River

W&GN

Curlew
Lake

S&BC

MARCUS

River

REPUBLIC

Columbia River

Railways of the Boundary District
and Adjoining Territory in the United States

—— CPR Controlled Trackage
········ GN Controlled Trackage
---- Kettle Valley Lines (KRVR-S&BC)

0   5   10   15   20

Miles

been issued by a Canadian court and therefore was meaningless in American territory!

Hill was of the belief that an injunction should be enforced—at least when it applied to someone other than himself—and on the morning of Sunday January 5, 1902, when things at Curlew were shut down for the Lord's Day, a force of W&GN men raided the R&KR land and began pulling down the offending trestle. The few R&KR men on the site promptly ran back to the nearby construction camp, and in a matter of minutes a sizeable crew of men, who no doubt were eager for any diversion of greater excitement than the visiting preacher's Sunday sermon, arrived on the scene and lost no time in repelling the W&GN attackers. In the event Hill's forces tried to return with reinforcements, the R&KR armed a number of its men to guard what remained of the trestle. Thus, the first round ended with the newcomer making it clear it too could play the game by Hill's rules.

Those few minutes of physical warfare generated enough legal paperwork to keep the lawyers on both sides busy for many months. The legal tangle halted all railway construction at Curlew, and with Hill blocked both from entering Grand Forks and reaching Republic, railway work in the area came to a virtual halt. This situation greatly alarmed James Anderson, the mayor of Grand Forks. Anderson recognized that Hill had far greater financial resources than Holland's syndicate and thus was ultimately bound to win the battle for Republic. He also believed Hill was the type of person who, should too many obstacles be thrown in his path, might retaliate against Grand Forks by deserting the community and shipping all the Republic ore to the American smelter at Northport. To counteract these concerns, Anderson made an offer perhaps unique in the annals of Canadian political history: if Holland would surrender the injunction blocking Hill's VV&E from reaching the Granby smelter, Anderson would step down in the race for re-election as mayor of Grand Forks and let his only opponent, the KRVR's Tracy Holland, win by acclamation. Holland agreed. He became mayor and Hill got his line to the smelter.

This move by Holland, as unprecedented as it was, by no means signified a mellowing of relations between himself and Hill. The KRVR continued to possess an injunction prohibiting the VV&E from crossing its railway and supporters were equally determined to block Hill's expropriations south of town. Perhaps fearing he was actually losing ground to the

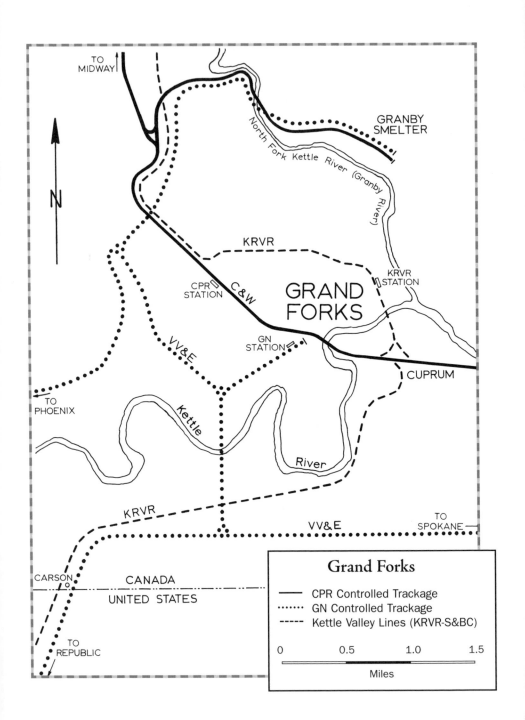

smaller company, Hill offered to call off the war at Curlew, where he had definitely gained the upper hand. However, Holland believed this was nothing more than an attempt by Hill to loosen the KRVR's choking grip on him in Canada. Thus Holland snubbed the offer; indeed, he indicated he was prepared to fight all the more vigorously. Despite an impressive display of legal pyrotechnics by Hill's lawyers at a Victoria court session on January 24, 1902, the KRVR managed to counteract Hill's efforts to dissolve the injunction prohibiting the VV&E from crossing the KRVR. Thus, Hill was still held in check while R&KR rails pushed onward to Republic.

Angered by the KRVR's tenacity, Hill publicly announced on February 8, 1902 that he was giving up the Boundary District entirely and would build only his rail line to Republic, not a line to Grand Forks. He added that all Republic ore would be shipped past Grand Forks to the Northport smelter. No doubt, Hill's announcement was merely a ploy to bring local pressure to bear on KRVR management, but the KRVR accepted it as a formal surrender by Hill, and the next week the KRVR surveyors laid out a set of survey stakes over the newly completed VV&E roadbed from Cascade City, claiming the "discarded" right-of-way for its own line.

This time Hill lost his temper completely. A crew of VV&E men promptly arrived on the spot and, to quote the newspaper report covering the incident, ". . . impressed upon the surveyors the desirability of quitting work."[4] Hill also loudly announced he would bypass the blockade set up by the KRVR sympathizers on the south side of the Kettle River by jumping to the north side of the river, thus paralleling the CPR into Grand Forks. Holland must have laughed over this threat because he knew the CPR would resist such a move even more strenuously than he and his associates were resisting Hill on the south bank of the river. Holland no doubt gained considerable delight in seeing Hill squirm from plan to plan in an attempt to match wits with the KRVR. Finally, on April 5, 1902, Hill gave in to the smaller company, dropped his expropriation application and paid the king's ransom demanded by the KRVR supporters for the right-of-way land. The high price the Kettle River Valley Railway had been able to extract from Hill for right-of-way could scarcely have dented the Great Northern's treasury; however it did put a considerable dent in Jim Hill's pride, and won for the KRVR-R&KR the precious commodity of time in the race for Republic. The delays enabled the R&KR to sprint ahead in tracklaying, and as of April 12, 1902, Holland formally declared his railway complete.

The opening of the railway was a major event for Grand Forks and Republic. Both cities that day were gaily decorated in Union Jacks and Stars and Stripes, and a special train, with some 300 passengers on board, ran over the line to introduce local people to their new railway. Before the wildly cheering crowd of Americans and Canadians thronging the copper camp at Republic, Tracy Holland personally drove a gold spike into the track. So enthusiastic was the crowd, in fact, that nearly everyone was willing to overlook Holland's eagerness in calling the railway complete. The "last" spike had actually been driven into a single pair of rails in the centre of Republic, five miles from the nearest piece of trackage on the remainder of the railway! However, the railway was actually completed a short time afterwards and Republic ore was soon flowing down the rail line to the Granby smelter, just as Holland had once dreamed.

Despite seeing the nominal achievement of his objective, Holland was hardly comfortable about his situation. With Jim Hill breathing down his neck, Holland could scarcely have been expected to feel elated, but he was greatly discouraged by his dealings with the Republic mine owners. Although they were shipping healthy volumes of ore over his new railway, they refused to commit themselves to long term shipping contracts as long as competitive transportation, in the form of Jim Hill, loomed on the horizon. The railway thus had an uncertain future.

Nevertheless, Holland took to the offensive. Three days after the celebration at Republic, he slapped yet another injunction on the VV&E. By this time, Hill was completely fed up with the KRVR, and he openly ignored the injunction by having his crews continue grading the VV&E roadbed while his lawyers appealed the court ruling. On April 29, Hill succeeded in having this latest injunction dissolved. The next morning the KRVR submitted an affidavit to have Hill indicted for contempt of court for ignoring the injunction. This new court case would harass Hill, but the last of the obstructions blocking him from reaching Republic had been removed. On June 9, 1902, the dominion government railway inspector approved the VV&E's completed railway between Cascade and Carson, and shortly afterwards the W&GN section of the line south of Carson to Republic was opened for operation, with through service provided between Republic and Spokane.

Hill had thus reached Republic. He still did not have his planned spur into Grand Forks proper and, on October 28, 1902, application was made to the Railway Committee in Ottawa for permission to cross both the

KRVR and CPR with an extension of the VV&E. The KRVR, with unrelenting stubbornness, sent a party to Ottawa to attempt blockage of the VV&E and the CPR naturally sent its usual contingent of obstructionists. But the fierce battle that ensued was short-lived and the Railway Committee granted the VV&E approval. Despite the defeat for the KRVR, the company's principal representative at Ottawa, George Cowan, left the meeting shouting, "Railway Committee or no Railway Committee, we still have our injunction!"[5]

Cowan may have had his injunction but Hill believed the Railway Committee had granted him all the authority he needed to build his railway. In a move characteristic of Hill's method of doing business, a diamond crossing was laid across the KRVR shortly after dark on Sunday, November 9, 1902, and the residents of Grand Forks awoke the next morning to find Hill's railway on their doorstep. Of course, the KRVR did not sanction Hill's action in the least and, immediately after discovering the offence, it positioned one of its locomotives squarely in the middle of the diamond crossing, blocking any train movements by the VV&E. When VV&E crews arrived in large number, violence seemed imminent, but sanity prevailed and the day passed quietly with the VV&E men packing supplies by hand around the parked locomotive, under the watchful eye of the KRVR employees. Late in the day, the KRVR removed the locomotive after Hill threatened to resurrect the Curlew lawsuit.

Hill's forcible entry into Grand Forks marked the end of the "hot war" between the VV&E and the Kettle River Valley Railway. Outright confrontation between the two never again occurred and there were no further court flare-ups, at least not that year. In fact, four days after the crossing incident at Grand Forks, both sides dropped their injunctions and lawsuits. But the battle for Republic was far from ended. The Kettle River Valley Railway and Republic & Kettle River Railway, which by this time had been considerably simplified by the vesting of both charters into a single holding company called Kettle Valley Lines, had given Jim Hill an unaccustomed thrashing and Hill's policy towards the KVL reflected his continuing desire for revenge against his troublesome rival. Hill set his rates for hauling Republic ore to the Grand Forks smelter at a low level, distressingly low for the Kettle Valley Lines considering the VV&E had its own spur line into the Granby smelter whereas the KVL had to turn over its cars to the CPR at Cuprum for delivery to the smelter, with subsequent switching charges. In addition, Tracy Holland, the driving force behind the railway since its conception, found the competition with Hill too great a personal strain and resigned late in 1902 without a replacement of similar calibre to take over the railway's management. Worse still, the Republic ores had proven difficult to smelt using conventional copper smelting processes and Granby was reluctant to accept the Republic ore except at a higher charge. The increased cost naturally reduced the demand, which in turn cut deeply into the principal traffic the railway had been intended to serve.

Having found the end of the rainbow at Republic a good deal less golden than anticipated, the Kettle Valley Lines management turned its attention to the earlier dream of a railway north from Grand Forks along the North Fork of the Kettle River to Franklin Camp. It was hoped this rising mining community would provide a transportation market profitable enough to offset the ailing Republic line. Early in 1903, the company appealed to the federal government for financial aid to build the 50-mile branch, and later that year it was granted the government's standard cash grant of $3,200 per mile with a proviso to increase the aid to as much as $6,400 per mile if unusually expensive construction conditions were encountered. The opportunities for outside financing appeared good because of the rich potential of the North Fork country; at least until Hill, who never seemed to forget a grudge, sabotaged any investment interest by announcing he would build his own line up the North Fork. While Hill probably never intended to build a railway along the North Fork, his announcement certainly hurt the KVL's chances of building a line of its own.

In 1904 the management of the Kettle Valley Lines resurrected the North Fork proposal and, to combat the effects of Hill's announcement the previous year, proposed the line extend beyond Franklin Camp through Fire Valley to Vernon, and west from Vernon across the Nicola Plateau to Quilchena, near the present town of Merritt. At Quilchena, the line was intended to connect with the not-yet-built line of the Nicola, Kamloops & Similkameen Coal & Railway Company. The KVL management even went so far as to secure statutory permission to run trains over the NK&S line from Quilchena to the Nicola coalfields, despite the fact both the North Fork line and Nicola line existed only on paper and in the minds of the promoters. Nevertheless, the proposal had merit. Coal was very much in demand at the three Boundary smelters and Nicola had coal in abundance. The railway was thus reasonably assured of a potentially lucrative trade. Moreover, the line would shorten the route from the Boundary District to the coast by several hundred miles, which would bring significant traffic and revenue.

On July 31, 1905, work began on grading the roadbed for the projected rail line starting from the CPR junction at Cuprum and extending towards the city centre of Grand Forks. Construction lasted only briefly before being halted, but following a local bylaw the next spring—passed by an impressive 231 to 9 majority and granting the railway free right-of-way through the City of Grand Forks—the "first" sod was once more turned on June 16, 1906. Work this time advanced at a steady pace, although it was hardly impressive.[6] Not until a year later, on June 24, 1907, did the first train run over the line through Grand Forks and, by the end of summer, when work on the extension ceased entirely, track had been laid only to Lynch Creek, 18 miles north of Grand Forks. This was less than half way to the first destination of Franklin Camp and an extremely discouraging distance from the promised goal of Nicola.[7]

With their dreams of a railway westward seemingly shattered, the officers of the Kettle Valley Lines struck out boldly in another direction by legally changing the name of the Republic & Kettle River Railway to the Spokane & British Columbia Railway. Besides indicating ambitions to reach southward to Spokane, the name change added an eighth name to the already well-endowed 35-mile section of track between Grand Forks and Republic.[8] The name change was followed a short time later by the purchase of several large parcels of land just outside Spokane and formal announcement of the company's intention to build to the Inland Empire capital. Quite probably the announcement was made solely to increase the attractiveness of the charter for a sale to either the Union Pacific or Milwaukee Road, newcomers to the Spokane area. However, no such interest was ever shown. Moreover, Jim Hill was not about to peacefully accept the entry of any more railways into his territory and his corps of lawyers soon had the S&BC so tied up in litigation it was not moving anywhere even if the envisioned purchase had materialized.

Incredibly, the Kettle Valley Lines would carry on the legal battle with Hill for nearly a decade, ultimately managing to exhaust him into surrender. However this fact was of rather slight consequence in the battle for Republic. By 1907, Hill had all but crushed his smaller rival. He had unyieldingly applied the thumbscrews of harsh free enterprise competition, coupled with a generous helping of personal vengeance, on the tiny corporation that had obstructed the expansion of his rail lines in southern British Columbia. No doubt Hill delighted as the financial plight of the Kettle Valley Lines grew more and more perilous. The Republic line was withering, and without the anticipated return in revenue, interest on the construction debts of the North Fork extension mounted. To make matters worse for the KVL, copper prices sagged badly during 1907 under the generally depressed business conditions of the time. Regular service on the Republic line was suspended and the track became overgrown with weeds.

The end of its short existence seemed imminent for the Kettle Valley Lines. A scant eight years, and the fateful hand of J.J. Hill, had turned Tracy Holland's golden dream into a nightmare, with only a near-bankrupt derelict company remaining. Hill probably felt satisfied no further retribution was necessary; the Kettle Valley Lines was a railway seemingly destined to pass into oblivion.

However, the financial ledger could not tell the complete story. There was a man associated with the Kettle Valley Lines who believed this small railway had an important future in southern British Columbia, a future he considered would not be complete until the dream of a Coast-to-Kootenay railway had become a reality under his leadership. He was not the first to dream of his own railway to the Kootenays. But Hill might have done well to pay attention to him. In part, because of this one determined man, a railway that had all but died would return to haunt Hill and, in the end, it was this dreamer who would help make the dream of a Coast-to-Kootenay railway come true.

5: Makeshift & Visionary

The Midway & Vernon Railway
builds part of the Kettle Valley Railway

The response of the citizens of Grand Forks to Tracy Holland's plan to connect their community with Republic was one of great enthusiasm, and from the moment of its conception the Kettle River Valley Railway was a source of great pride to the people of that Boundary community. Even the "Hot Air" appellate the people of Grand Forks had given their local enterprise was more often said with affection than malice. Such enthusiasm did not escape the attention of the citizens of Greenwood, 20 miles to the west. With both admiration and jealousy, they decided not to be outdone by Grand Forks: Greenwood would champion a railway of its own.

Unlike the broad, open valley of the Kettle River surrounding Grand Forks, which permitted numerous construction opportunities, the rugged hills thrusting upward from Boundary Creek left the residents of Greenwood only two possible options for railway construction—east or west. The first option could be discounted immediately because the CPR had built into Greenwood from the east. The CPR had also built west of Greenwood, but its westward extension covered only the ten miles to Midway. Beyond the end of track at Midway lay nearly 300 miles of untapped territory reaching all the way to the coast. Of course, Greenwood residents were not the first to look longingly westward from Midway. But for them the lack of direct coastal rail connections was particularly distressing. Geographically, the Boundary District was closer to the coast than the Kootenays, yet in terms of rail distance and travelling time it was actually more remote. To reach the coast Boundary residents faced either a rough horseback journey to the CPR lakeboats at Penticton or a circuitous journey by train east to the Kootenays then north to the CPR mainline or south to the American lines. To make the complete journey on the CPR required a minimum of four changes of travel mode, more in winter. Travel via the American rail lines was not a great deal better. Although the Great Northern system crossed the border at several points, passenger service on most of its Canadian lines was anything but frequent. Therefore, it was small wonder residents of the Boundary District were anxious to see a railway built westward.

Robert Wood, the leading citizen of Greenwood, was one of the chief advocates of rail connections to the west. Wood recognized that a rail line west from Midway to the coast would be a costly undertaking, especially because only ten miles west of Midway a mile-high ridge of mountains blocked the potential route. But Wood had an idea. Instead of trying to cross this mountain barrier headed westward, he proposed to build a railway skirting along the edge of the mountains following the Kettle River northward. Such a route could cross to the Okanagan Valley via a relatively low divide and ultimately reach Vernon. Vernon was the end of the CPR's subsidiary Shuswap & Okanagan Railway, built in the early 1890s to reach Okanagan Lake from the mainline at Sicamous. A rail connection between Midway and Vernon would mean the Boundary District could access the CPR mainline without having to first route back to the Kootenays. While such a rail line would not be a direct link with the coast, it would reduce by more than 200 miles the journey to the coast via Revelstoke and would eliminate the cost of transferring goods from boat to boxcar at the many connections. The fact the route involved little heavy construction was especially appealing to Wood.

In Greenwood, Wood found his idea universally accepted. Before long he had secured enough support to petition the provincial government for a railway charter. Backing him, among others, were Thomas McDonnell, a Greenwood mine operator; John Senkler, a Vancouver lawyer; James Kerr and James Dale, owners of the Carmi townsite and Butcher Boy mine along the proposed railway route; and Ralph Smailes of Greenwood. At Wood's prompting, Senkler and two others petitioned the provincial government early in 1901 to grant them authority to construct a railway west from Midway to Rock Creek then north along the Kettle River and its West Fork to the Okanagan Valley at Vernon. Their venture was to be called the Midway & Vernon Railway.[1]

In the provincial legislature the Midway & Vernon Railway proposal did not meet with the margin of support it had enjoyed in Greenwood, mainly because the M&V was not the through line to the coast the majority of members wanted. Wood argued that the M&V would open territory none of the proposed Coast-to-Kootenay railways had planned to traverse and even if a direct line were later built the M&V would remain in competition to such a line. The magic word "competition" had the desired effect upon the reluctant politicians, and on May 11, 1901 the Midway & Vernon Railway charter was granted. The company was also granted a cash subsidy of $4,000 for each mile of rail line completed. That same week James Kerr left for London with the intention of securing financing for the undertaking.

During the summer of 1901 the M&V undertook extensive surveys along the Kettle River, but no construction work was done. In fact, the M&V faded from the press limelight until December, when Wood announced that controlling interest in the company had been sold and surveys would resume within two weeks, under engineer James Coyle, in preparation for a start on construction in the spring. The announcement spurred speculation that ex-Rossland railway baron "Fritz" Heinze was the unknown purchaser of the M&V because Coyle had long been associated with Heinze. However, in time it became obvious Heinze was not involved with the M&V. Quite possibly the announcement was intended solely to keep the Midway & Vernon Railway in the news because it was apparent Kerr had returned from England empty-handed. Kerr publicly accused the CPR of scaring off British investors to prevent the rival railway from being built. His accusations probably had no basis in truth; the phenomenal financial success of the CPR was actually far more of an aid than a hindrance in the securing of foreign capital for Canadian railway speculations. A more plausible explanation for Kerr's failure was Britain's involvement in the bloody South African war at that time, which had prompted a deliberate government policy of discouraging the outflow of capital from the country.

Having failed to secure outside financing, the M&V promoters showed up on the legislature doorsteps in the spring of 1902 seeking a larger subsidy. Member D.M. Eberts, who introduced the M&V aid bill with an impressive speech expounding upon the railway's virtues, found the opposition members firing back painfully embarrassing questions directed at the railway's failure to begin construction after the granting of the previous subsidy, an almost certain sign of financial incapacity on the part of the promoters. Nevertheless, the bill eventually passed. In addition to an increased subsidy of $5,000 per mile, the Midway & Vernon Railway was granted free right-of-way through crown land and a ten-year exemption from taxes. Work was required to begin within six months of the granting of a dominion subsidy, or January 1, 1904, whichever came first.

Wood and Kerr immediately set forth again in an attempt to secure financing but met with no more success than previously. By mid-December 1903 it became obvious to them the provincial government subsidy would be lost if construction did not soon begin. Thus, they hired A.E. Ashcroft, a civil engineer of considerable reputation in the Okanagan, to prepare a portion of the right-of-way near Vernon for construction. Upon receiving instructions, Ashcroft came to Vernon with Robert Wood on December 28, 1903 and immediately began surveying a railway route from the outskirts of town southward along the west side of Kalamalka Lake. By the end of the following day he had completed the centre-line location for the first mile or so of the railway. In the meantime, Wood had persuaded one landowner along the projected railway route to permit the railway to commence work on a portion of his property pending its acquisition by the M&V. Wood had also buttonholed a man, Henry Seydel, off the streets of Vernon and appointed him superintendent in charge of the construction forces. Two days later, on January 1, 1904, the final day by which work on the railway could be started under the terms of the 1902 subsidy statute, Price Ellison, the Vernon member of the provincial legislature, fired a blast of black powder in a rock bluff on the west side of Kalamalka Lake before a large crowd of onlookers, signifying the commencement of construction.

Preservation of the Midway & Vernon Railway subsidy was thus assured. Afterwards, Wood invited all in attendance at the ceremony that afternoon to a gala dinner party back at the Kalamalka Hotel. The following week, Henry Seydel, superintendent and sole member of the M&V construction force, pushed his wheelbarrow through town to the spot where the celebration had been held the week before and began shovelling out a railway roadbed in keeping with the statute provision requiring the railway to begin construction and to ". . . prosecute the same until completed."[2] It was a meagre beginning for the "Makeshift & Visionary," the name some local resident had attached to the railway. By the end of the month the work force had doubled with the employment of a Mr. Gilroy, and the two men continued building the roadbed towards Midway. Astonishingly, they kept at it for several years. During that time, Seydel and

Gilroy managed to complete about a quarter mile of railway roadbed, all of which for almost a century remained intact on the rocky hillside above Kalamalka Lake, a forgotten monument to the Midway & Vernon Railway's perseverance.[3]

The leisurely pace set by Seydel and Gilroy might have been enough to technically fulfill the statutory requirements, but Wood knew it was hardly enough to get the railway completed in any realistic time period. In May 1904 he therefore entered into an agreement with the Atlantic Contracting Company to complete the construction work, in return for all the railway subsidies, amounting to $8,200 per mile, and 75% of the M&V stock. Atlantic Contracting failed to undertake any construction, and Wood subsequently made a similar arrangement with the New York firm of H.W. Poer & Company. One of the officials of the New York firm, A.A. Arthur, organized the Okanagan Construction Company. On July 5, 1905, Ralph Smailes signed an agreement to have the railway built by Okanagan Construction under terms similar to those signed with Atlantic Contracting the previous year. The signing of the agreement was typically "Makeshift & Visionary" in its timing, as there remained only three weeks before the expiry of the dominion government subsidy.

Within two weeks the Okanagan Construction Company awarded a subcontract to a familiar trio, the McLean Brothers, to grade the first 12 miles of roadbed from Midway to Rock Creek. On July 28, 1905—three days before the expiration of the federal subsidy—Lachlan McLean arrived in Midway. With neither plans nor surveys of the railway route, Lachlan set to work the next day at the edge of a small ridge a mile and a half west of town, no doubt hopeful this spot could be incorporated into the railway route. At first it looked as if Lachlan was heading towards Vernon at the same pace as the two men at Vernon were "racing" towards Midway. Within a few weeks the McLean work force had been enlarged to more than 200 men and grading work was proceeding along the north back of the Kettle River at a rate of several hundred feet per day.

With the rapid progress being made by the M&V, it became unpleasantly obvious to the CPR the upstart Makeshift & Visionary might indeed be able to complete its rail line. Not only did the CPR not relish the thought of future competition, it was riled by the M&V survey location west of Midway. The CPR, having learned a technique from J.J. Hill, decided physical intervention was quite appropriate under the circumstances.

The survey line the Midway & Vernon Railway crews had laid out in

October 1904 stretched from the end of the CPR track at Midway to the point where construction was started in July 1905, then continued to Rock Creek. Partway between Midway and the construction site, the M&V survey crossed the line the CPR had surveyed in 1899 as part of its own potential route through to the coast. The CPR recognized that once the M&V built over its surveyed route the CPR, if it built westward to the coast as it had promised, would be forced to either adopt a new route west of town or erect and maintain a diamond crossing with the M&V. To ensure neither possibility would occur, the CPR dispatched a work crew to Midway late in October and, without having either filed plans with government authorities or acquired right-of-way land, the crew graded a railway roadbed from the end of its trackage to a point where the CPR survey crossed the Kettle River two miles west of town. The crew laid down enough trackage on the roadbed to establish CPR priority over the M&V. However, the CPR's move to squeeze its less pretentious rival backfired rather embarrassingly: the slough grass meadow over which it had so freely graded its roadbed had been previously acquired by the M&V. This left the CPR to be packed off to court, as reported by one newspaper editor, ". . . to deal with the company upon which they were trying to play one of those smart tricks for which the C.P.R. is noted."[4]

The Midway & Vernon's action in upstaging Canada's largest corporation earned the tiny company a great deal of respect in provincial circles. Newspaper editors who had long written off the M&V as merely another of the many "paper railways" suddenly found it expedient to give the railway front-page coverage. In its headline of November 21, 1905, the *Vancouver Province* even speculated the M&V would soon build a line to Vancouver. Indeed, the M&V had officially announced it would build branch lines to Penticton and Kamloops. In October, when A.A. Arthur toured the M&V route with a large party of mining and agricultural experts, he said a line to Vancouver was not beyond consideration, a statement accepted as certain assurance the Midway & Vernon Railway would rise to become one of British Columbia's major railways.

By the end of November 1905, the McLean Brothers had completed grading from Midway to Rock Creek and sent their bill of $67,728 to the Poer Company in New York. Within a week a cheque for $10,000 arrived. A note attached to the cheque promised the balance would be forwarded immediately, along with a new contract for grading north to Westbridge. The McLean Brothers used the money to make partial payment to their workmen. But when neither the outstanding payment nor the promised contract arrived by December most of the men drifted away to other railway work. Initially, the McLean Brothers were not concerned about this delay, as there was a rumour prevalent in railway circles that J.J. Hill was negotiating to buy out the M&V, thus forestalling all the company's business pending the finalization of the sale. However, late in January 1906, the editor of the *Vancouver World* made the shattering accusation that the delay had nothing to do with J.J. Hill. The editor opined that the New York backers of the M&V had been scared away as a result of private statements by a government minister that the provincial government would not honour the M&V subsidy. Even without waiting to find out if these allegations were true, the citizens of Midway, Greenwood and Vernon were ready to scalp the minister responsible. Only by some tactful political manoeuvres by Premier McBride was a major government crisis averted. McBride recommended the question of the subsidy's validity be referred to the Supreme Court, promising to honour the subsidy if the court rendered a favourable verdict.

On March 27, 1906, the Midway & Vernon Railway subsidy case opened in the Supreme Court in Victoria. The crown prosecutor argued the single blast at Vernon on January 1, 1904, and the meagre exploits of Seydel and Gilroy, did not meet the government's idea of serious railway construction. The M&V counsel rebutted that the amount of work done was immaterial; the railway had, strictly speaking, been under continuous construction since January 1904. More importantly, the company had recently stepped up construction to a rate comparable to railway work undertaken by the CPR or GN. A.E. Ashcroft, Henry Seydel and Lachlan McLean were called to give testimony regarding their contribution to the railway work. The chief justice was obviously impressed by their statements and the following day rendered judgement in favour of the company. Smailes and Wood left the courtroom gleefully promising active construction would resume within 60 days. It was said the saloons in the Boundary District remained open all that night in celebration.

The next 60 days passed without resumption of construction. A short time later, on June 8, 1906, Smailes and Wood announced that 14,000 tons of rails, sufficient for the entire railway between Midway and Vernon, had just been ordered from the Dominion Iron & Steel Company in Nova Scotia. The announcement further stated that grading would be resumed by the end of June. The news was reassuring to residents of the Boundary

District, but June passed into July and July passed into August without any work being done. The M&V stayed in the news throughout the fall as a result of repeated rumours that other railways were attempting to buy out the line. In reality, the rumours were merely the twitching convulsions of a railway corporation that had died. The New York backers of the M&V, either as a result of the alleged statements or some other unknown reason, never fulfilled their promised contract, nor did they repay the McLean Brothers the money earned. Work never resumed.

In the several years that followed, the graded roadbed west of Midway deteriorated. Most of it would later be repaired and incorporated into the Kettle Valley Railway when that company built from Midway to Penticton, although portions of the original M&V roadbed are still visible almost a century later.[5] The Midway & Vernon Railway Company itself ended its days in the Defunct Railway Companies Dissolution Act of 1927; there, its name lies thoughtlessly thrown in among the scores of now-forgotten railways lining the pages of the act. Most of those railway companies never advanced beyond their statute of incorporation. For them, no further epitaph is warranted. Perhaps the Midway & Vernon Railway deserves at least a footnote. This was one "paper railway" that almost made it.

6: Steel Trail to Nicola

The CPR builds the Nicola Branch, later part of the Kettle Valley Railway

West of Grand Forks and the Boundary District where Tracy Holland was building his Kettle River Valley Railway early in the twentieth century, another region began attracting the interest of railway builders. Like the Boundary and Kootenay Districts before it, the drawing power of this new area—called the Nicola District—was the bountiful mineral wealth of a generous Creator. Here in the Nicola District, 200 miles west of the Kettle Valley Railway's birthplace, another line of that railway's later empire was to be constructed.

The Nicola District, comprised primarily of high, rolling hills and jack-pine-dotted plateau country, is loosely snuggled between the rim of the Okanagan Valley on the east and the Cascade Mountains on the west. The district's principal river, like the region itself, takes its name from an aberrant tribute to N'Kwala, an early chief of the Okanagan tribes, and cuts a natural pathway through the plateau in its relatively brief 50-mile journey north and west to the Thompson River at Spences Bridge. At several points along the river, tributary streams have also cut through the plateau, creating other pathways and exposing the deep seams of bituminous coal underlying the valley basin. Thus, the railway builders were provided with both motive, in the form of coal, and natural pathways, created by the river valleys, to spur their enterprise.

Long before recorded history, the native inhabitants of the Nicola Valley were aware of the region's coal outcroppings and did not need the white man's instruction to recognize that this "black earth" was useful. Gold rush miners also used the coal in their blacksmith shops. However, the coal exposures escaped official recording prior to 1872, when members of the Sandford Fleming survey expedition stumbled across the outcroppings while seeking a route for the proposed transcontinental rail-way. For Fleming, the find was significant. It was obvious to him the pro-posed railway would need coal for its locomotives, coal that would have to come from Alberta or Vancouver Island if a coal source contingent to the railway could not be found. Shipping the coal such a distance was an extra cost the railway no doubt would wish to avoid. Thus Fleming had reason to be encouraged by the discovery of coal on one of the potential railway routes. He was especially encouraged by the fact the coal lay on the short-est of all routes surveyed across British Columbia, that via Nicola Lake and Coquihalla Pass.

These two considerations led Fleming to return to the Nicola Valley in 1874 for a much more detailed survey. However, the results of this new survey were disappointing. Despite the easy character of much of the pro-jected route, the 35-mile steep descent through rugged Coquihalla Pass was deemed to make it less suitable for the transcontinental railway than the longer water grade route along the Thompson and Fraser Rivers. So the latter route was ultimately adopted. The CPR also decided that coal for its locomotives would come from the Vancouver Island mines of the Dunsmuir family or the mines of Lethbridge, not from the Nicola Valley.

Nevertheless, interest in a railway to the Nicola Valley was not lost. Early in 1891, a group of mainly Ontario businessmen submitted a peti-tion to the provincial government requesting the incorporation of their Nicola, Kamloops & Similkameen Coal & Railway Company, with author-ity to build a railway south from the CPR at Kamloops through the Nicola Valley to Princeton and Osoyoos. Included in the list of petitioners were John Fall Allison, a leading Princeton citizen; A.E. Howse of Nicola Lake; Charles Keefer, a noted civil engineer; and Sandford Fleming, who was the first to recognize the potential of the Nicola coal fields. William Hamilton Merritt, a mining engineer for whom the principal community of the Nicola Valley would later be named, was also a member of the syndicate. Completing the list were numerous other engineers, financial agents and lawyers with an enviable list of achievements. Much impressed, the provincial government granted the group their charter on April 20, 1891.

That same day, the government also chartered the Nicola Valley Railway. This was a hastily conceived proposal, apparently put forth by an agent of the CPR in answer to the challenge of the NK&S. The Nicola Valley Railway was authorized to build a 50-mile branch line from the CPR mainline at Spences Bridge up the valley of the Nicola River to the

Nicola coalfields. Also authorized was a 20-mile extension southwest up the valley of the Coldwater River to Voght Creek, where another coal seam had been discovered. This simultaneous chartering of two rival corporations made a race for the Nicola Valley appear to be imminent. However, when it became obvious the NK&S was having difficulties securing financing, the Nicola Valley Railway adopted the "hurry up and wait" policy often displayed by its sponsoring corporation. No action was taken. Two years later, when the 1893 depression hit Canada, the CPR promptly abandoned any interest in the region and ungratefully tossed the Nicola Valley Railway charter back to the promoters who had secured it on the CPR's behalf.[1]

In the midst of a severe depression, the Nicola Valley Railway promoters were left in an unenviable position, but they boldly announced in December 1893 that construction of the railway would soon be started. Surprisingly enough, they were correct. On April 17, 1894, just three days before the construction deadline of the Nicola Valley Railway charter, a prestigious ceremony was held on the outskirts of Spences Bridge, at which R.A. Anderson turned over a dusty clump of dry-belt bunch grass to herald the promised commencement of construction. Thus began—and ended—the story of the Nicola Valley Railway. Nothing more was ever done. The NVR charter, saved by that single sod turning, was left to expire for want of further construction.

During the next decade nothing positive was done towards securing rail access into the Nicola Valley, but not because interest in a Nicola Valley railway had waned. With each year, agitation for railway connections grew more vocal, and the mere sight of CPR engineers laying out the survey line from the Kootenays through the Nicola Valley to Spences Bridge in 1900 was enough to triple real estate values throughout the valley. This presence also spurred the dominion government to conduct a detailed geological survey of the valley's mineral resources. After a major drilling program, the government announced that numerous seams of high quality bituminous coal had been located at shallow depths. Probable coal reserves were set at 175 million tons, an impressive statistic for the railway advocates. Significant copper finds at Aspen Grove, on the lip of the plateau south of Nicola, and at Guichon Creek, west of Nicola Lake, were also reported. The many ranches of the plateau country, most notably the great Douglas Lake Ranch, added to the potential rail business.

Early in 1903, increasing demands for a railway into the Nicola Valley led William Hamilton Merritt, who was one of the few remaining members of the original Nicola, Kamloops & Similkameen Coal & Railway Company syndicate, to petition the provincial government for revival of his company's charter. In addition, Merritt requested statutory authority to add a Nicola Lake-Spences Bridge line to the list of projected undertakings of the NK&S. Although Merritt was in no better financial position than he had been 12 years earlier, he at least recognized the potential value of an active charter. This the CPR did not. It had neglectfully allowed the powers of the Nicola Valley Railway to lapse and ignored the pleas of Nicola Valley residents for a rail connection. Ignored, that is, until one spring morning in 1905 when James Dunsmuir vengefully locked out his Vancouver Island coal miners when they dared to seek a 25-cents-per-day increase in wages, thus threatening to leave every CPR locomotive firebox in the province stone cold for want of coal. That afternoon the only sound louder than the noise of trainloads of Alberta coal rumbling into British Columbia was the noise of CPR executives rapping on Merritt's office door.

Merritt knew the CPR faced a long wait before it could secure government resurrection of its expired Nicola Valley Railway charter. Thus, he coolly refused the CPR's offer to buy out his railway charter. Likewise he refused the CPR's second and third offer. Only after the CPR had raised its offer to several times its opening position did Merritt consent, and even then he would only give the CPR a lease of his charter, not an outright sale.[2] Because of this stance, Merritt retained his official position with the NK&S, but effective control of the company passed to the CPR. Within two weeks, crews were at work resurveying the line established in 1900. Tenders for construction contracts were also quickly called.

Simultaneous with its call for contract tenders, the CPR filed legal notice it intended to seek dominion government approval to extend the line from its authorized, but not built, eastern terminus at Osoyoos to a connection with its own line in the Boundary District, an announcement heralded with great excitement in Vancouver. When questioned, CPR president Thomas Shaughnessy affirmed the company's intention to build: "...preparations are being made for a gradual extension through the Similkameen Valley with the ultimate intention of reaching Midway."[3]

However, Shaughnessy emphasized the words "gradual" and "ultimate" in his statement. He said immediate attention would be given only to construction of the line as far as Nicola Lake, adding that the contract for construction of the entire 47 miles of railway had been awarded.[4] Although a few sections of heavy rockwork and one tunnel were involved in the first 20 miles from Spences Bridge, and eight crossings of the Nicola River were required, the line was projected to be of generally moderate construction. Maximum grade for the line was to be 1.0%, relatively light for British Columbia's rugged terrain.

Shortly after the contract had been awarded, men began arriving at Spences Bridge to work on the railway's construction. On June 20, 1905, the second sod on the Spences Bridge-Nicola railway was turned, 11 years after the first, at the west face of the bluff through which was to be driven the line's only tunnel. Within a month, more than 1,500 men were at work. Ironically, many of the railway workers were locked-out Vancouver Island coal miners who hoped to get back at Dunsmuir by helping build the railway designed to end his lucrative coastal coal monopoly. This action spurred James Dunsmuir to visit the Nicola Valley early in the fall, amid speculation he was there to buy out the coal basin and thereby eliminate any threat to his coastal coal business. But Dunsmuir declined to purchase any coal properties. After his visit he declared that the Nicola Valley possessed no future whatever. This pronouncement earned Dunsmuir a hot editorial from the local newsmonger, who predicted that Dunsmuir's "three hour careful examination" of the Nicola Valley was hardly sufficient for him to properly appraise a community whose thousand coke ovens would soon be supplying fuel for a dozen copper smelters.[5]

Grading work on the railway continued steadily through the fall and winter. On January 8, 1906, tracklaying began at Spences Bridge, using CPR locomotive 25, a derelict 4-4-0 that had been mothballed in the Vancouver yard for some time.[6] Track was quickly pushed up the first ten miles, where it was delayed until the middle of March while boring of the tunnel was completed. Once through the tunnel, tracklaying crews should have had an easy task. However, an acute shortage of both labour and crossties seriously curtailed the rate of progress and, even by very widely spacing the ties, the railway did not reach Alexander Coutlee's ranch at mile 37 until early June.[7] The fact that Dunsmuir's mines had resumed supplying coal to the CPR seemed to lessen the urgency of completing the railway.

That summer, with track as far as Coutlee, the residents of the Nicola Valley were confident the remaining ten miles of line to Nicola would soon be complete and the line in operation. Opening of the railway for regular service had to be delayed until sufficient ties could be found to bring the line up to standard for government inspection. Therefore, it wasn't until October 31, 1906 that the government approved the Spences Bridge-Coutlee section for operation, and even then the approval was only for freight service. Two days later, tracklaying on the entire line was completed to Nicola, but the Coutlee-Nicola section had also to be upgraded before approval for operations could be granted. The entire railway did not open for regular freight and passenger operation until early in April 1907.[8]

Simultaneous with the completion of tracklaying in November, the CPR announced that when the projected extension along the shore of Nicola Lake to Quilchena and eastward to Midway was undertaken, the community of Nicola would be made a divisional point on the railway. In fact, a station, freight shed, wye, water tower and two-stall engine house were already under construction. To the citizens of Nicola, the promise of becoming a railway divisional point, combined with the frequent appearances of survey crews along Quilchena Creek, was enough to offset the fact that Merritt, seven miles to the west, was rapidly denigrating Nicola to second place as the principal community of the Nicola Valley. The survey work was also assuring enough to Joseph Guichon that he erected a plush hotel at Quilchena in the belief the railway would soon provide him with ample patronage. Until the day of the railway's arrival, Guichon too would have to wait and watch while Merritt dominated the valley's trade and commerce.

The reason for Merritt's rise to prominence in the Nicola Valley was its bountiful coal resources. By the time the CPR's branch line was completed, four coal companies had been incorporated to exploit the newly accessible resources. The first company to actually undertake any physical work in the Nicola Valley was the Diamond Vale Coal & Iron Mines Limited, which had acquired large coal holdings throughout the valley. Early in 1906, the company did major prospecting work on its claim on the south side of the railway line, about a mile east of Merritt. Shortly afterwards, work was begun in cutting a shaft. The next company to begin work was the Nicola Valley Coal & Coke Company. In November of 1906, a syndicate headed by John Hendry—J.J. Hill's right-hand man in the province—bought out the Nicola Coal & Iron Company, which had been incorporated several years earlier but had not done any work on its holdings. The syndicate reorganized it as the Nicola Valley Coal & Coke

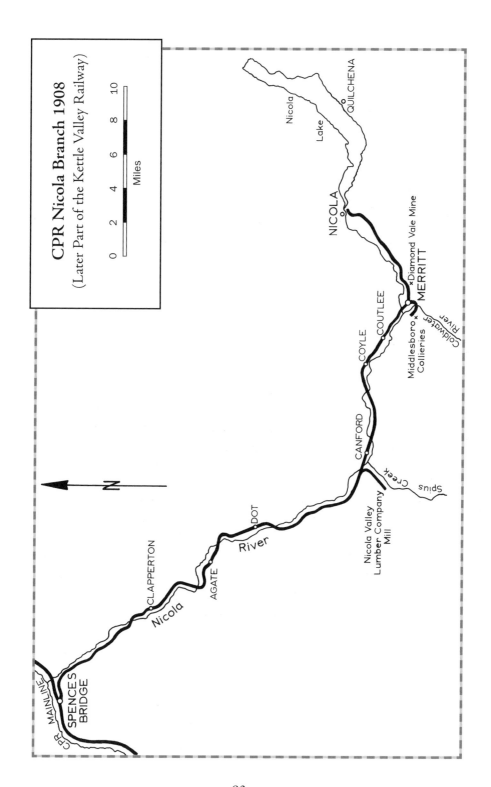

CPR Nicola Branch 1908
(Later Part of the Kettle Valley Railway)

Miles
0   2   4   6   8   10

N

SPENCES BRIDGE
MAINLINE
CPR
CLAPPERTON
Nicola
AGATE
River
DOT
Nicola Valley
Lumber Company
Mill
CANFORD
Spius Creek
COYLE
COUTLEE
Middlesboro
Collieries
MERRITT
Diamond Vale Mine
Coldwater River
NICOLA
QUILCHENA
Nicola
Lake

Company and opened a mine at Coal Gully, on the hillside across the Coldwater River from Merritt. This shaft quickly proved very promising and, by early January 1907, enough coal was being taken from the main shaft of the Coal Gully mine to supply the town's winter fuel needs.

On January 8, 1907, a special train brought a sizeable group of CPR and mining experts to the Nicola Valley Coal & Coke Company mine and, as a demonstration, a sample load of coal was tested in a CPR locomotive for the first time. The locomotive crew pronounced that the coal was the best they had ever used. Consequently, as of January 22, 1907, when the first load of coal left the Nicola Valley, the CPR did its best to secure the mine's entire output for its coal chutes on the mainline as far east as Revelstoke and for its boats on Okanagan Lake. Because the mine was located across the Coldwater River from Merritt, loading cars posed somewhat of a problem at first. But the CPR soon built a bridge and spur line to the mine tipple. By the year's end the Coal Gully mine, or Middlesboro Collieries as it soon became known, was turning out 225 tons of coal per day.

Quickly following the growth of the Merritt coal mines was the industry that was ultimately to usurp coal mining as the principal industry of the Nicola Valley, lumbering. The demand for railway crossties and mine timbers provided an instant market for the products of the interior forests, and numerous sawmills quickly sprang up along the railway. The largest and most important of the mills was the Nicola Valley Lumber Company. Begun by a Connecticut immigrant named Henry Meeker, who would dominate the lumber industry of the Nicola Valley for a quarter century, the Nicola Valley Lumber Company opened a large mill in May 1908 on the south side of the railway at Canford, ten miles below Merritt. This site was chosen for the proximity of Spius Creek, which could be utilized for floating logs down to the mill from the higher elevations, where the more plentiful rainfall produced larger trees. Logs were also floated down the Nicola River to the mill, although to a much lesser extent. The ease with which the rivers could be used in this manner obviated the need for transporting logs by rail. Not until about five years later, when most of the easily accessible timber had been cut, did the railway secure any appreciable volume of log traffic.

The forest industry of the Nicola Valley assured the CPR of about ten cars of sawn lumber per day. The coal industry provided about the same number of cars of coal. Along with the seasonal movement of cattle from the plateau ranches, this traffic made the daily mixed train between Merritt and Spences Bridge both lengthy and slow. The citizens of Merritt constantly campaigned for separate freight and passenger train service, but except for a brief period of CPR benevolence during the construction of the Kettle Valley Railway from 1911 to 1914, mixed train service was the only regular passenger service that would operate throughout most of the line's history.

Because of Merritt's rapid growth, the CPR let contracts in February 1908 for the construction of a station at Merritt to replace the boxcar that had served as the railway office for the first ten months of the operation.[9] Several spur tracks, wye and a locomotive water tank were also built. Despite these moves, the citizens of Nicola did not lose hope of seeing their community outgrow Merritt once Nicola became the promised divisional point on the railway extension to Midway. Hopes were especially high during the spring of 1908 because the CPR resumed survey work east of Nicola. But the Merritt newspaper editor, who had no further use for Nicola after having moved his presses to the larger community, merely ho-hummed, "Construction is once more an assured fact" and continued about his daily business of reporting the local gossip.[10]

Of much more interest to the citizens of Merritt early in 1908 was the news that John Hendry and W.H. Armstrong, of the Nicola Valley Coal & Coke Company, had been granted a railway charter by the provincial government to build their proposed Vancouver & Nicola Valley Railway from Merritt through Coquihalla Pass to the coast. This news probably excited the general populace unnecessarily. The chartering of the railway was almost certainly a ruse by Hendry to lever the CPR into lowering its rates for hauling coal to the coast to enable Nicola Valley coal to be competitive with coal from Dunsmuir's mines. Hendry no doubt reasoned that the threat of bringing his ally, J.J. Hill, into Merritt would pressure the CPR into lowering its rates. The tactic was partially successful, as the CPR promptly slashed rates on nearly everything into and out of Merritt. However, the coal rate was not reduced. The CPR held its rate firmly at $2.00 per ton to the coast. Many people, especially those with an interest in the Nicola Valley coal mines, accused Dunsmuir of influencing the CPR decision. A far more plausible explanation was that the CPR kept up its coal tariff to ensure access to most of the coal produced by the Middlesboro mine for use in its own locomotives rather than consignment to the coast for sale there. The generous rate reduction on other commodities probably resulted from a fear Hill might indeed get a railway into the one region of southern British Columbia the CPR could call its own.

Hill never did build into the Nicola Valley. During 1909 both the Canadian Northern Pacific Railway and the Grand Trunk Pacific Railway investigated using the Nicola Lake-Coquihalla Pass route laid out by Sandford Fleming as a possible route to the coast, but they too never built trackage there. Thus, unlike most of the territory of southern British Columbia, the Nicola Valley was one region of southern British Columbia that Canadian Pacific never had to share with any rival.

Despite the CPR monopoly, the Nicola Valley prospered as a result of its railway. It prospered even more when, true to Shaughnessy's earlier promises, the CPR rail line in the Nicola Valley was extended through to Midway as part of the Kettle Valley Railway after the CPR acquired, renamed and expanded the old Kettle River Valley Railway centred at Grand Forks. When the rail line was extended, it was built southward from Merritt up the Coldwater Valley, not eastward from Nicola via Quilchena Creek. Because of that decision, the seven-mile section of track between Merritt and Nicola fell into disuse while through trains bypassed it on their way east or to the coast. Nicola, with its dream of becoming an important divisional point on the CPR shattered, gradually passed into virtual oblivion, a forgotten remnant at the end of a discarded railway.[11]

Despite that rejection, Nicola remains. Many of its original buildings are still standing, and many are occupied and well maintained. The Quilchena Hotel also remains, with Joseph Guichon's portrait still hanging by the staircase just as it did a century ago. Majestically, his hotel remains open for business, with most of its original furnishings just as they were when he first installed them. It is a magnificent heritage preserved in suspended animation, untouched by the passage of so many years. Perhaps—just perhaps—it is still waiting for the railway that will now never come.

Slide Creek Bridge at mile 31.8 Coquihalla Subdivision under construction, September 1915. The wooden falsework will support the steel truss members until the entire span has been completed, after which it will be removed. This through truss span was 320 feet long, making it the longest single span on any bridge on the KVR. PHOTO COURTESY ANDREW MCCULLOCH FOUNDATION

Snowsheds in Coquihalla Pass, December 1915. Shed 1 at mile 23.8 Coquihalla Subdivision appears near the centre of the photo, with Sheds 2 through 4 to the left. PHOTO COURTESY ANDREW MCCULLOCH FOUNDATION

The winter of 1915-16 produced the heaviest aggregate snowfall ever recorded in Coquihalla Pass—67 feet. In this photo taken in December 1915 workers struggle to clear away a snowslide at partially completed Shed 12 at mile 26.6 in hope of completing the snowshed—and the railway—that year. They were successful at neither; a few days later construction work was abandoned until May 1916. PHOTO COURTESY ANDREW MCCULLOCH FOUNDATION

The severity of the winter of 1915-16 is clearly evident in this photo taken in Coquihalla Pass in early July 1916, just three weeks before the Coquihalla line officially opened. Snow from the previous winter still covers Shed 12, which was damaged by a snowslide that struck it in December before it had been completed.
PHOTO COURTESY ANDREW MCCULLOCH FOUNDATION

The bridge over the Coquihalla River at mile 49.7 Coquihalla Subdivision between two of the Quintette Tunnels. This deck truss span was salvaged from another rail line, as wartime shortages forced the KVR to use a "temporary" bridge until better times. In reality the bridge was never replaced, and it is now a footbridge in Coquihalla Canyon Provincial Park. PHOTO COURTESY ANDREW MCCULLOCH FOUNDATION

"Rough quarries, rocks and hills whose heads touch heaven" Shakespeare's words so inspired Andrew McCulloch that the passing track immediately east of this location was named Othello in honour of the Bard's immortal work. Here the Quintette Tunnels pierced the "rocks and hills" of Coquihalla Canyon in perfect tangent alignment.

The bridge over the Coquihalla River at mile 49.7 Coquihalla Subdivision, the same bridge that appears on a previous page. The west portal of Quintette Tunnel 12 appears on the right. This area is now part of the Coquihalla Canyon Provincial Park, and the impressive nature of the canyon in this photo makes it obvious why the park is one of the most popular in British Columbia. PHOTO COURTESY ANDREW MCCULLOCH FOUNDATION

Coquihalla Pass looking eastward along the railway towards Tunnel 7 at mile 27.6 Coquihalla Subdivision. This photo was taken before the rail line opened in July 1916 because the telegraph line has not yet been installed. PHOTO COURTESY ANDREW MCCULLOCH FOUNDATION

This photo of the magnificent deck truss and timber frame trestle across Bridalveil Creek at mile 21.2 Coquihalla Subdivision amply portrays the extreme beauty and ruggedness of Coquihalla Pass. This bridge was one of the longest surviving structures following the abandonment of the rail line, collapsing sometime between September 1995 and May 1996.

PHOTO BY BARRIE SANFORD

Following the officially opening of the KVR in May 1915 mixed freight and passenger train service was the only passenger service offered for much of the first year. In this photo an eastbound mixed train crosses the trestle over No Name Creek near Jellicoe. PHOTO COURTESY PROVINCIAL ARCHIVES OF BRITISH COLUMBIA

Crews install telegraph poles at mile 21.4 Coquihalla Subdivision, 1916. Tunnel 4 was planned at this location but poor rock conditions resulted in the KVR excavating an open cut instead. The site later became known as Hayden's Cut, after Augusto Taylor Hayden, the first KVR operating employee killed in Coquihalla Pass. PHOTO COURTESY ANDREW MCCULLOCH FOUNDATION

Incola Hotel, Penticton. This was the only hotel owned or operated by the Kettle Valley Railway and was patterned after the very successful CPR resort hotels of the Rocky Mountains.
PHOTO COURTESY ANDREW MCCULLOCH FOUNDATION

Fraser River Bridge at Hope, looking towards the townsite. Trains used the lower deck of the bridge and roadway traffic on the Trans-Canada Highway the upper deck. The mile 163 marker on the bridge reflects the fact mileages on the Coquihalla Subdivision were originally measured from Penticton, not Brookmere as was later adopted. PHOTO COURTESY ANDREW MCCULLOCH FOUNDATION

An eastbound Kettle Valley Railway passenger train poses for a photo on West Fork Canyon Creek trestle at mile 87.9 Carmi Subdivision in Myra Canyon on its way from Penticton to Midway about 1918.

Not all of the Kettle Valley Railway passed through rugged mountain canyons. This view of the tracks and Otter Lake near Tulameen about 1918 shows the subdued beauty of the land in the lee of the Hope Mountains. PHOTO COURTESY ANDREW MCCULLOCH FOUNDATION

One can almost sense the feeling of frustration in maintenance crews faced with repairing the bridge over the Kettle River at mile 15.5 Carmi Subdivision in the spring of 1918. Logs floating down the river jammed up against the bridge and caused the river to undermine the east abutment of the bridge, allowing the end of one of the spans to fall into the river. PHOTO COURTESY PENTICTON MUSEUM

Fill being placed on the Copper Mountain line, probably 1918. Although a dinky gasoline engine appears to be assisting the men, the work is still being done primarily by human and animal labour, just as the earlier portions of the Kettle Valley Railway. PHOTO COURTESY ANDREW MCCULLOCH FOUNDATION

A work train poses on the 765-foot long wooden frame trestle over Smelter Flat at mile 10.0 Copper Mountain Subdivision about the time of the line's opening in October 1920. PHOTO COURTESY ANDREW MCCULLOCH FOUNDATION

Honeysuckle Creek bridge at mile 11.9 Copper Mountain Subdivision, 1920. The area near here was one of the most problematic on the Kettle Valley Railway because of unstable ground.
PHOTO COURTESY ANDREW MCCULLOCH FOUNDATION

Tunnel Bluff on the Copper Mountain rail line, viewed looking north, 1920. Tunnel 4 appears near the centre of the photo, with Tunnels 2 and 3 in the distance. This photo shows the difficult terrain traversed by the Copper Mountain branch line. PHOTO COURTESY ANDREW MCCULLOCH FOUNDATION

Coquihalla Pass, May 1921, following one of many perilous winters. The view is looking westward towards Shed 12 as crews hike through the pass to determine if it is safe to begin clearing the rail line. The man in the photo may be Andrew McCulloch, who was leading the expedition. PHOTO COURTESY ANDREW MCCULLOCH FOUNDATION

Crews battle to clear snow from the east portal of Shed 14 following the big snow of January 1935. The wooden box beside the locomotive likely contained explosives for loosening ice and hard packed snow.
PHOTO FROM THE COLLECTION OF BARRIE SANFORD

Crews take a moment to pose for the camera at the west end of Shed 3 at Romeo while salvaging the contents of a derailed boxcar, January 1935. The cable in the photo holds the boxcar from falling into the canyon. Bill Presley, who sits facing the camera, rose to the ranks of a general manager of the CPR.
PHOTO FROM THE COLLECTION OF BARRIE SANFORD

Kettle Valley Railway employees pose on engine 3454 in the Penticton yard about 1922.

7: The Battle of Midway–and Elsewhere

Southern British Columbia 1904 to 1909

Following the CPR's arrival at Midway in 1900, the passage of nearly a decade had measured little progress in the task of completing a Canadian-controlled rail line across southern British Columbia. True, there were some concrete achievements. The Kettle River Valley Railway had constructed modest track mileage in the Grand Forks area, the CPR had nudged a rail line east from Spences Bridge to Nicola, and the Midway & Vernon Railway had graded ten miles of railway roadbed in the Boundary District, all of which would ultimately form part of the rail system stretching across southern British Columbia. But these railway contributions were minor compared with the nearly 300 miles of rugged mountain terrain separating Midway from the coast. They were minor, too, when compared with the progress the American, J.J. Hill, had made in strengthening his position in southern British Columbia.

Hill's railway construction in the province, like that of the CPR, had temporarily peaked at the turn of the century, and then languished, partly as a result of the unstable political atmosphere. But early in 1904, Hill forcefully and dramatically ended the lull in the province's railway construction.

His first construction effort was to extend the tracks of his New Westminster Southern into Vancouver from where it has dead-ended in 1891 on the south bank of the Fraser River opposite New Westminster. By the end of the year, Hill was also into the Crows Nest with a railway. He then pushed his trackage into the copper camp at Phoenix and bought heavily into the Granby Consolidated Mining & Smelting Company, which controlled the principal Phoenix mine and Grand Forks smelter. In response, the CPR slashed its Phoenix ore rate from $1.00 to 25 cents per ton, but it never recovered the business taken by Hill. Using the easier grades of his Great Northern mainline, Hill also snatched away the CPR's highly profitable business of hauling Fernie coal to the Grand Forks smelter. Thus, in a span of less than six months, Hill had acquired the best of the CPR's southern British Columbia freight trade. Not content with this savagery of the CPR, Hill announced in December 1904 that he would immediately start construction of his projected railway along the Kettle River from Curlew west to the coast.

After a decade of great effort and expense on the part of the CPR to win the Kootenays and the Boundary District at least partly over to Canadian control, its management was highly alarmed by the dramatic return of virtually complete American domination. Surprisingly, the first public reaction came not from the CPR but from a virtually forgotten man, Daniel Corbin. Of course, the CPR did not consider Corbin one of its best friends. But Corbin had a personal score to settle with Hill and he believed the CPR's current hatred for Hill would overshadow any lingering resentments against himself. More specifically, Corbin believed the CPR would now take a radically different view towards a railway connection with Spokane than it had a decade earlier.

What Corbin envisioned was a railway between Spokane and the Kootenays, not for carrying away Kootenay ore but for carrying Spokane trade to the CPR, thereby allowing Spokane to break free from the effective monopoly which Hill's GN and NP held upon the Inland Empire capital. On January 19, 1905, Corbin formally announced he would charter and build just such a railway from Spokane to a connection with the CPR's Crows Nest line west of Cranbrook. Corbin chose for his railway the stately name the Spokane International Railway. True to his prediction, the CPR received his proposition with enthusiasm. Hill's "theft" of its best trade had given the CPR a thirst for vengeance, and caution was thrown to the wind. The CPR immediately advanced funds to Corbin. The little war that Hill had started at Sandon a decade earlier had suddenly become very big.

The CPR's open alliance with Corbin was quickly countered by Hill's reaffirmation of his promise to push the VV&E line through to the coast. His son, Louis Hill, telegraphed the Victoria Board of Trade on April 14, 1905 assuring the line would be completed to Princeton by the end of summer and shortly thereafter pushed through to the coast. In his telegram Louis Hill casually added that "for the purpose of avoiding difficulties in construction" it would be necessary to divert a portion of the railway between Midway and the Okanagan Valley through the United States.[1] He further stated that an application for approval of the proposed diversion was being submitted to Ottawa.

James and Louis Hill may have expected universal approval from British Columbians for their commitment to push ahead with a railway connecting the coast and the Kootenays. However, actual response was noticeably lukewarm. The Great Northern's "theft" of the CPR's coal and copper traffic was proving to be more than just a deserving loss to a heartless corporation, which had been the opinion of some British Columbians at the time. The loss of trade represented a genuine privation to the economy of southern British Columbia, and a personal hardship to each of the many Canadian railroaders who had been laid off as a result. Many British Columbians feared that Hill's request to build a portion of the Coast-to-Kootenay line through the United States would only amplify the loss of Canadian trade. The fact that construction of the line between Princeton and the coast was promised only after completion of the line in the Similkameen Valley, not simultaneous with it, generated fears Hill might build only enough of the railway to make the Similkameen tributary to Spokane without completion of the line through to the coast. The *Victoria Colonist*—the same paper that had previously termed Hill's entry into southern British Columbia an invasion—described the Great Northern's rapidly expanding lines in the southern interior "like so many fingers on a hand, with the State of Washington as the palm."[2] The paper recommended Ottawa completely reject the proposed amendment to the VV&E charter permitting the American diversion.

In May 1905, the bill proposing amendment to the VV&E charter was placed before the House of Commons Railway Committee. It was obvious many of the Committee members shared the fears expressed by the *Victoria Colonist*. But J.J. Hill also had supporters. Most British Columbians had come to realize from the years of railway wars that when Hill built a rail line the CPR was invariably right behind with a railway of its own. Therefore, if it came down to a choice of two railroads or none, Hill had their vote. Residents of the Similkameen Valley in particular were solidly behind Hill. For them, a railway was a railway, and they were considerably less fussy about who built it than the armchair critics of the coast cites, most of whom were well served by several railways and marine services. Of course, the CPR did its best to block the bill's passage. But Hill merely left the charter amendment matter in the hands of his lawyers and set to work building the railway with his usual crass confidence that his lawyers would get the necessary approvals. On May 24, 1905, while the Parliamentarians in Ottawa debated the virtues of his railway, Hill awarded the first contract to have it built.

Hill's opponents cited his blatant contempt of formal procedures as justifiable cause for rejection of his request. However, on June 27, 1905 the bill passed the Railway Committee, with all British Columbia members in support. A group of British Columbians petitioned Prime Minister Laurier, asking him to require Hill to build through to the coast before allowing him to connect with lines in the United States, but because Hill sought no government assistance in building his rail line, Laurier moved to allow Hill a free hand. Late in July, despite three months of delaying tactics by the VV&E's opponents, the bill finally passed Parliament. By this time the legal authorization was only academic; Hill's construction crews were already across the boundary into Canada!

Also late in July, Hill awarded a second contract for the construction of a portion of the rail line between Curlew and the coast. On September 29, 1905 he made a personal appearance in Vancouver, promising to have the VV&E across the Hope Mountains ahead of any line the CPR might build. In his lengthy address to the citizens of Vancouver, Hill assured them the frequently expressed fears of the continuation of American domination of southern British Columbia were unfounded. What had prevented the natural gravitation of inland trade to the Vancouver tidewater terminus, Hill asserted, was the lack of a direct rail connection with the interior. His VV&E would soon provide that connection. "It will be an all-Canadian line, with terminals at Vancouver," he pledged, adding, "Mark my word: We will do more to upbuild Vancouver than any railway corporation has done yet."[3]

Strictly speaking, Hill was not correct in stating his VV&E rail line would be an all-Canadian line because it would have a number of short diversions through the United States between the coast and the Kootenays. That minor discrepancy did not deter Vancouver's wild jubilation over his announcement. The *Vancouver Province* headlined in its largest type: "Hill Says Vancouver will be the Terminus!" That same day, in its editorial, the paper further wrote of Hill: "He speaks in a low tone and with the directness and precision that indicates a mind that knows its mental processes and is sure of its facts."[4]

The obvious snub of the CPR in Hill's Vancouver speech did nothing to ease the bitter feelings existing between the Great Northern and the CPR. This bitterness became even more acute barely a month later when the greatest outburst of violence in the gang war history of the two rivals occurred near Midway. The episode started on September 30, 1905 when a crew of CPR men erected a fence of heavy timbers, liberally posted with signs prohibiting trespass, across the railway grade being built by Hill's VV&E about four miles west of Midway, at a point where the line was within a few hundred feet of the international boundary. The CPR alleged the VV&E grade at this point was being constructed across a small parcel of land the CPR received as part of the Columbia & Western Railway land grant, land the VV&E had neglected to secure from the CPR before proceeding with construction. Later that day, a squad of VV&E men who discovered the fence pulled it down. When they returned the following morning, they discovered the fence had been reconstructed and was now guarded by some 50 armed CPR men. After viewing this armed encampment the VV&E's chief engineer, James H. Kennedy, decided the grading work a few miles up the line was suddenly more pressing, and he ordered his crews transferred. He also wired Hill.

Upon receiving Kennedy's report, Hill went through the legal formality of requesting that the CPR sell the VV&E the disputed property. Since he already knew what the CPR's answer would be, he simultaneously filed an application for expropriation. The CPR legally could not stop Hill from expropriating the tiny plot of land in question, but it undertook every possible means to drag out the necessary court proceedings. Hill promptly struck back by buying out several pieces of land strategically located along the CPR's survey line near Princeton, and threatened ". . . that some sweet day he may use these to retaliate for obstructive methods adopted at Midway and elsewhere."[5]

It took the VV&E over a month to secure the expropriation order and, even when it was finally granted on November 4, 1905, Hill found the CPR unwilling to order its men to vacate the disputed land. The CPR claimed the order specified a parcel of land different than the one being disputed. Hill concluded the CPR was merely being obstructive. Perhaps purposely, he waited three days until November 7—a day sacred in CPR annals because of its association with the driving of the last spike at Craigellachie, in this case the 20th anniversary of the historic event—then struck with vengeance. That afternoon, more than 100 VV&E men poured onto the disputed property where they gave the CPR men exactly one minute to vacate the land. Vastly outnumbered, the CPR men were impressed with the merits of the suggestion and vanished in a twinkling.

It is unlikely Hill believed his forcible ejection of the CPR men from the property would end the matter. But he probably did not anticipate the retaliatory actions his move precipitated. Within minutes of the arrival of the CPR men back at Midway station, the telegraph wires were clicking out an order calling for every available man on the Canadian Pacific system in the province to report to Midway. Of course, southern British Columbia was full of railway construction workers eager for any excuse to down their tools and partake in any kind of diversionary excitement that would liberate them from their toil. Response was immediate. Word the CPR was calling in reinforcements naturally prompted the GN to conscript its own "army" of workers, and within hours scores of men from both sides were pouring into the Kettle Valley. Midway's small police detachment did everything possible to avert the seemingly inevitable clash. All efforts ended in failure late in the afternoon of November 9, 1905, when more than 300 CPR men, armed with shovels and grader's picks, thundered across the Kettle Valley like some barbaric invading horde of the ancient Roman Empire and fell upon the lesser forces of the VV&E guarding the treasured property.

At first, the violence was confined exclusively to VV&E property. Several hundred feet of light tramway track, used for hauling spoil from a nearby tunnel, were quickly pulled up and wrapped around trees adjacent to the right-of-way; liberal threats were offered that the same fate awaited any VV&E men foolish enough to interfere. But the CPR soon found the VV&E men stepping in to accept the challenge. In an instant, axes and shovels were clanging against each other in wild fury. Revolver shots also filled the air. In truth, the gunfire was purely a scare tactic on the part of a small band of VV&E employees hoping to frighten off the CPR men; most of the workers accepted the situation for what it really was—an authorized opportunity to let off steam—and efforts were directed more at securing tactical gain than inflicting bodily injury upon rival workers whose ethnic background and living conditions were really not too different from their own. Thus, while bruises were many, and a few bones were broken, serious injuries did not occur.

The lateness of the day helped restrict the duration of the battle and at sundown a temporary peace descended upon the scene, as the more than

500 rival workmen set up camp on opposite sides of the disputed territory. The fact that the parcel of property was only large enough to allow 50 feet of "no man's land" between the combatants did not seem to bother either side particularly; the rival workers merely settled around their campfires to enjoy dinner within hailing distance of the "enemy." Camp cooks reported a significant jump in food consumption, indicating more than one worker ate meals in both camps. Unfortunately, the peace was quickly broken, but not by the CPR or VV&E. The Midway police had decided the delicate peace would be impossible to preserve without their assistance, and they arrived upon the scene with warrants for the arrest of CPR land agent F.W. McLaine and the CPR construction foreman, judged by the police to have been responsible for the attack on the VV&E.

The two CPR men went willingly back to the Midway jail with the police, but became riled when it became apparent no warrants had been issued for any of the VV&E leaders. Not that it would have made any difference. The VV&E leaders, anticipating arrest, had merely retreated a few hundred feet south of their camp into a grove of trees on the American side of the international boundary where they could claim immunity from arrest by a Canadian law enforcement officer. The Midway police, perhaps recognizing the problems they had caused, released the two CPR leaders later that night after extracting a promise from them they would refrain from causing further trouble. Despite the pledge, the CPR men were heard to vow they would carry on the fight more vigorously than ever.

In the VV&E camp that night, preparations indicated no lack of willingness to oblige the CPR. Earlier in the evening, Hill's forces had received a special train of supplies and reinforcements from Spokane, including an entire boxcar of barbed wire. The wire was promptly laid out in long sections along the right-of-way. On the few remaining sections of tramway trackage, trees were laid across the rails and weighed down with massive boulders to prevent easy removal. In other areas the VV&E men had chained the rails to the mountainside using massive steel anchor bolts driven deeply into bedrock. Everything was readied for an anticipated morning attack.

When dawn broke, the CPR men once more advanced upon the VV&E right-of-way just as expected. After seeing the glistening rows of barbed wire Jim Hill's men had erected around the disputed property during the night, they decided to postpone any attempt to forcibly secure possession of the occupied territory. Instead, they turned their attention to an invasion of more attractive territory—the Midway saloons—while they awaited delivery of the dozens of wire cutters the Midway telegraph operator had instructed to be sent.

When the Midway police saw the CPR men coming, they took the logical precautionary move of ordering the town saloons closed. But as a means of preserving the delicate peace, the closure had no measurable impact, for just half a mile away in the Washington State community of Ferry, beyond the jurisdiction of Canadian authorities, the liquor was flowing more freely than the waters of the Kettle River. The CPR men merely marched out of town, crossed the international boundary en masse and filed into the Ferry saloons to secure the spirits they had been denied in Canada. The fact that saloons in Ferry were already packed to overflowing with VV&E men did not deter the CPR crews in the least. They merely pushed through the doors and drank away the afternoon shoulder to shoulder with the same men they would have cheerfully belted with a shovel handle the day previously. Needless-to-say, Ferry was a teeming place that afternoon. One sage reported that the only one of the Ten Commandments not broken in the town that day was the second, that relating to the making of graven images.

The free flow of liquor in Ferry soon took effect. Late in the day, three VV&E men crossed back into Canada and kidnapped CPR agent McLaine because, in their own colourful words, "He was a menace to their well being and would look well as an interior decoration for a dinky little powderhouse which had been run up near the mouth of the tunnel."[6] When the VV&E chief engineer, James H. Kennedy, heard of the episode, he personally freed McLaine and demanded the three men apologize to McLaine for their ill treatment of him. Fighting with the other roughnecks was one thing, Kennedy warned, but mistreatment of senior railway officials was definitely off limits. Perhaps Kennedy's working philosophy was based less on his belief in kind treatment of CPR personnel than the knowledge he was the top-ranking Great Northern official within 100 miles.

The three men obediently apologized to McLaine, but without waiting for his reply they raced to the Midway police office and wrote out a charge that McLaine ". . . did threaten to moove (sic) men by violance (sic) of the VV&E rightaway (sic)."[7] The spelling on their affidavit did not say much for the three men's schooling. Nevertheless, it represented something of a formal charge and an officer was immediately dispatched to re-arrest McLaine. The officer did not have to leave the police station because

McLaine showed up to lay a charge of his own against the three for kidnapping him. The officer on duty, in disgust, jailed all four men. By morning, the four had mutually agreed to drop all charges in order to escape the cramped quarters of the jail's single cell and each other's distasteful presence.

The provincial police soon arrived in force to ensure no further violence would occur but what had thus far transpired was more than enough to place the tiny town of Midway in the press limelight of the world. The *Toronto Globe* termed the incident: ". . . a disgraceful substitution of mob law for British justice in connection with railway enterprises in Canada."[8] Even in faraway London the episode rated editorial comment. Several British writers expressed dismay that in the advanced year of 1905 such barbaric incidents could actually have occurred within the British Empire. Obviously they did not know Hill and the CPR!

Immediately afterwards the dispute went before the courts and at the initial hearing it was discovered that, just as the CPR had alleged, the property specified in the expropriation order was different from the one over which blood had been shed. On November 14, 1905, the CPR was granted a new injunction prohibiting the VV&E from further work on the property pending the issuance of the correct papers. Hill resubmitted an application for expropriation, and in December the VV&E was finally granted the correct possession order. Undaunted, the CPR promptly sued the VV&E for trespass upon its lands prior to the granting of the proper order. The trespass suit, unbelievably, continued for years afterwards, with both Hill and the CPR pouring enough money into the rat hole of revenge to build at least a dozen miles of railway. Somehow the Battle of Midway would never quite be forgotten—or forgiven—by either side.[9]

The day after the court session—as if revenge was the driving motive—Hill's grading crews roared across the border northwest of Oroville, steamrolling up the Similkameen Valley towards Princeton. Simultaneously, Hill announced surveys would immediately commence eastward from Cloverdale to link his Seattle-Vancouver rail line with the line being built west from Oroville. A promise was made that work on the line would start with the return of good weather in the spring. Princeton, Hill assured, would be hearing the whistle of through trains from Spokane within a year.

Hardly surprisingly, the CPR was not about to let Hill capture either new territory or public sympathy. Thomas Shaughnessy retorted that Hill might have his railway into Princeton by year's end, but if he did, the people there to greet Hill's first train would have arrived the week before on a CPR train. To back his word, Shaughnessy dispatched a CPR land agent to the Princeton area to write out cheques for right-of-way land the entire length of Summers Creek, along which the CPR surveys had been located in 1899-1900. The CPR agent believed it was his corporate duty to also buy up any land Hill might find useful. But Princeton residents knew this action was simply the way Hill and the CPR did business, and contented themselves with the likely prospect their community would soon have not one, but two, railways.

Princeton was not the only community eagerly awaiting the arrival of a railway. Ever since Daniel Corbin had announced his plans to build the Spokane International in 1905, the citizens of Spokane had been awaiting the completion of the CPR-backed SI with great enthusiasm. As the new railway neared completion in the spring of 1907, Shaughnessy made sure there was no doubt left in anyone's mind that the CPR meant business in Spokane. Six luxury passenger trains were being delivered to the CPR for express passenger service to and from Spokane. West of Spokane to Portland, the trains would be handled by the Oregon Railway & Navigation line; east from Spokane, trains would be routed via the SI, the CPR's Crows Nest line, the CPR mainline to Moose Jaw and the Soo Line right into the heart of Hill's empire, Minneapolis-St. Paul. The initial reaction to the CPR announcement was that Shaughnessy was crazy to attempt this direct competition with the Great Northern. But Shaughnessy was quick to point out that the CPR route between Spokane and St. Paul, because it closely followed a "great circle" of the globe, was actually shorter than any of the American rail lines. CPR trains soon proved to be the fastest too. In fact, shortly after the *Spokane Flyer* and the *Soo Express* made their inaugural run, the American government dropped Hill's contract for handling Unites States mail between the Twin Cities and the Northwest and awarded it to the CPR. It was an insult-to-injury coup that Hill would never forget.

For its dagger thrust into the American Northwest, Hill struck back at the CPR with an announcement in April 1907 that he would push the Great Northern Railway into all of western Canada. He stated the VV&E would be immediately completed across the Hope Mountains, and the GN's line into Crows Nest Pass would be pushed both eastward across the Canadian prairies to Winnipeg and northward to Calgary, Edmonton and the Peace River. By connecting the VV&E on the west with the Grand Trunk Pacific at Winnipeg, Hill claimed he would give Canada a second transcontinental railway. He promised his lines in Canada would soon total more than 3,000 miles. That same month, Louis Hill succeeded James Jerome Hill as president of the Great Northern Railway and in his inaugural speech added to his father's promise: "If our Canadian plans do not miscarry, I expect within the next ten years to have a railroad system there which will be almost an equivalent of the Great Northern system as it is today in the United States."[10] Within a week of assuming office, Louis Hill had trackage across the border northwest of Oroville bound for Keremeos and the coast.

Unfortunately, the Hills were unable to advance as quickly as they had promised. Shortages of men and materials slowed tracklaying well below the planned pace. Construction crews then went on strike. Later that spring a newly completed bridge below Keremeos was washed out by high waters. Following a long delay the bridge was rebuilt, but no sooner had it been completed than a locomotive crew carelessly dumped firebox ashes on it, causing severe damage by fire. Not until July 10, 1907—without any of the public fanfare the Hills had wanted—did Great Northern rails reach Keremeos. The other GN lines promised were even less material. Late in 1907, owing to the sudden downturn in the economy, survey work on the projected line to Calgary, Edmonton and the Peace River was cancelled, and the planned extension through Crows Nest Pass to Winnipeg stopped at Michel, only 20 miles beyond Fernie.

The depression continued on into 1908 and resulted in the cancellation of many of Hill's railway undertakings in the Canadian and American west. However, work on the VV&E did not stop. James J. Hill, who continued to dominate the affairs of the Great Northern despite the official transfer of power to his son, gave the VV&E high priority in the allocation of GN's limited construction funds. Although the rate of construction was far from impressive, it never stopped all through the depressed years of 1907 and 1908. CPR expansion did not match Hill's during this period. Thus, when the depression began to break in 1909, Hill had considerably strengthened his already powerful hold on southern British Columbia.

In January 1909, the VV&E line between Cloverdale and Huntingdon was approved for operation by the federal government. Two months later, Louis Hill visited Princeton and had a long meeting with Ernest Waterman, manager of the Vermilion Forks Mining & Development

Company. Samples of the mine's 20-foot thick coal seam, located only 50 feet below the surface, were inspected and Waterman modestly assured Hill the mine could supply any amount of coal the GN wished to purchase. Hill, seemingly impressed, promised to speed the railway to completion. By late July the roadbed from Keremeos to Princeton was ready for rails.

The following month, A.H. Hogeland, the GN's chief engineer, appeared in Vancouver to discuss business matters with his counterpart in the VV&E, J.H. Kennedy. During his visit, Hogeland publicly hinted that J.J. Hill was preparing to make a major announcement in regards to his Coast-to-Kootenay railway. In light of Hill's steady progress on the VV&E, considerable attention was given to Hogeland's prophecy. However, British Columbians were electrified beyond belief when, two weeks later, on September 2, 1909, Hill announced he had rejected the original surveyed route—crossing the Hope Mountains with more than 30 miles of difficult 2.5% grade—and instead had chosen a new route involving an eight-mile tunnel under the east ridge of the Hope Mountains. In his announcement, Hill stated the tunnel would shorten the railway by more than 30 miles compared with the earlier planned line and would reduce both the length and the severity of grade in both directions. It would be the longest railway tunnel on the North American continent, a monument amply testifying to Hill's conviction that the greatest long-term economy was to be found in building fine quality rail lines. Within two weeks of the announcement, survey crews were readying the ground to begin work.[11]

By the end of autumn 1909 a station, water tank and two-stall enginehouse had been erected at Princeton and the grade for both a loop track and a spur to the Vermilion Forks mine, just east of the townsite, had been finished.[12] Tracklaying was likewise complete, but a strike by GN switchmen in November caused the inauguration of regular train service to be put off indefinitely. Thus, when the first passenger train finally rolled over the line on December 23, 1909, no one was even at the station in Princeton to greet it, the citizens being unaware the strike had been settled. Notwithstanding this poor beginning, the citizens of Princeton lost no time in turning out to jubilantly celebrate the first train's arrival. A gala party was quickly organized and, as a grand Christmas present to Jim Hill for his gift of a railway, the Similkameen River was unofficially renamed the Jimhillkameen River.

Hill's railway was thus into Princeton. Perseverance through the lean years of 1907 and 1908 had given him sole possession of Princeton and the Similkameen Valley and had brought the VV&E ever closer to a meeting point in the Hope Mountains. Hill, therefore, was closer to securing a rail line across southern British Columbia than was his long-standing rival, whose tracks at Midway still lay separated from the coast by nearly 300 miles of rugged wilderness. As the first train puffed into Princeton that December, contractors were also readying bids in answer to Hill's call for tenders for the construction of the 16-mile section from Princeton to Tulameen, near the eastern portal of the projected eight-mile tunnel, and for the 50-mile section from the VV&E at Abbotsford to Hope.[13] Once these two sections were completed, the gap between their end points would be narrowed to less than 40 miles. Those 40 miles of track would then be all that was needed to complete the Coast-to-Kootenay railway.

Hill also knew those 40 miles of track would then be the only thing preventing him from securing complete control of southern British Columbia. With his VV&E across the Hope Mountains, Hill could snatch from the CPR the last vestiges of trade his Spokane rail lines had been unable to capture, trade too heavily taxed by customs duties to be economically carried across the border. It was all so simple. Freight not hauled to Spokane over Hill's feeder lines radiating from the capital of the Inland Empire would be hauled to Vancouver over his VV&E. The CPR, with a much longer route from the Kootenays to either tidewater or a Canadian centre equivalent in commercial stature to Spokane, would be driven from southern British Columbia. This extrication of the CPR was undoubtedly what Hill wanted. Personal vengeance had given his VV&E a priority economics at the time could not justify.

As the year 1910 began, British Columbians seemed on the verge of having their long-held dream of a Coast-to-Kootenay railway brought to reality. Never before had they come so close. Yet never before were British Columbians so uncertain of the future. Why did Hill really want the VV&E? Was he building it for the dedicated purpose of carrying southern British Columbia's trade to the coast? Was it Hill, the Canadian-born genius of the Great Northern, who would return to his native land and build the railway upon which the aspirations of an entire generation of British Columbians depended? Or would Hill carry only enough trade over the VV&E to starve out the CPR then direct all the rich trade of the province's interior to Spokane?

Hill's personal intentions will, of course, never be known for certain.

But British Columbians realized one thing: the CPR was not about to allow Hill sole control of southern British Columbia. In fact, it was rapidly mounting forces to build its own rail line across the mountains separating the southern interior from the sea to meet the challenge of "Empire Builder" Jim Hill for supremacy.

8: Disciples of Destiny

James Warren and Andrew McCulloch
take charge of the Kettle Valley Railway

Early one afternoon in February 1906, a cold east wind was blowing sharply down from McRae Pass when a stocky, warmly dressed man stepped off the CPR train in Grand Forks. No one in the crowd thronging the station platform recognized this stranger. Nor did any of them know he would soon rise to a prominent position in southern British Columbia's mining, smelting and railroad industries and hold that position for the next third of a century. Similarly, no one knew this man's visit to Grand Forks was about to set into motion a chain of events that would alter the destiny of both Grand Forks and the rest of southern British Columbia.

The stranger's name was James John Warren. Born in Ontario on January 30, 1870, he had practised law there for several years after graduating from Toronto's famed Osgoode Hall law school. During his early years of private practice Warren had been invited by a friend, James Stratton, to join the fledgling Trusts & Guarantee Company, which Stratton had founded in 1897 with the help of Thomas Coffee, Frederick Holland and Christian Kloepfer—the same men who had supported Frederick's brother, Tracy Holland, in building the Kettle River Valley Railway.

Warren joined the company and quickly demonstrated his administrative ability, becoming manager of the Trusts & Guarantee Company on October 1, 1905. Because the Kettle River Valley Railway had been built largely with Trusts & Guarantee capital, it was natural the railway became one of Warren's chief concerns. His trip west in February 1906 was made largely to familiarize himself with the KRVR and its financial problems.

An inspection of the Republic rail line quickly convinced Warren the railway faced a dismal future under J.J. Hill's economic thumbscrews. He was also convinced the starry-eyed proposal of the railway's management to extend track to Spokane offered no hope of salvation. The most obvious solution to the Kettle River Valley Railway's financial dilemma, Warren recognized, was to sell the company to one of the larger railways in the hope of recovering as much from its bad investment as possible. But who would buy it? Certainly not Hill; he was more than happy to watch the KRVR's wheels rust off after all the trouble it had caused him. The CPR would not likely want the KRVR either because the railway's value as a branch line would be dubious, considering the original management's inability to make the line profitable. The possibility the CPR would buy the charter to reach Spokane had been quashed more than a year earlier when it joined with Daniel Corbin to build the Spokane International Railway.

Calculated reasoning told Warren that, failing a negotiated sale to the CPR or GN, the best alternative was for the railway to fold up completely before any further losses were incurred. However, calculated reasoning was not enough. Warren had seen too much of southern British Columbia to write off the KRVR's future. He had pioneered the White Bear mine in Rossland back in the bonanza days of the 1890s and became convinced a potential treasure house of mineral wealth lay untouched beneath the forested mountain slopes of southern British Columbia. What was needed to bring this potential wealth to commercial value was a direct rail outlet to the coast. Suddenly Warren perceived the destiny for his railway.

Warren may have dreamed he could turn the financially ailing Kettle River Valley Railway into a major rail line but he was clear-headed enough to realize the task would not be easily accomplished. To begin with, Warren was not even an officer in the KRVR. His only relationship with that corporation was through the Trusts & Guarantee Company to which the KRVR was indebted. Another obstacle was the immense cost of constructing a railway to the coast, a fact verified by the many derelict corporations that had attempted it. Even if finances could be secured, the KRVR would be forced into a close alliance with either the CPR or GN to secure connecting links with existing lines in the Boundary and Kootenays. In that respect the GN could be immediately discounted. Past relations between the KRVR and the GN aside, Hill was too close to achieving a Coast-to-Kootenay rail connection of his own to consider sharing the spoils of what appeared to be certain victory. That left the CPR as the only other possible ally.

Perhaps Warren had already singled out Canadian Pacific as his choice, believing that Canadian control of the Coast-to-Kootenay railway was essential to establishing economic unity within the province. While Hill was definitely ahead in the race to cross the southern interior, his actions did not indicate a sincere concern for the aspirations of southern British Columbians. He rarely stayed on Canadian soil longer than 24 hours during his visits. By contrast, the visits of CPR president Thomas Shaughnessy reflected his deep love for the province and its future. Shaughnessy had personally founded a number of business enterprises in southern British Columbia, including the Summerland Development Company, which became responsible for helping make Okanagan fruit world famous. These investments, Warren knew, represented an act of faith extending beyond mere corporate responsibility to foster trade for the CPR. Because he and Shaughnessy shared a common interest in southern British Columbia and the railway so vital to its future, it seemed natural to Warren the two of them should work together to weld the bands of steel between the coast and the Kootenays.

Late in 1907, J.J. Warren attempted to approach Thomas Shaughnessy to propose an agreement between the CPR and the KRVR to build a rail line to the coast on terms similar to the highly successful alliance between Daniel Corbin and the CPR in building a line into Spokane. At the time of his approach Shaughnessy was absent on business and Warren's suggestions met with a highly negative response from the lesser CPR officials. Nevertheless, Warren was not discouraged. He remained convinced Shaughnessy possessed a vision not shared by others within the CPR, and thus he bided his time, awaiting the chance to speak privately with Shaughnessy. That chance arose a few months later when Warren learned Shaughnessy had booked passage aboard the Canadian Pacific steamship *Empress of Britain* for Liverpool. Warren booked for the same sailing and, after the ship left Saint John on April 18, 1908, introduced both himself and his ideas to Shaughnessy.

At their meeting, Shaughnessy expressed great interest in the concept of an alliance between the two companies. The Kettle River Valley Railway—or Kettle Valley Railway as it had come to be called and would soon be legally named—represented a possible subsidiary corporation the CPR could use to expand its rail line west from Midway. Warren stressed that the gap in Hill's VV&E was steadily closing and, should Hill be permitted the only line between the coast and the interior, he would gain virtually complete control of southern British Columbia.

Shaughnessy agreed. He assured Warren that for many years he had wanted to push CPR rails west from Midway, waiting only for the proper economic climate to justify the high construction cost. Such time had not yet arrived, Shaughnessy suggested, especially with Canada in the midst of a severe economic slump. He further warned Warren that the majority of CPR directors favoured the east, and few would likely support the construction of a rail line recommended against in three separate surveys. Nevertheless, he agreed with Warren that the CPR had to push ahead with a railway to the coast to protect its existing rail system in southern British Columbia. He asked Warren to proceed with the initial preparations for extension of the Kettle Valley Railway westward to the coast while he sought the necessary funds for construction. History later revealed the strategic importance of the pair's visionary and daring decision.[1]

Even before his historic meeting with J.J. Warren in April 1908, Thomas Shaughnessy had taken a number of steps on his own towards bridging the gap in the CPR line across southern British Columbia. As early as 1905, Shaughnessy had assigned engineering staff the task of revising the survey done by CPR engineers in 1899-1900. He wanted to establish a satisfactory railway route between Penticton and Nicola in keeping with his promise the Nicola Branch would ultimately be extended to the Okanagan. The man Shaughnessy chose for this job was Henry Carry, the same engineer who had assisted Edgar Dewdney in his survey of the Hope Mountains during 1901. Carry was directed by Shaughnessy to omit the Similkameen Valley from the survey because Hill's VV&E was already being constructed over this route. Instead, the Trout Creek Valley was to be used to approach Penticton.

During 1905 and 1906, Carry staked his first survey. This line duplicated the Columbia & Western Railway survey southward from Nicola along Quilchena Creek and Summers Creek to Princeton, but instead of following the Similkameen River southeast it turned northeast up Five Mile Creek (now known as Haynes Creek) to Osprey Lake. At Osprey Lake it began the descent of Trout Creek to the Okanagan Valley just north of Penticton. After reviewing this survey, Shaughnessy decided to omit Princeton from the projected mainline, thereby reducing the line's length and gradients. Starting in September 1907, Carry staked two alternative survey lines, both based on omitting Princeton from the railway route.

One line followed his earlier survey from Nicola up Quilchena Creek,

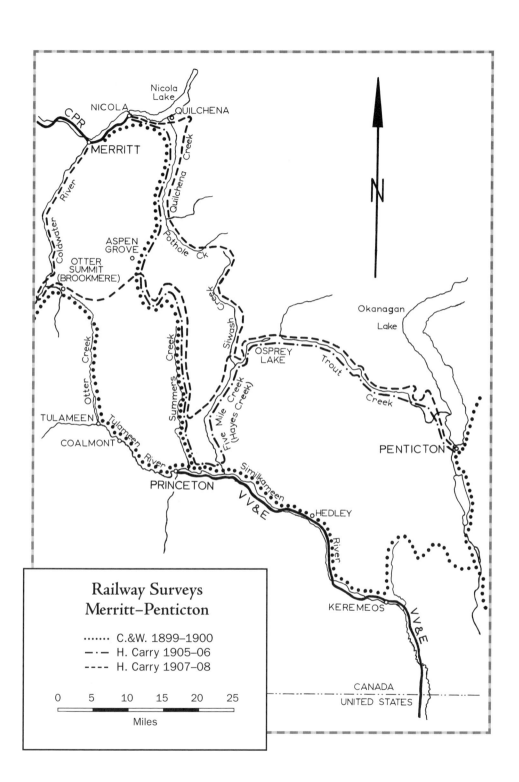

Railway Surveys
Merritt–Penticton

.... C.&W. 1899–1900
— ·— H. Carry 1905–06
---- H. Carry 1907–08

0   5   10   15   20   25
Miles

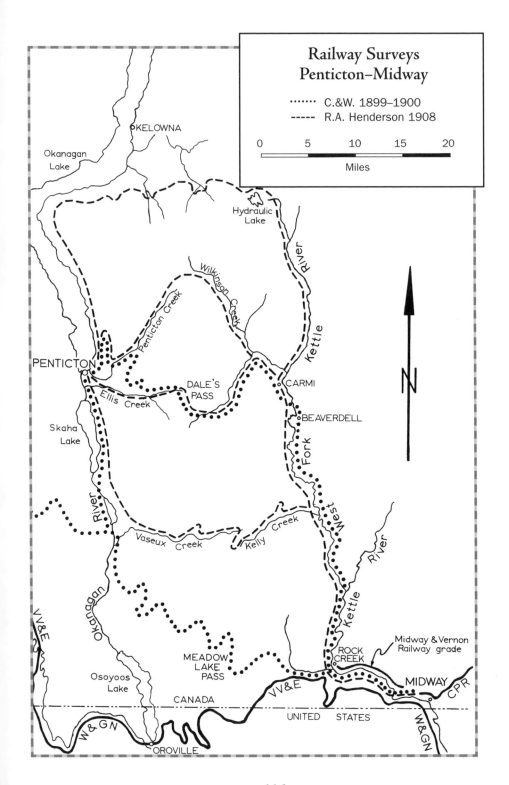

Railway Surveys
Penticton–Midway

······· C.&W. 1899–1900
- - - - - R.A. Henderson 1908

0   5   10   15   20
Miles

OKELOWNA

Okanagan
Lake

Hydraulic
Lake

River

Wilkinson Creek

Penticton Creek

Kettle

N

PENTICTON

DALE'S
PASS

CARMI

Ellis Creek

BEAVERDELL

Skaha
Lake

Fork

River

West

Vaseux   Creek

Kelly   Creek

Kettle

River

Okanagan

VV&E

Midway &Vernon
Railway grade

MEADOW
LAKE
PASS

ROCK
CREEK

Osoyoos
Lake

MIDWAY

CPR

CANADA

VV&E

UNITED   STATES

W&GN

W&GN

OROVILLE

then turned eastward on a tributary stream, Pothole Creek, and crossed over the 4,500-foot divide at its headwaters to join Siwash Creek, a stream leading to the original survey not far west of Osprey Lake. The second alternative line left Merritt and followed the Coldwater River southwest to Pass Creek (now known as Brook Creek) and Otter Summit (now the community of Brookmere). From Otter Summit this line climbed out of the Otter Valley south of Aspen Grove, but instead of dropping down Summers Creek into Princeton as Carry's first survey had done, the new line stayed high on the hillside above the streambed and crossed a saddle of land ten miles northeast of Princeton to the Five Mile Creek Valley, where it joined the earlier survey. This new line was somewhat longer than the other two, but it had a remarkably easy grade climbing out of Merritt—only 0.9%—and it provided direct access to Coquihalla Pass, through which the CPR mainline at Hope was less than 50 miles away.

During 1908 J.J. Warren also undertook a number of important steps in preparation for construction of the extension west from Midway. Warren had agreed with Shaughnessy that, while Carry established a suitable railway route from the Nicola Valley to Penticton, the Kettle Valley Railway would do the same between Midway and Penticton. In keeping with this understanding, Warren wired the Trusts & Guarantee solicitor in Grand Forks on June 18, 1908 to send engineer R.A. Henderson to Midway to determine what portions of the Midway & Vernon Railway grade, abandoned since that railway's collapse in 1905, could be utilized as part of the rail line westward.[2] Henderson filed his report on June 26 and was immediately assigned by Warren to establish a railway route location west from the end of the M&V grade at Rock Creek to the Okanagan Valley. Equipped with a complete set of surveys borrowed from the CPR, Henderson set to work under conditions that, as one newspaper reported, reflected "the most profound secrecy."[3] By the end of summer Henderson had completed his initial survey work and submitted a report to Warren outlining several possible routes.

The first route Henderson documented followed the Kettle River north from the end of the M&V grade for about 15 miles, swung westward and climbed Kelly Creek to its headwaters at the 4,700-foot summit with Vaseux Creek then descended the latter stream to the Okanagan Valley. The survey was 78 miles in length, with grades no greater than 2.2%.

The second route followed the Kettle River northward past Carmi, climbed the South Fork of Wilkinson Creek through Dale's Pass and descended Ellis Creek into Penticton. Unfortunately, while Penticton and Carmi are only 20 miles apart, the summit of Dale's Pass is more than 3,500 feet higher than Penticton and 1,800 feet higher than Carmi. This necessitated including 30 miles of difficult 2.2% grade and 11 miles of killing 3.4% grade.

The third route followed the second survey to the fork of Wilkinson Creek, then continued up the main body of that stream to the summit and down into Penticton.

The fourth and final survey continued north from Carmi to Hydraulic Lake, a small water body southeast of Kelowna, then descended into Penticton on a long line around the eastern edge of Okanagan Lake. Although this line was the longest of the surveyed routes, being about 130 miles in length, it crossed the divide to the Okanagan Valley via the lowest pass, 4,100 feet, and could be built with the easiest grades. Warren acknowledged Henderson's surveys and promised to review them with Shaughnessy.

Early in 1909, Shaughnessy wrote to Warren asking him to include in the KVR's projected undertakings a line branching off Carry's survey near Otter Summit and cutting through Coquihalla Pass to the CPR mainline opposite Hope. Warren was intrigued by the suggestion. He knew a line through Coquihalla Pass would shorten the route to the coast by more than 100 miles, significant if the KVR were left with the unattractive prospect of competing with a second line to the Kootenays—Hill's VV&E.

But Warren was cautious. Coquihalla Pass had earned a reputation as a difficult pathway through the Hope Mountains. Half a century earlier the brigade trail through the pass had been abandoned after only two seasons because the many steeply walled canyons and heavy snowfalls made travel exceedingly difficult.[4] Likewise the Sandford Fleming expedition of the 1870s, seeking a route for the transcontinental railway, exhaustively studied Coquihalla Pass hoping to make use of its extreme directness through the coastal mountains.

Fleming estimated as much as six miles aggregate tunnelling would be necessary to build a rail line through the Coquihalla Pass. Even with tunnels, he reported, "The gradients would still remain unusually severe, and the work of construction would be extremely troublesome and expensive."[5] When Henry Cambie explored the route in 1876 to authenticate this unoptimistic report he found the pass still blocked by snow from the previous winter, despite his journey being made in the early fall. Even J.J.

Hill sought to escape the terror of Coquihalla Pass by planning an eight-mile tunnel under the Hope Mountains.

Nevertheless, Shaughnessy confided to Warren his conviction that a rail line through Coquihalla Pass was essential to the success of the Kettle Valley Railway. With such a line the CPR could permanently fence Hill out of British Columbia or at least compete with him on equal terms if the VV&E also completed its proposed line to the coast. In Shaughnessy's view, the possession of all southern British Columbia was dependent upon gaining control of this narrow thread of river. For this reason in early 1909, he assigned CPR engineer W.I. Bassett to establish a railway location through Coquihalla Pass.

Bassett's arrival in Coquihalla Pass in the spring of 1909 marked the first time in nearly a decade a CPR survey crew was at work in the Hope Mountains. Extreme secrecy was observed; it wasn't until late summer the general public learned survey work was underway. The news made front-page coverage in coastal papers, as did Shaughnessy's arrival in Vancouver on September 21, 1909 on his way to Victoria for a private conference with Premier McBride to discuss the matter of the Coast-to-Kootenay railway. Upon intensive questioning by the press, Shaughnessy confirmed that Bassett was working for the CPR. He added that Bassett had laid out "a virtually direct route" across the Hope Mountains and construction of the railway would "soon become a live question."[6] Beyond these remarks, Shaughnessy said nothing. The press was well satisfied with the meagre tidbits it had obtained. The information he had divulged, plus the fact he was meeting with McBride, was all the evidence needed for the press to be convinced the CPR would not permit Hill to be the first across the Hope Mountains.

What transpired between Shaughnessy and McBride at their September meeting is a matter of conjecture. The brevity of their conference and the terms of an agreement that was signed shortly afterwards made it clear the two men shared many objectives. McBride had often expressed his intense desire to see completion of the Coast-to-Kootenay railway. Indeed, he said the only reason he had turned down so many previous proposals was the lack of proven construction abilities among the syndicates promoting construction. McBride was equally open in stating his apprehension that Hill had secured the VV&E solely to ensure continuation of Spokane's domination of the provincial interior. What was needed, McBride asserted, was a Canadian-controlled railway across the southern interior. In this regard, the plans of Shaughnessy and Warren fit in perfectly. A tentative agreement was made between Shaughnessy and McBride to have the Kettle Valley Railway, under the control and sponsorship of the CPR, complete the rail line from Midway west to the coast. Warren then met with McBride to formalize the terms in a written agreement.

Under the terms of the agreement, the KVR would acquire the assets of the Midway & Vernon Railway and pay its outstanding debts. The KVR would construct at least 25 miles of railway between Midway and the Nicola Valley in 1910, commencing work at no fewer than three places, and would complete the entire railway within four years. In return, the provincial government would give the KVR a cash subsidy of $5,000 per mile for the line between Penticton and a junction with the CPR's Nicola Valley branch. The remainder of the line was to be built without provincial subsidy, except for a free grant of right-of-way through crown land and a temporary exemption from certain taxes. Work was to begin within four months of a formal ratification of the agreement. The proposed line through Coquihalla Pass was not mentioned in the agreement because the KVR did not yet have statutory authority to build it.

Immediately following the conclusion of his agreement with Warren, McBride dissolved the Legislative Assembly and called an election. He publicly announced his agreement with Warren and also announced he had signed an agreement guaranteeing the construction bonds of Mackenzie and Mann's proposed Canadian Northern Pacific Railway. Subsidies were proposed for a number of other railways as well. In short, McBride's election platform was based entirely on railway development. The announcement prompted the resignation of two of McBride's cabinet ministers, who asserted the proposed railway subsidy program would bankrupt the province. When the votes were counted on November 25 it was obvious British Columbians thought otherwise. Not only was McBride personally returned to office by a landslide, his party won all except four seats in the Assembly. Given this endorsement by British Columbians, McBride formally signed the draft agreement with Warren and submitted it to the Legislature for ratification.

During the first reading of the bill, McBride was frequently interrupted by loud applause and he received a standing ovation as he concluded: "This valuable trade, which had gone heretofore to enrich the merchants and businessmen generally to the south of the international line, would now come, as was right, to build up our own coast cities and to, as should be, foster a closer relationship and sympathetic understanding between the people of British Columbia living on the coast and those residents of the interior of the province."[7] On March 10, 1910, the bill was ratified and the agreement bound into law.

Richard McBride had risked his political career on the Kettle Valley Railway. Thomas Shaughnessy had now to do likewise. The ratification of the agreement between the Kettle Valley Railway and the government of British Columbia left the KVR only four months to begin construction. Shaughnessy could therefore afford little delay in seeking the sanction of the CPR directorate to formalize his tentative agreement with the KVR. At a meeting in Montreal late in February 1910, he presented his proposal to the CPR board of directors.

Shaughnessy entered the meeting room armed with a telegram from W.I. Bassett, received on February 21, reporting that despite deep snow and subzero temperatures the railway survey of Coquihalla Pass had just been completed. Bassett reported that a successful location, with grades not exceeding 2.2%, had been achieved, a feat Hill's surveyors had been unable to match in the four years they spent in the Coquihalla. In spite of this triumph, Shaughnessy would need all the persuasive powers he could muster; when he presented his proposal to the board of directors not one single member offered support. Several directors cited the fact that every survey done by the CPR had recommended against extension of the rail line west of Midway and reviewed the problems; three major mountain ranges had to be crossed, and the rail line down Coquihalla Pass, despite Bassett's highly commendable survey, would still be a 35-mile long toboggan ride down one of the most rugged river canyons on the continent. They further pointed out that the Great Northern Railway already had a line from Grand Forks to Princeton that was 80 miles shorter than the proposed KVR route and with only 30 miles of westbound ascending grade—against the direction of the heavy ore traffic—in excess of 1%, and that being only 1.25%. The longer and heavier grades projected for the KVR dictated against hauling through freight and the sparse population along the route meant local traffic was unlikely to develop any time soon.

No doubt Shaughnessy hesitated in the face of such opposition. Then, with the same vision and fortitude his predecessor William Van Horne had shown in building the railway that had made Canadian Pacific world famous, Shaughnessy rose to his feet and asserted that the railway would be built. "Gentlemen, the people of Canada want an all Canadian line, and

I am going to give it to them."[8] Shaughnessy then sat down. All was quiet. His critics said nothing further and Shaughnessy proceeded to build the promised railway. History would reveal that had he not taken this forthright and daring step the great dream of a Coast-to-Kootenay railway would almost certainly have remained forever only a dream. History would also reveal that his decision was not to be without further controversy. From that day to the present—and likely long into the future—railway historians and transportation economists would debate the correctness of his action. Only one issue is beyond dispute: wisdom or folly, the decision to construct of the Kettle Valley Railway was ultimately Shaughnessy's and his alone.

Early in 1910 J.J. Warren, who officially become president and general manager of the Kettle Valley Railway, approached the federal government with a request for permission to add a line through Coquihalla Pass to the statutory powers of the KVR. This requested was assented to on March 17, 1910. With its passage, the last legal obstacle preventing the start of construction was removed.

A new and difficult problem now confronted Warren. As a lawyer and financier, Warren was competent to manage the KVR and assure approval of governing statutory regulations, but the actual physical task of constructing such a difficult railway demanded the appointment of a highly qualified engineer, a man possessing great skill, ability and daring. The Kettle Valley Railway would involve nearly 350 miles of construction through some of the most rugged terrain on the continent, part of which—the Coquihalla River canyon—would be one of the most challenging pieces of railway construction in the world. Warren was uncertain who should direct the engineering of such a construction project. But Shaughnessy had no hesitation; he named a man who not only would build the incredible railway but who would direct its operations for almost two decades after completion. That man's name would become synonymous with "The KV": Andrew McCulloch.

McCulloch was born in Lanark Country, Ontario on June 16, 1864, the oldest of five children whose parents were of Scottish descent. His parents were farmers who had settled in a poor and rocky part of Ontario and McCulloch's early days at home were a difficult struggle to help his family scratch an existence from the land. McCulloch was devoted to his parents and faithfully helped provide for the family's younger children. But his temperament was unsuited to farm life, and from an early age he longed to leave home. He nearly got that chance early in 1885 when the local militia unit to which he belonged was summoned to Kingston to go west over the new Canadian Pacific Railway to aid government forces in putting down the Riel Rebellion. Just as his train was ready to pull away from the station, word arrived that the rebellion was over, and McCulloch, a thoroughly dejected young man, was forced to return home.

McCulloch later enrolled in the Dominion Business College at Kingston, graduating on June 6, 1888 as (so read his diploma) an "Intelligent and Competent Accountant," having achieved a school average of 93%. Following his graduation, he was offered a secure job in a local business. However, when one of McCulloch's free-spirited friends, Angus Nicholson, suggested the two of them give the new upstart city a whirl out west—Vancouver—McCulloch abandoned his accounting career. On March 25, 1889, he left his Ontario home for the west, possessing only, as McCulloch himself later said, ". . . abundant health, all the strength usually given to one man, a little education, a love of the great outdoors and a willingness to work."[9] McCulloch's first ride over the Canadian Pacific Railway made an indelible impression upon him. From the entries in his diary and his activities in later years, it was obvious his heart had found a place it would never again leave.

Positive initial impressions aside, McCulloch and Nicholson found they could not secure employment in Vancouver and they were forced to accept work in a sawmill near Seattle. They remained there until April 1890 when McCulloch secured what he called "a pretty good job" clearing survey lines along the switchbacks of J.J. Hill's Great Northern mainline through Stevens Pass.[10] When the railway was completed in 1893 McCulloch was laid off and, with a depression starting, he was forced to return home for the winter. But mountains and railroads coursed through his blood and at the first sign of spring McCulloch once more headed west.

McCulloch's return to the west in 1894 was interrupted by the GN strike that year when the train crew simply walked away from the train, leaving McCulloch and some 100 fellow passengers stranded in the middle of the Montana badlands where they would remain until the strike was settled three weeks later. The delay worked somewhat to McCulloch's advantage. At least he received free food from the railway. When he reached Seattle, McCulloch found jobs virtually non-existent because of the depression and had to endure some rather rough times until he later landed a job in a nearby lumber mill. Even during hard times McCulloch had high spirits and ambitions. He was an avid reader, devouring books in prolific proportions. And when the day's work was done, while his fellow workers headed for the nearest saloon, McCulloch would set out in a small dinghy to row across the choppy waters of Puget Sound to attend the live theatres of Seattle, especially to relish the great Shakespearian performances of his day. When the play had ended he would return to his dinghy and row until sunrise in order to be back in time for another day's work. Ironically, McCulloch's love for Shakespeare—gained from the hard times of the depression—was to produce a legacy that would outlive his railway.

In July 1894, McCulloch heard the CPR was hiring men to repair its mainline after the massive spring floods that year, and he had no difficulty securing a job working with a bridge gang along the Thompson River. When this was finished he headed home for winter. However, he never made it. He stopped in Michigan and was given a job on the construction of the Lake Superior & Ishpeming Railway. Before the end of a year, he had been promoted to resident engineer on the project. Subsequently, McCulloch returned to British Columbia to work on the construction of a portion of the Nakusp & Slocan Railway. When that project was completed, he casually walked over 100 miles in three days to secure a job surveying the CPR's Crows Nest line. So satisfactory was his work on this project the CPR promoted him to assistant engineer on the Columbia & Western Railway work, westward from Robson. His railroad career took him to the prairies for several years but he returned to British Columbia in 1905 to play a key role in the location of one of the best-known pieces of railway engineering in Canada—the Spiral Tunnels in the Rocky Mountains near Field.[11] His contribution here was recognized by his appointment on May 1, 1907 to the position of Division Engineer of Construction: Eastern Lines, with headquarters at Montreal. This was one of the top engineering positions in the Canadian Pacific Railway.

McCulloch accepted his new position with relish and did a superb job constructing many of the CPR lines in Ontario, Quebec and New Brunswick. However, it was obvious from the notations in his diary that his heart was neither in the east nor the office, a fact Thomas Shaughnessy seemed to recognize in the clear-headed, sharp-witted McCulloch. Thus, when Warren telegraphed Shaughnessy early in May 1910 that work on the Kettle Valley Railway could begin, Shaughnessy had no difficulty in selecting the man for the job. On May 21, 1910, Andrew McCulloch was asked to accept the position of Chief Engineer of the Kettle Valley Railway; his answer, without hesitation, was yes. Shaughnessy then introduced McCulloch to J.J. Warren, the man with whom McCulloch would work to build the railway. McCulloch soon earned the nickname "Chief" and Warren became "J.J." Thus began one of the deepest of mortal friendships; it would be maintained for the next 30 years.

On May 25, Shaughnessy further spoke with McCulloch, explaining the guidelines he wished to set for the construction of the Kettle Valley Railway as a result of his review of Carry's and Henderson's surveys. The railway, after leaving Midway, was to pass through Beaverdell and Carmi, but must not go north of Hydraulic Summit. It was to pass through Penticton and the general area of Summerland. It was to connect with the existing railway in the Nicola Valley and with the proposed line through Coquihalla Pass. All grades on the railway were to be 1.0% or less except on the climb out of the Okanagan Valley east and west of Penticton, where steeper 2.2% "pusher grades" could be employed. McCulloch was free to take all existing survey documents and use them as he saw fit, the cost of construction being underwritten by the CPR in return for the bonds and debentures of the KVR. Other than these restrictions, Warren and McCulloch were on their own. Unlike any of the other CPR subsidiary rail lines in southern British Columbia, the Kettle Valley Railway would receive neither interference nor direction from the CPR. As Shaughnessy finished, he added one more restriction: the Kettle Valley Railway must be first class in every way, an enduring monument for all time to the CPR's faith and dedication to the service of the people of southern British Columbia. No compromise in that directive would be accepted.

After McCulloch's final meeting with Shaughnessy, the entries in his diary reflected considerable apprehension about his abilities to handle the great challenge put before him. His co-workers and fellow engineers of Windsor Station showed no such apprehension when, on June 1, 1910, they accompanied him to the train that would return him once more to the mountains of southern British Columbia. Before he boarded, they presented him with a magnificent engraved silverware chest in token of their appreciation for his many years of service and leadership. The gift was also their way of offering him encouragement and good luck. They, like Shaughnessy, knew the right man had been chosen to do the job.[12]

9: Bridging the Gap

The Kettle Valley Railway starts construction

Early in June 1910, as Andrew McCulloch's train carried him west to British Columbia, his thoughts undoubtedly were concentrated on the task which lay before him. He had sound reason to be apprehensive. Upon his arrival in British Columbia he would be faced with a task of Herculean proportions. The Kettle Valley Railway had been projected through some of the most difficult terrain in North America yet it would have to be built in record time to beat J.J. Hill's VV&E. Carry and Henderson had done only preliminary engineering work, and not a single location plan had been approved by the appropriate governmental authorities. Indeed, as yet there were no plans to submit for approval.

Moreover, the first decade of the century that Wilfrid Laurier said belonged to Canada had produced a boom in railway construction that strained the availability of men and materials. Qualified engineers were scare. Virtually every responsible contractor in the country was already fully engaged. Unskilled labourers—needed by the thousands in that age before mechanization—were in short supply. Steel mills were two years behind on their orders for rails. Spare freight cars were a rarity, spare locomotives non-existent. In fact virtually every commodity needed in railway construction was out of stock or in short supply. William Van Horne, in his typically colourful language, aptly summed up the problems of western Canada's railway construction boom: "The hopper is too big for the spout."[1] This assessment was of little consolation to McCulloch, who had only 40 days to begin construction of his railway.

Nevertheless, McCulloch was not discouraged. Before leaving Montreal he and Warren had carefully reviewed the existing survey reports and had already reached a number of conclusions regarding the construction of the Kettle Valley Railway. Shaughnessy's instructions required the railway to pass through Beaverdell and Carmi; therefore the only feasible route west of Midway was along the Kettle River and its West Fork. Once into Carmi the railway could not go through Dale's Pass or up Wilkinson Creek without the grades exceeding the 1.0% limitation specified by the CPR president, thus the only crossing of the divide between the Kettle River and the Okanagan that could be utilized was Hydraulic Lake Pass. The requirement that the railway pass through the general area of Summerland eliminated any route west of Penticton except via Trout Creek. Because the rail line was also to extend through Coquihalla Pass, there was little realistic alternative eastward from Merritt than to follow the Coldwater River to Otter Summit. These restrictions meant the only portion of the railway route not defined was the section between Otter Summit and the headwaters of Trout Creek at Osprey Lake. Of course, the finalization of the railway's specific position along the generally defined route—"locating" in civil engineering jargon—had still to be undertaken.

While in Montreal, McCulloch and Warren had also decided their initial attention should be given to settling the affairs of the Midway & Vernon Railway so the KVR could begin the relatively easy task of refinishing the existing grade from Midway to Rock Creek. In the agreement with the provincial government the KVR was to receive title to the M&V grade; in return the KVR would pay the government the cash equivalent of the roadbed's value, which the government would use to pay the outstanding wages of the men who had constructed the grade. The value of the roadbed was open to question because of deterioration so the statute provided for the establishment of a commission of three men to settle the price. One man was to be named by the railway, one by the government, and the third by the mutual agreement of the first two. On June 2 the provincial government named Robert Green, a Legislature member from the southern interior. A week later, Warren announced the KVR had chosen L.M. Rice, an engineer from Seattle who had worked with McCulloch on the construction of the Columbia & Western Railway. Subsequently John Forin, a Nelson magistrate, was named as the third man.

On June 15, 1910 the three men, accompanied by a host of government officials, inspected the railway grade.[2] Conflict soon arose. McCulloch and Rice walked the entire ten miles of line, carefully noting in their field books every minute detail of the line's construction. They arrived at a decidedly different value than the government's representative, who was reported to have merely ridden over a short portion of the right-of-way in his buggy. Rice and McCulloch set the value at $57,000. The government evaluator set the figure at more than double this amount. Judge Forin, skilled in the art of weighing the merits of conflicting evidence, leaned towards the more thorough analysis made by Rice and McCulloch and, with his urging, a compromise value of slightly less than $63,000 was reached. McCulloch enlisted J.A. Tuzo as the KVR's first assistant engineer to stake the grade in preparation for the necessary repair work.[3]

McCulloch then left Midway and went to Penticton, where he met Warren on June 21 to discuss railway matters with the local municipal council. A number of decisions between the railway and the council were quickly reached that day. It was agreed the railway would make Penticton its headquarters, with roundhouse and servicing facilities. In return, Penticton would grant the railway a section of municipal property on the shores of Okanagan Lake as the site for a depot and allow the railway an exemption from local taxes for a specific period. Penticton voters promptly ratified the agreement by a majority of 151 to 5. Although the agreement was later set aside by the courts because of a technical error in the bylaw, when voted upon again in 1911 it received a comparable margin of approval.

Following their Penticton meeting Warren returned east, and McCulloch proceeded to Vancouver where he planned to organize the men he expected to have responded to his request for engineering personnel. Upon his arrival at the CPR station in Vancouver, McCulloch found to his dismay that not a single man had responded. Even many of the less-skilled surveying positions, such as axemen and chainmen, had gone unfilled, despite McCulloch's generous offer of $2.00 per day. Frustrated by this poor response, McCulloch left the station and stalked up to the newly opened KVR office.[4] Charles Gordon, the young man whom Thomas Shaughnessy had sent west as secretary-treasurer of the KVR, related to the author in 1970 that McCulloch "slammed the door so hard behind him that the glass almost fell off the door." Like McCulloch, Gordon had been in the CPR's Montreal office prior to coming west, but the two men had never formally met because of McCulloch's frequent absences from Windsor Station. As Gordon remembers it, McCulloch's mood in Vancouver that morning did little to effect a congenial introduction.

McCulloch opened the conversation by demanding to know who this stranger was in the KVR office. Gordon politely introduced himself, but hardly had he finished before McCulloch retorted sharply, "Well, I'm the Chief Engineer around here, and how in hell can I build your damn railroad if I can't get anyone to help me?" Before Gordon could mutter a response, McCulloch demanded, "Where can I get a pair of work boots? I may be building this whole damn railroad myself!" Gordon meekly referred him to a shoe store several blocks away. McCulloch left, slamming the door behind him. Half an hour later he was back, fire on his breath. "These damn boots of yours just cost me eight dollars. Hell, in any other store I could have got them for three-fifty!" Gordon tried in vain to apologize for directing McCulloch to such an expensive store. Gordon reported: "He threatened that if I ever crossed his path again he'd make a whistle post out of me for his new railroad." Despite this unconventional introduction, McCulloch and Gordon—different in personalities as night and day—joined in a friendship that would outlast the boots by more than 30 years.

Following the unsuccessful attempt to recruit engineering personnel in Vancouver, McCulloch took the CPR train to Merritt. There on June 27, 1910 he opened the second office of the KVR with himself as the only staff member. Early in July, McCulloch's fortunes changed for the better when Edmund Coley, an engineer who had worked with McCulloch on several prairie locations, arrived at Merritt in response to McCulloch's earlier request. Coley immediately became the KVR's second assistant engineer.[5] That same week, McCulloch and Coley set to work lining a set of survey stakes southward from a junction point with the CPR's Nicola Branch.

On June 30 Warren let a contract for the clearing and grading of the 30 miles of railway projected from Merritt to Otter Summit.[6] The contract was awarded to the construction firm of Macdonell, Gzowski & Company, which had a year earlier completed the CPR Spiral Tunnel project.[7] Although the exact location had yet to be determined and the Board of Railway Commissioners still had to approve the location plans, it was imperative work begin quickly because of the time limitation in the agreement with the provincial government. On July 9, 1910—one day before the deadline in the agreement—a team of horses and a scraper were put to work grading the roadbed south of the Merritt yard.[8] Over the next few days, construction continued at a pace akin to the "mule and a bale of hay outfit" at Penticton back in 1898. By the end of July the contractors had added sufficient men that they could stay close on the heels of the surveyors progressing up the Coldwater Valley. McCulloch had also added two more assistant engineers.

McCulloch chose for the most part to follow Henry Carry's survey line along the east bank of the Coldwater River from Merritt to Brook Creek, although a few miles above Merritt he briefly diverted the line to the west bank and back to avoid an unstable clay bluff. Between mile 20 and 25.2 above Merritt, where the valley was much narrower than at lower elevations, McCulloch altered the survey to cross the Coldwater River six times in an attempt to avoid heavy rockwork and eliminate any severe curves in the rail line. At mile 25.2 the final crossing of the Coldwater River returned the railway to the east bank of the river and allowed it to turn back on itself in a giant loop that gave the line sufficient distance to climb to Otter Summit without exceeding a 1.0% ruling grade. From the end of this remarkable four-mile long curve, known as "The Loop" (later named Brodie), the short line to the coast would branch off for Hope, a scant 50 miles away through Coquihalla Pass.

Following the surveyors were the hordes of labourers whose muscles, with the exception of horse-drawn scrapers, the occasional steam shovel and liberal amounts of black powder, were the force that constructed the entire Kettle Valley Railway. The workers were representative of many nationalities, the only common trait among them being the inexorable toil in which they engaged. The editor of the *Merritt Herald* described them as "mostly foreigners."[9] However, that description did not mean their pay allotment was unwelcome in the community. The construction of the KVR caused a major building boom in Merritt. Throughout July and August, buildings appeared to be under construction everywhere. Real estate offices seemed second in popularity only to the saloons. Indeed, the same newspaper editor who disdained the intrusion of railway workers into his community boldly predicted trainloads of coke would soon be leaving for the Boundary smelters every hour while the Grand Trunk Pacific and Canadian Northern fought with J.J. Hill for right-of-way into the rising city of destiny.

Having started the construction at Merritt, McCulloch and Warren returned their attention to the Midway end of the railway. On August 11, 1910, the KVR awarded L.M. Rice & Company a contract for the complete grading and tracklaying of the first 35-mile section of railway from Midway to Bull Creek, including the repair of the M&V grade. Without the pressing deadline faced at the Merritt end, preparation work at

Midway progressed more slowly and active construction did not begin until October 4, 1910.

Penticton was the logical choice for the required third point of construction because of the relative ease of supply delivery via the CPR boats on Okanagan Lake. Unfortunately Penticton posed several serious problems for location of the railway. Both the east and west shores of Okanagan Lake were lined with high glacial terraces—locally known as benches—with relatively level, stable tops, but with edges that made an abrupt drop to the lake in the form of towering clay cliffs, prone to slumping when broken by any kind of cutting. This made it virtually impossible to obtain a stable roadbed directly from Penticton, at that time only a small village huddled on the shores of Okanagan Lake, up to the top of the terraces. For this reason, McCulloch decided to locate the railway yard and terminal a mile south of the town proper. There, the broad alluvial fan of Penticton Creek on the east side had produced a natural ramp up to the east bench, and Shingle Creek had cut a relatively stable draw through the west terrace. These geological graces gave the railway easier access to the benches and permitted the KVR to make use of a large meadow on Fairview Road as a railway yard. A short spur line was proposed to connect the yard with the station, which was planned for the waterfront property on Okanagan Lake deeded by the municipality.[10]

Throughout the fall of 1910 construction continued steadily. Because of the general shortage of labour in the west the number of men at work never exceeded 600, a modest work force indeed for such a major construction project. Even so, the crews made reasonable progress, and by mid-October about ten miles of roadbed had been completed southward from Merritt. As the work advanced further and further from Merritt, it became evident an early start had to be made in tracklaying to reduce the cost of hauling supplies to the centre point of construction. Unfortunately, Warren had been unable to secure any rails or locomotives for tracklaying. Even the CPR was so desperate for motive power it had suspended maintenance work on almost all its lines in western Canada while every locomotive worked overtime to move the largest wheat crop to date in Canadian history. McCulloch's comment on the matter was simply, "No ties, no locomotives, no nothing to work with."[11]

Warren subsequently reported that the Nicola Valley Lumber Company was willing to supply a limited number of ties from its mill at Canford and on December 9, the CPR telegraphed the lukewarm news it would provide a few more ties and a few miles of second-hand rails. Later that week the track material arrived and some token tracklaying was done by hand. But without a locomotive the task could not be tackled seriously.[12]

On December 18, 1910, the train from Spences Bridge brought with it a few more cars of rails, and by a miraculous feat of string-pulling on the part of J.J. Warren, a beat-up, cast-off 4-6-0 locomotive, 496, on loan from the CPR.[13] Despite its shortcomings, this long-awaited locomotive pleased McCulloch and his staff, and with its use the next day they set a new KVR tracklaying record of 1,300 feet in a single day, a record that was to remain intact for some time. The limited supply of ties and rails was exhausted by Christmas and, although a few more carloads arrived before the New Year, the work of laying them ceased once more when the 496 trapped itself above several derailed cars near the end of the line.

By mid-January 1911, trackage east from Merritt had reached mile 10, but halted again, this time for want of ties. One might suspect the crews were burning them to keep warm, as temperatures all that month hovered at 40 degrees below zero. The 496 reacted equally unfavourably to the cold and, when a fresh shipment of ties arrived the same day as the thermometer dropped to a new winter low, the 496 broke down, giving the tracklaying crews a respite from the harsh weather. Although the repairs to the locomotive did not take long, on February 16, 1911 the 496 broke down once more, this time necessitating that it be sent to Kamloops for major repair.

Unluckily for McCulloch, the roundhouse foreman at Kamloops was a conscientious man who, for the previous two months, had been making a strenuous effort to locate a "missing" locomotive, namely the 496. Following the discovery of his lost sheep, the foreman adopted an extremely fatherly attitude towards his flock of locomotives, which precluded the return of the 496 after the necessary repairs had been completed. Thus ended the 496's brief career on the Kettle Valley Railway. Without a locomotive of any kind at Merritt the KVR could not resume tracklaying, and with the harsh weather showing no signs of letup McCulloch was forced to halt all construction at Merritt until the spring.

Progress at Midway was also below original anticipation. Late in December the CPR made a Christmas present of a few derelict flat cars and cabooses to the KVR; all of them were of debatable value in railway construction work and absolutely useless without a locomotive.

Nevertheless, McCulloch accepted them gratefully and, following the episode with the 496 at Kamloops, had "Kettle Valley Railway" stencilled on them to ensure their permanent residence on the railway. On January 2, 1911, the Kettle Valley Lines 4-4-0 locomotive 1 was transferred from the Grand Forks operation to Midway and on January 17 a tracklaying machine finally reached Midway. Tracklaying was begun. By February 8 track had reached Rock Creek, and by month's end it stretched to mile 15.5, where a twin span wooden Howe truss bridge was being erected to carry the railway across the Kettle River to the west bank. Grading work northward had already stopped because of the harsh winter conditions and, with tracklaying forced to stop awaiting completion of the bridge, mile 15.5 was to remain the end of steel for several months.

Cold weather was not the only thing distressing McCulloch. In January he learned J.J. Warren and J.R. Stratton had been arrested on charges of fraud in connection with the collapse of the Farmers Bank, which left control of the railway largely in McCulloch's hands. Warren and Stratton were later exonerated of the charges, but the incident did little to add encouragement to the generally depressing state of affairs on the Kettle Valley Railway.

Despite the slow construction, that first winter was a time of extreme activity for McCulloch and his engineering staff because of the need to complete as much of the railway's location surveys as possible in readiness for construction in the spring. Of course McCulloch's assistants did the majority of this work, but McCulloch frequently played a direct role in the locating function. For example, on the Kettle River section, one of the assistant engineers, M.E. Brooks, had located the railway survey line north from the bridge at mile 15.5 along the west bank of the Kettle River and its West Fork as far as Carmi. This section was relatively easy except for a short piece near mile 30 where the West Fork of the Kettle River doubled back upon itself in a narrow constriction near the confluence of Bull Creek. At this point Brooks had proposed a tunnel several hundred feet in length to cut through the rocky ridge on the west side of the canyon. McCulloch disliked the prospect of delaying tracklaying while the tunnel was being drilled. Taking the surveying transit himself, he tested his own location ideas by carrying the survey line across the river at mile 26.6 and up the east side of the river. By approaching the canyon from the east bank and crossing the river again at a strategic point, McCulloch was able to squeeze the line through the canyon without a tunnel. To Brooks' amazement McCulloch's revised line was actually shorter than his original location. Moreover all tight curves had been eliminated. McCulloch had amply demonstrated the skill that had earned him his reputation as one of the country's most competent location engineers.

North of Carmi, McCulloch achieved a similar success. The preliminary surveys done by both the Midway & Vernon Railway and by Henderson had followed the floor of the West Fork of the Kettle River for 15 miles north of Carmi then climbed Kallis Creek, a small tributary stream forming a natural pathway to the summit. Unfortunately Kallis Creek rose too quickly to permit location of a 1.0% grade along its valley and was too narrow to permit the use of climbing loops in its lower reaches. C.J. Seymour, the assistant engineer assigned to this section, was quick to encounter this dilemma. After examining Seymour's preliminary work, McCulloch spent several days exploring the adjacent hills on foot and horseback. He returned to Seymour with the suggestion the line loop into Wilkinson Creek, just above Carmi—miles from the area where the problem was centred—thereby gaining enough elevation to slip through a previously undiscovered cut in the hillside near Arlington Lakes. The climb could then continue to the summit at Hydraulic Lake. Seymour followed this suggestion and discovered it produced a perfect 1.0% grade.

Impressive as these achievements were, even more resourcefulness would be needed west of Hydraulic Lake. On this section 3,000 feet of elevation had to be covered in the descent from the 4,100-foot summit at Hydraulic Lake to lake level at Penticton. Moreover, this descent was along the edge of rugged mountains cut by numerous transverse streams. At Canyon Creek (now known as Myra Canyon) the stream had eroded the mountain-face into a steeply walled canyon an unbelievable 2,000 feet in depth. Even McCulloch was stunned on first sighting the chasm. He estimated that five or six miles of extremely heavy construction would be necessary to permit bridging the canyon. Sawmill Creek (now known as Bellevue Creek), five miles to the west, posed another serious challenge.

Construction over this route was estimated to be so difficult that McCulloch was advised by his assistant engineers to locate the railway at lake level along the eastern shore of Okanagan Lake from Penticton to Kelowna, then make the 3,000-foot climb to Hydraulic Lake in a series of loops laid out on the easy hillside to the northeast of the summit. Although this route would avoid Canyon Creek entirely, it would result in a considerably longer railway. Mindful of Shaughnessy's directive that the railway must be first class in every way, McCulloch rejected this alternative and decided the railway must route through Canyon Creek. Early in 1911 he assigned assistant engineer William Gourlay the task of establishing a preliminary survey line to provide data for a decision regarding exact route location.[14]

As the winter of 1910-1911 gave way to spring, active construction work once more resumed on the Kettle Valley Railway. Unfortunately the shortage of locomotives continued to plague the KVR, and the completion of many miles of new grade that spring only served to make the locomotive shortage more distressing. In March, the CPR consented to transfer engine 149, which for most of the previous year had been assigned to switching duties at Middlesboro Collieries at Merritt, to the KVR to replace the 496 but the tenure of this locomotive was barely over a month and for several weeks there was no locomotive at all at Merritt.[15] On May 22, 1911, CPR 1284, ten years older and in worse mechanical condition than the previous 496, was delivered to Merritt.[16] McCulloch may have thought the arrival of the 1284 solved his locomotive problems at Merritt, but when the KVR crew tried to take a train down to the gravel pit at Coutlee, two miles below Merritt, McCulloch found to his amazement that the CPR refused to allow the derelict 1284 back on its tracks! After considerable argument a compromise was reached and the 1284, under the guiding hand of William "Smoky" Clapperton, was soon busy chugging up and down from Coutlee.

By late spring the overworked 1284 could no longer keep up with the combined tasks of tracklaying and ballasting the completed track, and in June another locomotive was added.[17] In July the 1284 broke down entirely and was dragged off to the repair shop, never to polish KVR iron again. The CPR begrudgingly sent the KVR another locomotive, 1330, to remedy the problem.[18] It was a husky 2-8-0 from the Kootenay Division and was not only relatively new and in good condition, but it could haul 13 loaded ballast cars at once, more than double the load handled by the 1284.

The operation of two locomotives naturally introduced the problem of controlling train movements, and it became necessary to build a number of short sidings at close intervals to allow two trains to pass. Upon completion of ballasting, the majority of these short sidings were removed, but some were extended as permanent passing tracks for the railway's regular operation. The first such siding was located 9.3 miles

above Merritt, at a point where the KVR passed through a large and excep-
tionally pretty glen bounded by groves of aspen trees. Warren and
McCulloch—who chose the names of all the stations on the Kettle Valley
Railway—named the site Glen Walker, after E.G. Walker, the owner of a
nearby ranch.[19] A second siding and a water tank to supply water for loco-
motives were built at mile 17.9 when the track reached that point in
August. This station was named Kingsvale, after another local rancher,
"Dell" King.[20]

East of Kingsvale, rails were laid across the last bridge over the
Coldwater River on September 20, 1911 and reached Otter Summit, 29.4
miles from Merritt, nine days later. An additional two months were needed
before the line was fully ballasted. When ballasting was completed, no time
was lost requesting approval from the dominion government to operate
the railway. On November 29 a dominion government inspector—best left
unnamed—arrived in Merritt in a condition McCulloch described in his
diary as "comfortably drunk," and promptly declared the railway to be satisfactory.[21] Any fear for public safety resulting from this dubious pronouncement was removed shortly afterwards when John P. Forde, a conscientious representative for the provincial government, inspected the
line. The exact words of the news report covering Forde's inspection were:
"He pronounced it to be the best section of railway he had ever examined,
thus reflecting great credit on the engineering staff of the railway company."[22] Few observant passengers who ever rode the Kettle Valley Railway
failed to share Forde's amazement at the work done by Andrew McCulloch
and his assistants.

Grading and ballasting on the section of the railway in the Kettle
Valley also resumed during the spring of 1911, although the general shortage of labour made the progress of construction very slow. In fact, one
subcontractor had been thrown in jail for illegally smuggling aliens into
Canada in an effort to have sufficient manpower to complete his contracted section. A second locomotive added at Midway had little effect
on progress.[23] Likewise, a contract awarded to L.M. Rice & Company in
July for the portion of the KVR line from the end of that firm's first
contract to the summit at Hydraulic Lake was of nominal significance
that summer. Early in the fall the bridge at mile 15.5 was completed and
track subsequently spurted up to the bridge at mile 29.8 near the end
of grading. Other than that, little progress was made in the Kettle Valley
during 1911. The year ended with rails reaching only to mile 35, a

disheartening distance considering over a year and a half had passed since work had begun.[24]

Even less progress was made at Penticton during 1911. Early in the year the Kettle Valley Railway began constructing a fine hotel—later named the Incola—and a wharf and short section of railway grade leading from the wharf through town towards the proposed railway yards were built.

Virtually no other progress was made there that year. Even the wharf was not begun until mid-year and the occasion of its start of construction did not rank high in the annals of Penticton's history. McCulloch's principal concern was to get railway work at Penticton underway as soon as possible after he had assembled a crew to do the job. Thus, not long after sun-up on June 10, 1911 a KVR crew set to work readying to drive piles for the wharf. To McCulloch such a task was purely pedestrian. Penticton's reeve, E. Foley-Bennett, thought the start of pile driving to be an occasion too important to pass without official sanction. Having been awakened just minutes before the work of driving the first pile began, he was unshaven and fastening his suspenders as he ran to the wharf, only to arrive at the lakeshore too late to bestow the municipality's formal blessing on the first pile. Local citizens on hand to watch the pile driving deemed the event had not been adorned with the dignity befitting either their reeve or the symbolic importance of the event, so a request was made for another, more dignified ceremony. In addition to the opening confusion, there was also some question as to whether or not the wharf construction constituted bona fide railway work under the agreement between the railway and the municipality because the pile had been driven out in the lake, which strictly speaking was outside the municipal boundary. Therefore it was decided there would be a new ceremony. On July 1, 1911, in front of a Dominion Day crowd of Pentictonites and with his suspenders properly fastened, Foley-Bennett turned the first sod on the KVR work at Penticton. The event was only ceremonial. The acute shortage of labour would delay the start of meaningful construction until well into the fall.

Construction work on the section between Penticton and the adjacent community of Summerland was also held up, partly by the labour situation and partly because of a dispute over the railway's location. The dispute had started when assistant engineer M.E. Brooks began staking a survey line up the south side of Trout Creek, across the canyon from the community of Summerland. This was taken as a certain sign in the minds of Summerland residents that the railway was bypassing their community. A loud volley of complaints ensued. Summerland residents demanded the KVR follow Carry's original survey, which had crossed Trout Creek and passed through the area above Summerland. The *Summerland Review* editorialized that if the railway stayed on the south side of Trout Creek the community would be short-changed from becoming a major metropolis on "the new transcontinental route" all because of an "infinitesimal" bridge.[25] James Ritchie, the town's reeve and chief promoter, met with McCulloch who agreed to have Brooks examine possible alterations in the route to accommodate Summerland. However, Brooks revealed what McCulloch already suspected: the line bypassing Summerland and avoiding a large bridge would be less expensive. On May 31, 1911, Warren officially informed Ritchie the KVR route would remain on the south side of Trout Creek.

Ritchie promptly rallied the proletariat to protest once more and a letter was sent to the minister of railways in Ottawa demanding he order the KVR route to be altered. The minister promised Ritchie a public hearing prior to a final decision on the railway route. In the meantime the KVR went ahead and awarded a contract to L.M. Rice & Company for the construction of the first five miles west of Penticton, as this section was outside the area of dispute. On August 14, 1911 the promised hearing was held at West Summerland. After each side had presented its case, the minister stated he did not think it fair to order the railway route to be changed. Instead he informally asked McCulloch and Warren to reconsider their decision in the interest of public goodwill and potential trade for the railway. McCulloch and Warren decided to abide by the Minister's request. A new line, the line the railway eventually built, was surveyed crossing Trout Creek on a 619-foot-long, 241-foot-high "infinitesimal" bridge—the highest on the Kettle Valley Railway and the third highest railway bridge ever built in the province—to rejoin the original survey line higher up the Trout Creek Valley.[26]

Not long afterwards the KVR awarded G.A. Carlson & Company a contract for construction of the remainder of the line from Trout Creek to Osprey Lake, a point 38.8 miles west of Penticton.[27] As with the other sections of railway, shortages of manpower and materials plagued both Rice and Carlson and for most of the winter fewer than 200 men were at work. There was also no motive power for the Penticton section. Thus, when the first shipment of rail cars reached Penticton on December 11, 1911, a pair of "hay burners" had to substitute for the preferred "coal burners" in moving the cars off the barge onto the short section of track on the new wharf.

It was essential Andrew McCulloch have a continuous overview of construction to ensure contractors were completing each phase of the work according to specification. This was a demanding job, compounded by the slowness of travel between the numerous areas of construction. Between Merritt and Penticton the journey entailed one of three different routes: an overland ride by horseback; a ride by horseback to Princeton then by GN train to Keremeos and by stage or horseback to Penticton; or by train and boat via Spences Bridge and Sicamous. The fastest method took two days; the slowest took nearly a week. Between Penticton and the Kettle Valley the journey took even longer. Therefore, it was hardly surprising that much of McCulloch's time was spent travelling. His work required certain members of his staff accompany him. A.A. Swift, his chief clerk, who had come from Montreal, was a constant companion, as was Charles Gordon, the KVR's secretary-treasurer. J.J. Warren, the railway's president, was also a frequent companion.

Swift, in an interview in 1969, related to the author a humorous incident that occurred one time when the four men spent the night in Beaverdell's sole hotel. After the night's lodging and breakfast the four men were preparing to leave when Warren approached the hotel manager to settle their account. The proprietor informed them the charge was 50 cents each or $2.00 in total. Warren reached into his bulging billfold and laid a crisp $20 bill upon the innkeeper's desk. The proprietor was aghast by the bill. Not in years, he explained, had he seen a bill of such large denomination. He could not possibly make change. Warren then turned to the others and asked if any of them might have a bill of smaller denomination. McCulloch stepped forward and dropped a few pieces of silver onto the hotel desk—but not before he turned and thrust a fistful of one dollar bills at Warren with the curt comment, "That's the third night in a row you've pulled that trick. I'm going to change that damn twenty of yours before it breaks the rest of us!"

McCulloch and Warren may have enjoyed humorously baiting each other in such ways but they were certainly never cheap with friendship, either between themselves of with the hundreds of others they met in the course of their years with the Kettle Valley Railway. At Christmas McCulloch always seemed to have a gift for everyone and, in return, as Swift related, "McCulloch practically needed a boxcar just to carry away the presents given to him by his many friends and admirers."

As the year 1912 dawned, McCulloch became increasingly concerned that construction progress on the Kettle Valley Railway was lagging well below original expectations. Despite some 18 months of work the railway was scarcely more than 20% complete. McCulloch was not alone in his frustration. All across Canada hardly a railway was being completed with any degree of rapidity owing to the continuing acute shortage of labour. So acute was the problem that early in 1912, the Canadian government moved to rescind all legislation restricting the entry of aliens into Canada in the hope of filling the many vacancies in western railroad camps. Some people feared the legislation would result in a wholesale invasion of Canada by Chinese and Japanese. However as a direct cure for the problem the legislation was profoundly successful. By the end of 1912 more than 5,000 men were at work on the Kettle Valley Railway, and for the first time since work had begun in July 1910 construction was able to advance as a rate commensurate with a project of such magnitude.

Throughout the spring of 1912, work was under way west of Penticton and on the West Fork. At the Merritt end, ballasting and trimming were underway to realign the tracks after the frosts of the previous winter.[28] By mid-June this work was completed for the first ten miles and on Sunday June 23, 1912 the KVR celebrated the occasion by running its first passenger train. CPR locomotive 131, assigned to switching at Middlesboro Collieries, was excused from its normal duties for the Lord's Day to provide the first train with its motive power.[29] The KVR had no passenger equipment, but a string of flatcars fitted with wooden benches was quite acceptable to the cheering crowd of Merritt citizens who, as a preview to their new railway, rode up to Glen Walker for an afternoon picnic.

The Kettle Valley Railway's first passenger train was a well-received adventure in public relations. But it certainly was no precedent for future months. The increasing availability of manpower allowed construction work to advance at an accelerating rate, causing the KVR's shortage of motive power to be more acute than ever. One borrowed CPR locomotive had to handle all work at Merritt, and the Kettle Valley Lines 2 was kept more than busy on the West Fork. Compounding this shortage, the locomotive based at Merritt seemed to disappear and reappear on a week-to-week basis depending on the vagaries of CPR traffic. As construction advanced further and further from the points of supply, Warren and McCulloch realized the situation was becoming intolerable. In March 1912

Warren instructed Fred Demuth, motive power superintendent, to purchase as many locomotives and cars as he could for use on the KVR. Demuth promptly went east to try and secure the required equipment, but everywhere locomotives were in short supply. It wasn't until May that he was able to acquire any equipment and even this acquisition amounted to only four used locomotives and a rag-tag collection of second-hand cars of various types purchased in Chicago. When Demuth tried to bring his stock across the border a squabble ensued with customs officials, and it was well into July when the only four locomotives ever to bear the Kettle Valley Railway name were received on construction sites. Two of the locomotives were put to work on the West Fork and the other two were sent to Merritt to assist in ballasting.[30]

Unfortunately, one of the locomotives sent to Merritt did not have the best of introductions to the Kettle Valley Railway. On July 26, 1912, just after its delivery to Merritt, the locomotive was sitting out the night on the KVR track south of the wye when a wiper, who had been cleaning the valve gear, moved the locomotive to expose parts of the running gear he had been unable to reach. In moving the engine he accidentally backed into a string of dump cars and a ballast plow, sending them loose down the grade towards Spences Bridge. The cars and plow accelerated downgrade before derailing into the ballast pit at Coutlee, smashing into complete ruin less than a week after arriving onto the KVR.

On October 26, 1912 the first locomotive arrived at Penticton. Locomotive 3 had been engaged in ballasting completed track on the West Fork but, with ballasting operations there finished for the winter, the engine was hauled over the CPR to Okanagan Landing and sent by barge to Penticton. George Nadan, the KVR's first locomotive engineer assigned to Penticton, had the honour of driving KVR 3 off the barge into the Penticton wharf that day and he made sure the arrival of that community's first locomotive was the gala occasion the gathered throng of Pentictonites expected. He and his fireman provided KVR 3 with a good head of steam so that after Mrs. Warren had been given the honour of blowing the whistle for the first time, eager Penticton citizens could take turns doing the same and riding in the cab while the engine ran back and forth over the few hundred feet of trackage then constituting Penticton's railway. As soon as the locals had finished their fun the locomotive went to work unloading the work cars and the accompanying cars of rails. The following day it was laying out steel on the completed grade through town.

The addition of the locomotives, along with the greatly increased work forces, allowed work on the West Fork section to advance rapidly during the summer of 1912. This progress in turn dictated that McCulloch commence construction on the Hydraulic Lake-Penticton section. Unfortunately McCulloch was extremely disappointed with the location survey Gourlay had prepared during the previous winter. It wasn't that Gourlay had done a poor job; on the contrary it was Gourlay's clear delineation of the difficulties involved that caused concern. McCulloch had hoped to utilize a continuous 1.5% grade in dropping the 3,000 feet from Hydraulic Lake to Penticton. Gourlay's survey had shown that use of a 1.5% grade would force the line around the outside of the mountain ridge east of Okanagan Lake for the entire 60 miles, with numerous expensive tunnels and bridges. McCulloch was also disturbed that the route required a large number of tight curves, which destroyed much of the operating advantage of the moderate grade. Even so, Gourlay advised, the route would have to be accepted. The only alternative was to cut through the narrow pass at Chute Lake just above the falls where Chute Creek cascades over the lip of the mountain ridge to Okanagan Lake. While this alternative route was easy for much of the way, the exit point at Chute Lake was only 15 miles from Penticton and nearly 3,000 feet above it. Thus the railway could not connect Chute Lake and Penticton with grades less than 4.5%, well above the limit specified by Thomas Shaughnessy.

McCulloch spent nearly a month covering the territory east of Penticton in an attempt to resolve the dilemma of route location. The longer he spent hiking in the hills above Okanagan Lake the more intrigued he became by Chute Lake Pass. McCulloch recognized that locating the railway via Chute Lake would not avoid the inevitable heavy expenditure of building through Myra Canyon but the wooded valley of Chute Lake Pass was very direct and involved far lighter construction than Gourlay's line around the mountain edge. Moreover Chute Lake and Hydraulic Lake were at practically the same elevation; the 30 miles of track required between them could be nearly level. If only the railway could reach Chute Lake from Penticton on a reasonable grade he would have his answer.

Then McCulloch hit upon a bold plan. Drawing upon his experience in surveying the Spiral Tunnels at Field, McCulloch decided to utilize a 2.2% grade for 15 miles northeast from Penticton. There he would have the line double back on itself in a huge loop, head south for several miles all the while maintaining the 2.2% grade, then double back again through a spiral tunnel, exiting just below Chute Lake. The long 2.2% grade would be steeper than the 1.5% grade originally proposed—indeed it would be the longest stretch of ruling grade over 2% on any railway in Canada—but McCulloch believed the increase in grade would be compensated by a considerable reduction in the number of curves in the climb out of the Okanagan Valley. When Gourlay did a survey of the huge double loops and spiral tunnel McCulloch had proposed, this not only proved to be true, but the new line was shorter, eliminated all but four tunnels and worked out to be 25% lower in estimated construction cost, a savings McCulloch had predicted before Gourlay began his survey. The astonished members of the engineering staff were already calling the Kettle Valley Railway "McCulloch's Wonder."

On August 3, 1912 the KVR awarded a contract to Grant Smith & Company for construction of the Hydraulic Lake-Penticton section, which ultimately was 57 miles long when completed. Because of litigation over right-of-way, construction work could not be started in Penticton proper, but camps were quickly established on the east bench. On September 24, 1912 grading of the newly contracted section began three miles east of town.[31]

With the award of the construction contract for the Hydraulic Lake-Penticton section, the only portion of the KVR between Midway and Merritt not either complete or under contract was the section from Otter Summit to Osprey Lake. McCulloch and Warren had purposely deferred a decision on this section in the early stages of construction because of the section's isolation from supply points. However, with rails already into Otter Summit and extending westward from Penticton, any delay in commencing work on the intervening section could only delay final completion of the railway.

Even so, commencement of work on this section was not merely a matter of awarding a contract. During 1910 and 1911 the community of Princeton had undergone a major coal mining boom, spurred by the arrival of J.J. Hill's VV&E. And Coalmont, 12 miles west of Princeton on the VV&E's projected route to the coast, was showing signs it would become an even greater coal producer once it secured rail connections. The growing trade of these two communities, especially compared with the largely barren Nicola plateau country through which Carry's survey had been projected, made Warren seriously consider altering the KVR route to put Coalmont and Princeton on the railway mainline. The KVR had already formally requested statutory approval to construct a branch line to Princeton from the projected KVR mainline. If the railway was going to build to Princeton anyway it might just as well continue through to Otter Summit with trackage, thought Warren. Such a route would mean Princeton and the rich Tulameen Valley could be on the railway mainline and the construction of some 75 miles of trackage through largely unproductive territory could be avoided.

Warren first presented his major route revision idea to McCulloch on July 29, 1911. During early August that year both men spent several days covering the newly proposed route. McCulloch quickly concurred with Warren that the suggested route was vastly superior in terms of traffic potential, and because it was only slightly longer than Carry's 1907-08 survey it represented a genuine possible alternative. McCulloch assigned an engineering crew to undertake a detailed survey. By December a preliminary line had been located.

The new survey line followed Carry's survey west from Osprey Lake for a distance of about ten miles. Instead of levelling off and crossing the divide between Five Mile Creek and Summers Creek, the new line continued down Five Mile Creek into Princeton on a steady 1.0% gradient. Five Mile Creek, for much of its descent, drops more than the 1.0% grade of the survey. Thus, the survey was forced to locate high on the face of a rock bluff where Five Mile Creek joins the Similkameen River just east of Princeton. It also forced the survey to pass slightly above the town of Princeton proper. Missing the townsite was not entirely detrimental. The survey's location on the north side of Princeton would prevent the railway from running into conflict with Hill's VV&E at river level. Also, on the west side of Princeton the surveyed route would enable the railway to follow the Tulameen River while keeping to the north bank, which obviated a bridge and avoided the high bluff just west of the townsite through which Hill, with his usual brash disregard for geography, had tunnelled.

West of that point the KVR's proposed route location was not so simple. From Princeton to Coalmont, Hill had already constructed his railway along the narrow floor of the Tulameen Valley, skipping his line from one side of the river to the other to secure the best alignment. This effectively excluded the KVR from utilizing a river level line. Of course, the KVR could choose a higher alignment and keep above the VV&E, an alignment the KVR survey did in fact follow, but a higher line would be much more costly to construct than the low level line the VV&E had built, which had been costly enough. A higher line would also surely meet with opposition from the Great Northern magnate because of the likelihood of snow and slide debris from the KVR landing on his tracks.

As winter turned to spring a confrontation between the two railways over the proposed KVR route revision seemed increasingly likely. Indeed, the confrontation became a certainty on April 10, 1912 when Warren publicly announced the Kettle Valley Railway was adopting its newly projected survey route via Princeton and the Tulameen Valley as the official route of its mainline instead of the originally proposed route via Aspen Grove.[32] Hill was quick to react. Reprisals for the KVR's invasion of his territory, he said, would be forthcoming. And Hill's threat was not without potential clout, based on his progress in pushing the VV&E towards completion during the previous two years. Despite the same labour shortages that had plagued all railroad builders, Hill had pushed his tracks ever closer to a meeting point in the Hope Mountains, eastward from Abbotsford and westward from Princeton. In fact by 1912 virtually all that remained to be finished on the VV&E was the short section centring on Coquihalla Pass. Here Hill had hesitated, almost as if transfixed by the gaping chasms and roaring abysses of the Coquihalla River. Yet he pushed on. Too much was at stake. He knew Coquihalla Pass was the key to the treasure house of southern British Columbia, the one missing link between the rich mines of the interior and the tidewater of Vancouver.

But Coquihalla Pass was also a canyon so rugged and difficult in character that the first railway through its narrow defile would virtually exclude the possibility of construction of a second railway. Thus, the first railway through the pass would have a strategic advantage of immense magnitude. The battle between the KVR and the VV&E for Coquihalla Pass was therefore not simply the next theatre of battle in the long war Hill and the CPR had been waging for nearly a quarter of a century. This battle would be the most important of them all, the final and conclusive battle of the longest and most bitterly fought railway war in the province's history. It would be, predicted one seer, the corporate death duel of the century.

10: Death Duel at Coquihalla Pass

The Great Northern concedes southern British Columbia

When J.J. Hill first crossed the Canadian border with his subsidiary New Westminster Southern Railway in 1891 he started an intense war between the Great Northern Railway and Canadian Pacific Railway for the rich freight trade of southern British Columbia. The two decades that followed produced some of the most intense and violent rivalry in railway history. During that time neither company had been able to successfully exclude its rival. As rapidly as one company extended its trackage, the other generally followed, ensuring the balance of power remained delicately poised between them. This mutually competitive survival was the prime contributor to the vast railway development—over-development might be a better term—in southern British Columbia, with a per capita investment perhaps unequalled in the world. At the time per capita investment did not concern either Hill or the CPR. Their only desire was to tip the delicate scales of balance in their own favour. As the two giants approached the strategic gap at Coquihalla Pass in the race to secure Coast-to-Kootenay rail connections, the power struggle became even more intense.

Hill had concretely acknowledged the importance of a rail line across the Hope Mountains by persevering with construction of the VV&E during the depressed years of 1907 and 1908, when economic conditions dictated against heavy capital investments. This perseverance had put his railway to the edge of the Hope Mountains. Therefore when Richard McBride announced late in 1909 that his government was backing the CPR in a bid to push its new subsidiary Kettle Valley Railway across southern British Columbia, it was obvious there would be a major confrontation between the CPR and GN in the mountains east of Hope. No subsidy was offered to Hill. However, being accustomed to both hard knocks from Canadian politicians and to funding his own railway projects, Hill accepted the KVR challenge in the same manner which he accepted any other threat to his empire—he went railroad building.

On February 21, 1910, VV&E crews commenced digging the tunnel just west of the Princeton townsite as the first step on the extension through to the coast. Almost simultaneously work was started at Abbotsford pushing the VV&E grade eastward. In the provincial Legislative Assembly, Hill's men were equally busy. Three of the VV&E's principal officers had petitioned for incorporation of the Penticton Railway, which Hill proposed to build north from the international boundary just north of his railway at Oroville along the valley of the Okanagan River to Penticton. Hill also sent a survey crew to locate a railway from Tulameen north into Merritt, with the designated intent of breaking the CPR's monopoly on the Nicola Valley coal mining industry. A lesser GN official was even more assertive: "We will be in Merritt next summer. Take that from me for it is a fact."[1] People with more objectivity might have questioned whether even Hill could build the promised line so quickly, considering the acute shortages of labour and materials all railroad builders faced, but in Merritt doubters were in a distinct minority. The general citizenry in that community lapped up the GN promises like a thirsty kitten would lap up a saucer of warm milk.

Throughout the summer of 1910 construction of the VV&E west of Princeton continued as rapidly as conditions would allow, and by the end of August the entire 16-mile section of grade from Princeton to Tulameen, with the exception of the 1,062-foot-long tunnel at Princeton, was complete and ready for tracklaying. Tracklaying west of Princeton could not be started until the tunnel was complete and, with winter approaching, Hill chose to put off further work until the following spring. Thus he withdrew all construction forces except those actually working on the tunnel. The citizens of Princeton did not share such logic. Rather than consider the high costs of moving supplies to Tulameen for further construction prior to the advancement of track, or the engineering difficulties involved in driving the Princeton tunnel through the loose rock encountered, most Princeton citizens preferred to believe Hill was reneging on his promise to complete the VV&E as quickly as possible. The editor of the *Similkameen Star* accused Hill of "inviting both opposition and competition by his dallying policy."[2] Subsequent editions headlined such mundane comments as

"VV&E takes nap after five years building 150 weary miles."[3] As unfair as these criticisms may have been, work on the VV&E section east of Abbotsford had also been curtailed as a result of a dispute over right-of-way lands. This unfortunate coincidence gave editors more ammunition with which to barrage J.J. Hill.

In truth, there was a great deal more than just a short tunnel and right-of-way dispute preventing Hill from reaching the coast. The towns of Tulameen and Hope, the end points of the portions of the VV&E under contract in 1910, may have been only 32 miles apart by direct distance, but they were separated by one of the most rugged mountain barriers in the world. Despite more than five years of exploration work, Hill's surveyors had been unable to establish a railway location across that barrier with grades of less than 2.5%, except by utilizing a projected eight-mile tunnel. Hill recognized that such a long tunnel, as desirable as it was from an operating viewpoint, would take many years to construct. Those years he no longer had now that the Kettle Valley Railway was out to beat him to the coast. Therefore, Hill decided late in 1910 that his priority would be to complete the VV&E as quickly as possible; the tunnel could be added when time permitted.

On November 22, 1910, it was publicly announced that survey work on the proposed tunnel had been suspended and VV&E chief engineer J.H. Kennedy had been instructed to prepare for construction of the railway over the original survey line of 1905 via Otter Summit and Coquihalla Summit.[4] The press release stated that the 40-mile section from Tulameen to Coquihalla Summit had already been successfully located, with a maximum westward grade of 1.2%.[5] It also stated plans were being filed with the Board of Railway Commissioners to enable work to begin when good weather returned in the spring.

Hill's decision to revert to the originally surveyed VV&E route made the narrow gap at Coquihalla Pass all the more strategic. Prior to the change, the VV&E survey had avoided significant conflict with the Kettle Valley Railway by not entering the main canyon of the Coquihalla River until below the exit point of the proposed eight-mile tunnel under Railroad Pass; on the remaining section between that point and Hope the VV&E had been staked on the south bank of the canyon, across the river from the KVR. However, the route change meant both surveys were on the same side of the river through the much more rugged upper canyon of the Coquihalla River, where construction of two independent lines would be exceedingly difficult. Thus possession of the first line through Coquihalla Pass had suddenly become a matter of unprecedented importance to both companies.

Fortunately for the VV&E, Hill had stubbornly insisted the original location survey done by his staff be filed with the Board of Railway Commissioners in Ottawa for approval, and although he had publicly announced in September 1909 that the route had been dropped in favour of the long tunnel, formal application to change the route had not been pursued. Therefore the VV&E possessed valid claim to the first route through Coquihalla Pass. In March 1911, when KVR crews returned to work in Coquihalla Pass for the first time since the VV&E announcement in November 1910, Hill was waiting with a court injunction prohibiting the KVR from interfering with the VV&E survey.

Hill's move, judging from past episodes, was a certain sign a battle would ensue. Warren chose to instruct the KVR surveyors to obey the injunction order and limited his reaction to a letter of protest to the Board of Railway Commissioners. Hill threatened that if Warren actively pursued the protest he would immediately push his tracks into Tulameen. To this Warren gave no reply. Warren's lack of response, coupled with Hill's shortage of labour and an order from the BRC postponing approval of either the VV&E or KVR survey lines through Coquihalla Pass until the claims of both companies had been reviewed, forestalled much of Hill's hurry. The promised tracklaying did not begin until July 1911.

Although the BRC order deferred confrontation, it did nothing to reduce the importance of Coquihalla Pass to either railway; it merely caused both railways to focus their immediate attention on the approaches leading up to Coquihalla Pass. Hill pushed ahead, constructing an extraordinarily fine roadbed eastward from Abbotsford. The CPR's Mission-Huntingdon branch and the interurban line of the British Columbia Electric Railway had both been crossed on an expensive overhead structure, rather than a less costly level crossing and along the rugged northern shore of Sumas Lake the line had been laid out using long tangents and easy curves despite the considerable extra rock removal required to secure a superb alignment.[6] East of Sumas Lake the line had been laid out with numerous tangents more than a mile in length, further evidence that Hill wanted a quality railway requiring minimal maintenance.

The VV&E survey location between the Sumas River and Hope was virtually identical to that of the present Canadian National Railway mainline. This fact was not merely coincidental; survey crews of Mackenzie and Mann's Canadian Northern Pacific Railway—ultimately part of the Canadian National system—had simultaneously staked the same right-of-way. The simultaneous surveying of the same right-of-way J.J. Hill happened to be claiming would normally have been adequate cause for a good scrap. On this occasion Hill had not even time to raise his eyebrows when Mackenzie and Mann came forth in February 1911 with an offer to allow Hill rights to run his trains over the completed line of the CNPR between Sumas River and Hope, thereby avoiding the cost of constructing his own line and the possible delay that could result if they got into dispute over right-of-way.

It was both a surprising and generous offer. Indeed it was almost without precedent in the annals of Canadian railway history. However, Hill had been in the railroad business too long to think such a generous offer had been made without ulterior motive. Hill knew that what Mackenzie and Mann wanted was terminal land in Vancouver for the transcontinental railway they were building, and Hill and the CPR had already acquired all suitable land in that city. Because they had antagonized the CPR by building a competing Canadian transcontinental railway, Mackenzie and Mann recognized that their only hope of securing terminal land was to butter up Hill into parting with some of his acreage on Vancouver's False Creek. Hill also suspected the twosome was hoping for trackage rights over his railway into Vancouver. Despite such misgivings, Hill sat down with his former partners in the VV&E and in record time a deal was finalized. On May 22, 1911, it was publicly announced an agreement had been signed giving the CNPR exclusive ownership of a railway from Sumas Landing to Hope, with the VV&E being given rights to use the line for its own trains.[7] The press release made no mention of any compensation to be given the CNPR for the concession it had granted.

Hill's sudden alliance with Mackenzie and Mann to put the VV&E into Hope—and later to let the Canadian Northern into Vancouver over Great Northern trackage—brought an immediate reaction from the CPR president, Thomas Shaughnessy. It was bad enough Jim Hill was spiking a steel trail for Coquihalla in an attempt to force the CPR and its subsidiary Kettle Valley Railway out of southern British Columbia, but Hill's move in letting the CPR's rising transcontinental rival into Vancouver made the great railway battle west of the Rockies more significant than ever. The alliance at the coast meant it was entirely possible Mackenzie and Mann's announced plan to push a railway from Kamloops down through the Okanagan Valley to Penticton was being formulated in connection with Hill's own plan to push a railway north from Oroville. Indeed, speculation was rampant that Hill and the Canadian Northern syndicate were working hand in hand to cut up the southern British Columbia pie for themselves.

Shaughnessy issued his own press release stating that within two months the CPR would begin double tracking its mainline from Vancouver eastward to a point across the Fraser River from Hope, near the proposed junction with the KVR, in preparation for handling the large volume of Kootenay goods the CPR expected would soon be coming down Coquihalla Pass. To taunt Mackenzie and Mann as well as Hill, Shaughnessy said the double track would afterwards be extended across British Columbia and eastward to the Great Lakes, giving the CPR an added operating advantage over the Canadian Northern system.

In an attempt to further strengthen its position, the CPR issued maternal directions despite earlier assurance that the KVR had outgrown parental guidance; in reaction to the possibility of a joint Hill-Mackenzie & Mann rail line down the Okanagan Valley, J.J. Warren was instructed to apply to the dominion government for authority to build a railway between Penticton and Vernon. In all likelihood, Shaughnessy never intended the KVR to actually build the railway, as the CPR lakeboats represented a far more economical means of transportation, but McCulloch's surveyors promptly secured the best right-of-way to discourage any competitive inroads. The work of building a double track on the CPR mainline eastward from Vancouver also proceeded that spring, as promised by Shaughnessy.

Hill and Mackenzie and Mann countered with assurances they would push work on their joint railway to Hope, but work on this line was hit by unexpected delays. Although a reasonable amount of grading was done in 1911, the year ended with track reaching only to Kilgard, five miles east of Abbotsford. Westward from Princeton, five bridges had to be constructed over the Tulameen River and as a consequence the tracklaying that began in July was not completed to Coalmont until November 10, 1911.[8]

The arrival of the VV&E proved to be an integral part of Coalmont's development. During the 1880s the town had gained some distinction in a brief gold flurry on nearby Granite Creek, but it was the Tulameen Valley's fine bituminous coal deposits, disregarded by the early miners in their feverish search for gold, that were to have a much greater influence on Coalmont's economy. By the time Hill's railway arrived, the Columbia Coal & Coke Company had already actively begun operating its first mine, and the town's newspaper, the *Coalmont Courier*, was publishing full-page advertisements proclaiming the town to be located on "The Largest Body of Coal yet Discovered in North America." Indeed, only the name Coalmont was appropriate for a community located so close to such a mountain of coal. Inflated as these boasts may have been, Hill knew tests conducted on coal from the Columbia mine had rated it as one of the finest steam coals on the continent and quickly signed a contract with the company for the delivery of 500 tons of coal per day to feed the ravenous appetites of the Great Northern Railway's many steam locomotive fireboxes.

Hill's arrival into Coalmont pushed him ever closer to Coquihalla Pass. However, his eagerness to carry away Tulameen Valley coal to fuel American locomotives again aroused suspicions among British Columbians that completion of the Coast-to-Kootenay railway was lower on Hill's priority list than directing traffic to his GN mainline. Such suspicions were supported by the fact that work on the joint CNPR-VV&E line between Sumas River and Hope continued to lag through the latter part of 1911 and no work whatsoever had been done in starting the all-important link across the Hope Mountains. This lack of progress in British Columbia contrasted sharply with Hill's very active work in constructing a line between Wenatchee and Oroville, which would open up a direct downhill run for trainloads of Coalmont coal to reach the GN mainline at Wenatchee.

These fears were reinforced by Hill's refusal to publicly comment on a report, received from Kennedy in November 1911, of the survey revisions done in Coquihalla Pass. L.C. Gilman, assistant to the president of the GN, also refused to comment on the survey report when he visited Vancouver on December 15, 1911. The provincial newspaper editors thus continued to grind out editorials criticizing Hill and the policies of the Great Northern Railway in British Columbia. Two weeks later Hill announced he had accepted Kennedy's survey revisions, and work on the VV&E would resume in the early spring. Hill added that an appeal would be immediately made to the Board of Railway Commissioners for approval of the VV&E survey and for an order revoking the earlier ruling prohibiting the VV&E from commencing work in Coquihalla Pass. This ruling, said Hill, was solely responsible for his delay in construction.

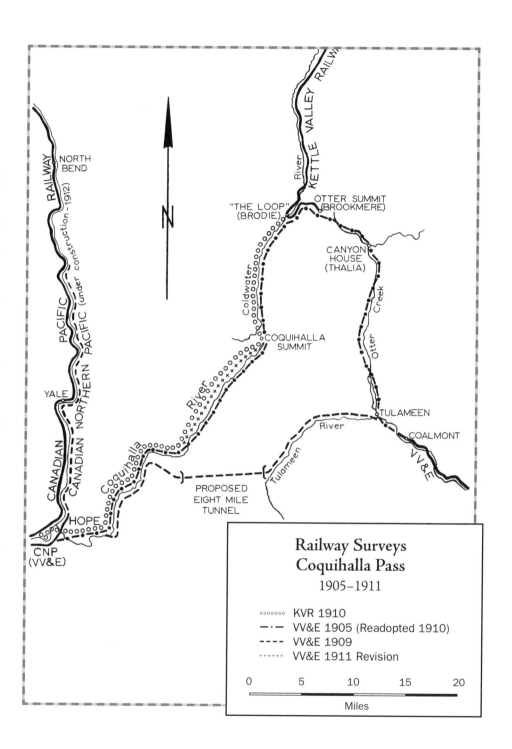

Railway Surveys
Coquihalla Pass
1905–1911

ooooooo KVR 1910
—·— VV&E 1905 (Readopted 1910)
---- VV&E 1909
++++++ VV&E 1911 Revision

0   5   10   15   20

Miles

Hill's announcement evoked a strongly worded New Year's address from J.J. Warren to a Penticton audience in which he promised rapid completion of the KVR and a strong counteroffensive to Hill's renewed efforts. Warren's assurances, along with considerable work by the CPR in upgrading the Crows Nest line and the Columbia & Western, precipitated the rumour that the CPR was planning to replace the Fraser Canyon-Kicking Horse Pass line with the KVR as its principal route across the province. It was further rumoured the CPR would operate the new mainline with electric locomotives using power from the Bonnington electric plant below Nelson. Although the CPR would not confirm either rumour, the absence of confirmation did not stop real estate promoters in the southern interior from using the rumours to enhance the sale of properties.[9]

On January 26, 1912, the VV&E formally applied to the Board of Railway Commissioners for approval of its location survey through Coquihalla Pass, an application as complicated as it was contentious. The original VV&E location survey, approved by the BRC in 1906, had utilized a continuous 2.5% grade along the south side of the Coquihalla River canyon from Coquihalla Summit to a point 10.5 miles west, where it had been proposed the line would cross the river on a low bridge and follow the north bank the remaining 28 miles into Hope. The KVR's survey maintained a continuous 2.2% grade located entirely on the north bank. The respective locations meant that in the lower canyon the VV&E would be below the KVR and consequently subject to debris from the KVR right-of-way during snow or slide clearing. The VV&E representatives at the hearing no doubt believed this concern would be justifiable cause for the BRC to rule against the KVR because the VV&E survey had been filed first. In an unusually cordial move for the two corporations, the VV&E representatives declined to press the matter.

The reasons for the VV&E grace were not altruistic. Subsequent to its original survey, the VV&E had discovered that the south bank along which their survey was located was more prone to snow slides than the north bank because the mountain peaks above the south bank faced away from the melting rays of the spring sun. For this reason the VV&E had surveyed a new location on the north bank, virtually duplicating the KVR location. Because the right for this location rested with the KVR, the VV&E representatives, out of fear of losing any chance to secure the superior north bank location in the difficult upper section of Coquihalla Pass, chose to avoid a direct confrontation with the KVR over the lower portion of the Pass, where on a pinch two rail lines could be built.

After hearing the evidence, George A. Mountain, the BRC's chief engineer, presented the opinion the KVR survey should be approved from the proposed junction with the Merritt-Midway line to the first point of conflict with the original VV&E survey, 10.5 miles west of Coquihalla Summit. This represented a total distance of 24.5 miles. The VV&E claim, he stated, was valid only for the 1906 approved location line; it was not a blanket reservation on Coquihalla Pass. Therefore, the KVR should be granted first claim to the north side survey location. To resolve the dispute in the lower reaches of Coquihalla Pass, Mountain suggested a full Board of Railway Commissioners hearing be held. The Board's chief commissioner agreed and on February 13, 1912, an order was issued approving the KVR location. A hearing was also called for March 14 in Calgary.

The KVR might have appeared to win the battle for Coquihalla Pass as a result of the BRC decision. This appearance was purely illusory. The VV&E still held control of the north bank in the lower section of the Coquihalla River canyon, where the KVR survey location was too high above the river to bridge the canyon to the south bank and escape the VV&E. Thus each railway held the other in check. This was a condition which, based on past relations, was certain to create trouble. Mountain recognized trouble was precisely what was bound to occur once the winter snow was gone, and he tried to dampen the fires of rivalry by pushing for an immediate BRC order that would be acceptable to each side. In a letter to his chief commissioner Mountain wrote: ". . . the nature of the country is such that it will be impossible to get two rights-of-way down the Coquihalla . . . and in my opinion, the Chief Engineers of both roads should get together and plan a double track joint location for this distance."[10]

If Mountain seriously believed the KVR and the VV&E would voluntarily agree to construction of joint trackage through Coquihalla Pass—thereby giving both companies a Coast-to-Kootenay rail line—he did not know the personalities involved. While McCulloch and Kennedy were personal friends and concurred privately, Hill vetoed the idea. The Calgary hearing of March 14, 1912 consisted of little more than an exchange of the usual contempt each railway's masters held for the other. Indeed, the BRC delegates at the hearing were so overwhelmed by the allegations that they adopted the usual committee approach and referred the matter back to the BRC chief engineer. He in turn replied that nothing could be done until an inspection had been made of the location surveys. With Coquihalla Pass 30 feet deep in snow, that inspection would be delayed for some time.

The BRC's dubious verdict, if intended to help cool the friction between the two railways, failed. Indeed, the long war between the two railways became even more bitter early in 1912 when British Columbia's premier, Richard McBride, called the fourth election of his political career and once more based his election platform on a railway aid plan. McBride's railway program called for the formation and government backing of a new railway, the Pacific Great Eastern Railway, to build northward from Vancouver to the Peace River. It proposed giving government aid to the Canadian Northern Pacific Railway for several branch lines in the province, along with aid concessions to a number of smaller railways. Also included was a subsidy of $10,000 per mile for the Kettle Valley Railway to build its proposed line through Coquihalla Pass, with an added $200,000 grant for the construction of a combined rail and general traffic bridge across the Fraser River at Hope. Nothing was offered Hill. Naturally, McBride's announcement generated criticism from Hill, but McBride countered that the VV&E could have been across the Hope Mountains five years earlier if Hill had not procrastinated in construction. McBride also noted that Hill had made no attempt to rebuild the Kaslo & Slocan Railway after it had been destroyed by a forest fire in July 1910 and had maintained only those GN subsidiary lines in British Columbia that were profitable ore hauling routes. McBride's members passed the KVR aid bill into law and awaited the impending election.

McBride's stand in supporting the Kettle Valley Railway found strong sympathy in the province. Most British Columbians had long been suspicious of Hill, and many accepted McBride's position that Hill's VV&E, even if completed, would be used only to ensure continued American domination of the southern interior. One newspaper, in support of McBride, stated, "Until a Canadian railway crosses the Hope Mountains there is no possibility whatever that the Similkameen will cease to be a tributary to the city of Spokane."[11] Although opposition members argued that the subsidy was not in the public interest, this editorial statement accurately reflected the majority opinion in British Columbia. When the votes were counted on the evening of March 28, 1912, McBride had won all but two seats in the Legislative Assembly. Incredibly, not a single opposition member had been elected; the two lost seats were both taken by independents.

The assurance of the additional subsidy, along with BRC approval of its location survey in the strategic confines of the upper canyon of the Coquihalla River, gave the KVR a substantial advantage over the VV&E. Yet the Great Northern Railway could not be written off as a strong contender in the battle for Coquihalla Pass. Hill was well accustomed to building railways with neither government authorization nor government funds. When, two weeks after the election, Warren announced the KVR would build its mainline via Princeton and the Tulameen Valley—thus putting the entire 90 miles from Hope to Princeton in dispute—Hill made it clear he would forge ahead with the VV&E. To show the GN flag, Carl Gray, the man whom J.J. Hill had personally selected to succeed his unimpressive son as president of the Great Northern, made an immediate inspection trip of the entire VV&E route. Grey's tour included visits to Penticton, Princeton, Merritt and even remote Coquihalla Pass. Climaxing his visit to British Columbia, Gray announced on May 15, 1912 that contracts were about to be let for the clearing of the right-of-way from the end of track near Coalmont to Coquihalla Pass. The VV&E, he said, would not back down in the battle for Coquihalla Pass.

In June, Warren reacted to Gray's announcement by boldly going ahead and clearing a right-of-way westward from the Merritt line towards Coquihalla Summit. The KVR move prompted George Mountain to push for a firm directive from the Board of Railway Commissioners and, despite the fact a great deal of snow remained in Coquihalla Pass at the time, commencing June 28, 1912 Mountain's assistant, A.T. Kerr, carried out the requested inspection of Coquihalla Pass. Kerr rushed his report to Mountain but the findings cast no new light on the problem. Kerr reported that it would be an incredible achievement to build even one railway through Coquihalla Pass, let alone two, and the cost would be monumental. Kerr added: "It is my opinion there is no room for the two lines, even if the [Coquihalla] River was the dividing line between the two Companies. The country is very rough. The locations of these lines for long stretches are in many places on perpendicular rock bluffs from three to five hundred feet above the River, and in many instances much higher."[12]

Kerr recommended a single line of railway be constructed the entire distance from Coquihalla Summit to Hope, with both companies sharing its operation. In view of the difficulties the two companies had at making agreements, Kerr tactfully added that an acceptable alternative might be for each company to build an independent track on a common roadbed. His recommendations were merely that: recommendations. No formal order of any kind was forthcoming from the Board.

The Board of Railway Commissioner's decision—or more correctly, lack of decision—did little but sanction the traditional method the CPR and GN used in settling right-of-way disputes, through court injunctions and violent use of grader picks. Both railways were already actively clearing a right-of-way from their respective ends of track into Coquihalla Pass. On August 8, 1912, the KVR forged ahead by awarding a contract to the firm of Twohy Brothers for the construction of the 14-mile section of railway from the Merritt line to Coquihalla Summit. Not to be outdone by the KVR, Hill announced on September 20, 1912 that a contract had been awarded to Guthrie, McDougall & Company for the 42-mile section of the VV&E from the end of track just north of Coalmont to Coquihalla Summit. Both companies specified a July 1913 completion date. The contractors soon had a full force of men on the ground grading towards the narrow confines of Coquihalla Pass. The outcome of meeting seemed predictable: with the trade of all southern British Columbia riding on it, the impending confrontation in Coquihalla Pass would surely relegate the Battle of Midway to forgotten history.

What actually occurred in Coquihalla Pass in the autumn of 1912 was totally contrary to expectations. The fall turned out to be one of the quietest seasons on record between Hill and the CPR. The mutual harassment of the construction crews, so characteristic of past episodes, was totally absent. In fact, the rate of progress on both the KVR and the VV&E was allowed to drop well below that demanded by a struggle of such corporate importance. Jim Hill could not even be located for comment; it was rumoured he was on an extended fishing trip in New Brunswick. Without him, one newspaper reporter commented, the VV&E was "silent as a tomb."[13] The KVR was also strangely quiet. It had ceased pressing its earlier request to the BRC for immediate resolution of the Coquihalla dispute and now seemed more concerned with completion of the line between Merritt and Midway. The anticipated battle for Coquihalla Pass was an outright anticlimax.

The sudden paradox in the actions of the two corporations became even more confounding early in October when L.C. Gilman publicly offered to relinquish the VV&E's claim to the north bank location in the lower reaches of Coquihalla Canyon and allow the KVR to build the entire

Coquihalla line itself if the KVR would lease back trackage rights at a reasonable price. Gilman's offer marked a most profound revolution in the corporate relationship of the Great Northern and Canadian Pacific. At the invitation of Richard McBride, who offered free use of his legislative offices in Victoria as a meeting place, Warren and Gilman met early in November to discuss details of Gilman's offer.

Although the talks were brief, they yielded surprising success. On November 15, 1912 Warren and Gilman announced that the two companies had agreed to a general principle that unjustified duplication of expensive trackage should be avoided in the future. As evidence of their new policy, they stated that an agreement had been reached for the line east of Coquihalla Pass whereby the KVR would complete construction of its line in the Coldwater Valley to Coquihalla Summit and would grant the VV&E running rights over this trackage plus the four miles of already completed trackage between "The Loop" and Otter Summit. In return, the VV&E would grant the KVR running rights over the first eight miles of its track from Otter Summit eastward to Canyon House (now named Thalia) once the rail line was completed. This proposal allowed the VV&E to cancel the portion of its construction contract between Otter Summit and Coquihalla Summit duplicating the KVR line. Both railways agreed to double track the relevant sections of the joint line when traffic conditions justified.

Even if the major point of dispute, the right to build in Coquihalla Pass, had not been resolved, the November agreement marked an historic achievement and opened the door to continued negotiations. The progress of subsequent meetings was slow. However, on the evening of April 9, 1913 Warren and Gilman emerged from their conference suite in the Hotel Vancouver and announced that the battle for Coquihalla Pass was over. A mutually acceptable agreement had been reached for the construction and operation of a single line of railway, to be shared equally by both corporations, through Coquihalla Pass. Not that rivalry between the CPR and GN was over. Neither railway was about to surrender the battle for the transcontinental freight trade, nor was Jim Hill ready to personally make peace with Canadian Pacific. His hatred for that corporation would not be reconciled until he reached his grave. However, one part of the war—the celebrated battle for Coquihalla Pass—had ended peacefully. That peace, one observer suggested, was an achievement no less amazing than the railway it later made possible.

The announcement of the signing of the Coquihalla Agreement was one of the most important news items in the province during 1913. "Railways Bury Hatchet—Coquihalla Pass is soon to have one line!" head-lined one interior newspaper.[14] Other papers gave praise to Warren and Gilman for their efforts in reaching a settlement. British Columbians could now envision an end to their quarter century struggle to secure a direct railway from the coast to the Kootenays.

The agreement called for the Kettle Valley Railway to construct, own and maintain a 54-mile long line of railway from Otter Summit to Hope.[15] The Great Northern Railway, operating trains on behalf of the VV&E, was to be granted trackage rights over the line for 999 years in return for a basic annual rental fee amounting to 2.5% of the cost of construction, with additional charges to be levied depending upon the number of trains the GN operated over the line. The railway was to be built on the completed KVR location survey along the north bank of the Coquihalla River Canyon on a ruling grade against eastbound traffic of 2.2% over most of the 36-mile climb from near sea level at Hope to 3,646-foot Coquihalla Summit. Specified in the agreement was a completion date of December 31, 1914, an extremely short construction time considering the fact that, as one newspaper reported, "The Coquihalla section will probably be the heaviest railway work ever undertaken in British Columbia."[16]

Indeed, the 38 miles from Coquihalla Summit to the junction with the CPR mainline, across the Fraser River from Hope, would set more than one record for magnitude of construction. The work would require 43 bridges, containing 22 million board feet of timber and 4,500 tons of steel, 13 tunnels and 15 snowsheds, the latter totalling almost two miles in length.[17] Millions of cubic yards of earth and rock would have to be moved, virtually all of it by human muscle and sweat. The monetary costs of the construction would be a staggering $136,000 per mile, five times the average cost for Canadian railways in 1913. One mile in the upper canyon would cost $300,000, making it one of the most expensive miles of railway in history. Notwithstanding these difficulties, Warren and Gilman as-serted their determination to complete the railway within the proposed time limit. On August 6, 1913, the grading contract for the joint section from Hope to Coquihalla Summit was awarded to the American con-struction firm of McArthur Brothers and three weeks later construction began just east of Hope.

Parr Tunnel at mile 75.8 Princeton Subdivision under construction, 1948. This tunnel was constructed to eliminate two crossings of the Tulameen River. Construction methods had changed dramatically since the original line was built a third of a century earlier. PHOTO FROM THE COLLECTION OF BARRIE SANFORD

In March 1946 the trestle across Snowshoe Creek just east of Jessica collapsed as a result of earth movement. This was the fourth time the trestle had been damaged in this manner. When it collapsed again in March 1950 an earth embankment was constructed to replace it. PHOTO FROM THE COLLECTION OF BARRIE SANFORD

CPR engine 5134 passes Hope station with an eastbound freight train in 1948. The tail of the train is on the Hope Bridge. PHOTO COURTESY NORMAN GIDNEY

Brookmere station had the highly unusual feature of two through tracks on each side, whereas stations normally had through tracks on only one side so the public did not have to cross active tracks to reach the facility. This feature owes its origins to the fact Brookmere was intended to be a joint divisional point for both the KVR and Great Northern Railway. PHOTO FROM THE COLLECTION OF BARRIE SANFORD

Crews ready CPR locomotive 3401 in front of the Brookmere roundhouse. This photo was taken some years after the locomotive ran away on the Coquihalla grade in 1926 and crashed in the worst wreck in KVR history. PHOTO COURTESY JACK LESLIE

CPR locomotive 5178 with eastbound Train 12 poses on Trout Creek Bridge for this photo taken in the late 1930s or early 1940s. The smokebox number plate from this locomotive is now in the Penticton Museum where it was donated following the locomotive's scrapping in 1957, presented in memory of two men killed in a derailment of the engine at Romeo in November 1941. PHOTO COURTESY PENTICTON MUSEUM

In thrusting a railway across southern British Columbia Andrew McCulloch was called upon to use nearly every engineering technique known in railroad construction. This photo shows CPR locomotive 5258 leading eastbound Train 12 up one of the three giant loops needed to overcome the abrupt elevation difference between Belfort and Jura east of Princeton. PHOTO COURTESY CANADIAN PACIFIC RAILWAY

A pair of newly delivered diesel units pilot Train 12 along the shore of Otter Lake during the summer of 1953, shortly after the start of the conversion from steam to diesel power on the CPR's Kettle Valley Division. PHOTO COURTESY CANADIAN PACIFIC RAILWAY

Diesel locomotive 4104 and steam locomotive 5212 pose side-by-side in Penticton yard prior to 5212 leaving for Vancouver with the last official steam-powered train on the former Kettle Valley Railway, September 1954. PHOTO COURTESY PENTICTON MUSEUM RAILWAY

The Coquihalla line boasted four passenger trains per day when this photograph was taken of passenger Train 12 crossing Ladner Creek Bridge in 1953. However, within a decade both the train and railway would be gone.
PHOTO COURTESY CANADIAN PACIFIC RAILWAY

The same scene as appears in the photograph on the opposite page after the abandonment of the Coquihalla line in 1961. PHOTO BY BARRIE SANFORD

Diesel units suffered their share of mishaps as well as steam locomotives. CPR diesel 8715 shows the effects of hitting a rockslide at Osprey Lake in April 1959, two years after being delivered to the CPR from the Canadian Locomotive Company. Fortunately, none of the crew was badly injured in the incident.
PHOTO FROM THE COLLECTION OF BARRIE SANFORD

Tracks hang suspended across Tangent Creek at mile 38.3 Coquihalla Subdivision following the severe damage to the line in November 1959. This was the most severe of the many washouts that prompted the CPR to abandon the rail line through Coquihalla Pass. PHOTO FROM THE COLLECTION OF BARRIE SANFORD

Diesel unit 8603 with a short freight train emerges from "Little Tunnel" high above Okanagan Lake on the 3,000-foot descent from Chute Lake to Penticton. Shortly after this photograph was taken the last train ran over this section of rail line. PHOTO BY BARRIE SANFORD

On a beautiful Okanagan morning a lone "F-M" diesel unit pilots a short freight train along the shore of Skaha Lake bound for Osoyoos. The engine will return to Penticton in the afternoon with cars loaded with Okanagan fruit. PHOTO BY BARRIE SANFORD

The short length of this freight train crossing the bridge over West Fork Canyon Creek in Myra Canyon foretells that service on the Carmi Subdivision line will soon end. PHOTO BY BARRIE SANFORD

The "Second Mainline" of the CPR at Beaverdell in 1974, a year after the last train had operated over the railway. Rails in this section were removed in 1979. PHOTO BY BARRIE SANFORD

GP-38 diesels largely took over from "first generation" diesels on the remnants of the Kettle Valley Railway in 1976. Here two GP-38s pilot a trainload of lumber flats at Clapperton Tunnel between Merritt and Spences Bridge. PHOTO BY BARRIE SANFORD

Even into the 1980s much of the territory traversed by the former Kettle Valley Railway remained little changed from when the railway was built three-quarters of a century earlier. In the final months of operation this train climbs the valley of Spearing Creek just east of Brookmere. PHOTO BY BARRIE SANFORD

A small portion of the Kettle Valley Railway near Summerland remains in operation, using a two-truck Shay steam locomotive from the British Columbia Forestry Museum and several passenger and freight cars. In this photo Mayo Lumber Company 3 readies for the official opening of the revived railway on September 17, 1995. PHOTO BY BARRIE SANFORD

The legacy of the Kettle Valley Railway also continues in Myra Canyon, where planks and railings have been installed on the 17 remaining trestles to create a popular hiking trail. Here hikers pause for a picnic alongside the trestle that was once at mile 87.4 Carmi Subdivision. PHOTO BY BARRIE SANFORD

The agreement some people had called the "Compromise of the Century" hardly proved such when details of the Coquihalla Agreement were revealed. Gilman had not only signed away the VV&E's valid claim to the north bank location in the lower part of Coquihalla Pass but he had granted the KVR an option to use the VV&E trackage between Otter Summit and Princeton when that line was completed, thereby sparing the KVR from having to build a second line down the Tulameen Valley. Gilman had further given the KVR an option to run trains over the VV&E-W&GN line from Midway to Curlew. Exercising of this option would allow the KVR, by connecting with the Spokane & British Columbia Railway line at Curlew, to bypass the steep grades on the CPR line between Grand Forks and Midway. No similar concessions, such as GN trackage rights into Merritt, were required of the KVR. Therefore, the agreement was not a compromise; it was a major concession to the CPR by the Great Northern. Indeed, considering the formidable struggle Hill had made to push his trackage into British Columbia against the opposition of the CPR, the agreement was tantamount to complete surrender.

Nor was the signing of the Coquihalla Agreement an isolated instance of Great Northern withdrawal from the British Columbia scene. On the VV&E line between Coalmont and Otter Summit, the GN cut construction forces drastically, and by late fall 1913 only a few token crews remained on a project that had been assigned the highest priority less than a year earlier. On December 23, 1913—four years to the day after the first GN train had reached Princeton—train service to that community was cut from daily except Sunday to three trains per week. Service on other parts of the GN system in British Columbia was also cut.

In the Similkameen, no longer was the principal river called the Jimhillkameen River. The names now reserved for Hill and his railway were purely derogatory, the mildest of which was the reference to the Great Northern as the "Great Now and Then." Even the Board of Railway Commissioners could not fathom the sudden transformation in the GN's policy towards British Columbia; it issued an edict severely chastising Hill for his cuts in service and construction, but to no avail. Late in the year another construction crew on the VV&E was withdrawn.

To contemporary observers of the long supremacy war between the CPR and GN, it was obvious a strangely remarkable episode in the his-tory of British Columbia had transpired in the battle for Coquihalla Pass. The peaceful end to the long battle was, in itself, not unexpected. The general introduction of government regulation of railway rates and the rising power of the railway trade unions served to temper competition between all railroads, including the CPR and GN. In addition, the growing political tensions in Europe along with the slowing North American economy served to limit the sources of expansion capital upon which both railways relied heavily, making them more cautious about large capital outlays for new trackage. Also, James J. Hill was of advancing age and diminishing influence in the affairs of the Great Northern. Yet none of these factors could account for the abruptness with which J.J. Hill's reign in southern British Columbia had come to an apparent end. How could nearly three decades of the most bitterly contested corporate struggle in the province's history have ended so quietly? Why had the Great Northern virtually disappeared as an active force in British Columbia?

In reality, the demise of the Great Northern Railway in Canada resulted from the same political forces that two decades earlier had stymied Daniel Corbin, the man upon whose fledgling trackage Hill had built the GN's empire in southern British Columbia. What Hill had failed to fully appreciate, despite his Ontario birth, was the latent fear of American political annexation that haunted many Canadian politicians, and the impact this fear had on shaping government policy. At times the fears were well founded: military clashes between the two nations did occur in the early nineteenth century. But the invasion many Canadians had feared never came. Instead, by the late 1800s the Canadian and American people had come to realize they were each other's most important ally. The mutual isolation from other lands, a 3,000-mile common border, shared customs, language and business, and the similar hardships of a still-wild frontier continent gave Canadians and Americans a bond transcending the coolness of their official liaison in far away London.

Hill recognized this growing friendship as the genesis of a great potential trade market. Hill, who one contemporary described as "the most far-sighted and statesmanlike economist in America," believed such trade could be nothing less than spontaneous.[18] The same isolation and geographic interdependence that had brought the Canadian and American people together would make each the other's most prodigious customer in trade.

Hill's railways were testimony to his conviction. The rail lines of the Great Northern system entered Canada at 16 places, 12 of them in British Columbia. Yet Hill was not satisfied. He was convinced his freight traffic in the province could be expanded significantly with access to major markets.

With the exception of Vancouver, Canadian cities were either too small or too distant from the interior mines to provide effective markets, and Vancouver lacked the direct rail connections so necessary for successful commerce. In contrast, there were numerous cities in the American west with growing industries demanding the natural resources southern British Columbia gave forth in abundance. However, the well-fortified tariff wall Great Britain had erected around its North American colony, and the similar barrier the United States had erected effectively fenced off Hill from realizing his dream. Therefore, while Hill cautiously pushed his VV&E across southern British Columbia to connect the Kootenay mines with the tidewater of Vancouver, he also worked to pull down the tariff barriers between the two nations to expose these same mines to the vast markets of the American West.

Hill found a strong ally in Wilfrid Laurier, the man whom Canadians had elected their prime minister in 1896. Like Hill, Laurier could see the vast markets for Canada's raw materials in the United States. He could also see Canadians looking enviously across the border at the plentiful supply of consumer goods priced below those Canadians paid for similar goods that had made the long journey from Great Britain. Laurier worked diligently throughout his term of office to secure what he considered a satisfactory reciprocity agreement with the United States. Early in 1911, after a decade and a half of negotiations, he was able to announce his success. In April of that year, the United States government formally approved the terms of Laurier's personally drafted free trade agreement. His success made Laurier a hero. He returned to Canada from Washington and confidently called an election for September 1911 to seek the sanction of the Canadian people to ratify the agreement. Praise for his success was forthcoming from many Canadians, and there initially seemed little doubt he would win.

One Canadian did not join in the praise—William Cornelius Van Horne, the old man of the CPR. Van Horne had long left the management of the CPR when he spoke out against Laurier's reciprocity agreement in 1911 but his intimate association with the company in its formative years had instilled in him a deep concern for its affairs. He charged that the reciprocity agreement would cause the defeat of the CPR in its long war with J.J. Hill for southern British Columbia's rich mining trade. He further added: "Shall we be permitted to recede from reciprocity when Mr. Hill has extended his seven or eight lines of railway into the Canadian

Northwest—lines which have for some years been resting their noses on the boundary line, waiting for reciprocity?"[19] Free trade, Van Horne warned, would spell the end of the CPR, not only in the Kootenays but in the rest of Canada. With the tariff wall broken, railway traffic would become north-south, not east-west, and Canada would be broken into its original geographic fragments, each attached to adjoining sections of the American republic. The transcontinental railway, which Canadians had struggled so valiantly to build, would be destroyed. He called upon the Canadian people to rally against the treaty and "bust the damned thing."[20]

In older Canadians, Van Horne's warning resurrected the latent fear of American domination. In new Canadians, who found in twentieth century Canada prosperity unimaginable in their native European homelands, Van Horne's appeal had even greater impact. Few immigrants were willing to risk their newly found prosperity, a prosperity due largely to the railway built by the man who was now asking for their support. The Canadian people reacted to Van Horne's appeal by rising up and defeating Wilfrid Laurier's government by a resounding margin. In so doing, Van Horne stated, the Canadian people had once more demonstrated their resolve to remain one nation.

Laurier's defeat naturally ended any possibility the tentative reciprocity agreement would be signed into law. Laurier's defeat also ended J.J. Hill's dream of seeing trainloads of goods flow across the international border in both directions over his railways that followed the natural lines of continental geography. Hill would have to be satisfied with his Canadian rail lines carrying only those goods destined to remain within Canada, or those goods that could withstand the heavy customs duties at the border.

The only viable route for trade within Canada was the sole east-west railway James J. Hill had built in the dominion, the VV&E, and in this railway Hill lost little of his personal interest. In fact, until his dying day Hill maintained that Kootenay freight, if not hauled over the geographically logical route to the United States, could be hauled over the mountains to Vancouver on his VV&E better than the CPR's Kettle Valley Railway. However, the defeat of Laurier and of any reciprocity possibilities caused other members of the Great Northern Railway management to seriously question the wisdom of further expenditures on the GN's lines in Canada. With his advancing age and lessening influence in GN's management, Hill was unable to sway majority opinion. Against his personal wishes,

GN management ordered the many cutbacks in the province throughout 1912 and 1913 as a direct reflection of the loss of interest in its Canadian system. Indeed, it seems certain that Hill's begrudging approval of the Coquihalla Agreement had been given solely because he recognized that, having lost the support of GN's management for his Canadian enterprises, he could never defeat the CPR in southern British Columbia. Better, therefore, he share trackage through Coquihalla Pass than risk being unable to secure any line across the Hope Mountains at all.

Unknown to most people, Hill's dream of having the Vancouver, Victoria & Eastern Railway live up to its name in connecting Vancouver and Victoria with eastern British Columbia did come true. Unfortunately, Hill never lived to see its completion. Perhaps it was just as well he died only a few weeks before the VV&E was to be completed. The succeeding Great Northern management shared none of James J. Hill's faith in southern British Columbia, and it abandoned the VV&E almost the same day the line opened. In the years that followed Great Northern policy was even more regressive. All but two of the railways "Empire Builder" Jim Hill had so forcefully and cunningly pushed into British Columbia would be abandoned and the rails torn away, a sad end to the once magnificent empire built on one man's resolute and determined conviction that the forces of geography must ultimately triumph over the forces of politics.

11: The Dream Fulfilled

The Kettle Valley Railway is completed

The settlement of the Coquihalla Pass dispute, followed by the rapid demise of the Great Northern Railway as an active force in the development of southern British Columbia, left the task of completing the Coast-to-Kootenay railway solely to James Warren and Andrew McCulloch with their Kettle Valley Railway. Notwithstanding the progress made up to 1913, a great deal of work remained to be done before the dream of direct rail connections between the coast and the Kootenays could become a reality. In fact, at the start of 1913—two and a half years after work on the KVR had begun—only 82 miles of railway were operational. The graded roadbed on about 50 more miles was ready for rails, but even this brought the total distance to only slightly more than 130 miles, less than half of the 325 miles of railway required for the Kettle Valley Railway's construction. Of course, the poor progress made up to 1913 was exclusively the result of shortages of manpower and materials, not any unwillingness on the part of McCulloch and Warren to vigorously prosecute the railway's construction. During late 1912, and even more so during 1913, with more resources available, the rate of construction progress accelerated considerably.

The most visible progress on the KVR during 1913 was in the Okanagan Valley. On December 20, 1912 the KVR added a second locomotive for service at Penticton.[1] Three months later, on March 27, 1913, a third locomotive was added for ballasting the completed track to the site of Trout Creek Bridge, seven miles west of Penticton, and for delivering steel for the erection of the great bridge itself.[2] West of Trout Creek grading had been vigorously pushed. In fact, by late spring completion of the bridge was the only thing preventing the KVR crews from being able to lay track clear to the summit of Osprey Lake.

Trout Creek was no minor obstacle. Its gaping chasm required the highest bridge on the KVR, with an additional 400 feet of wooden trestle-work approaching the main steel span. So much timber was needed for the approach trestle and the wooden falsework to support the steel span during assembly that a sawmill was built five miles west of Summerland exclusively for cutting timbers. The construction of the falsework alone consumed two full months. No sooner was it completed than an irrigation dam on the upper portion of Trout Creek gave way on May 13, 1913 and the ensuing flash flood sent the whole structure crashing into the canyon. Although no one was injured in the incident, the trestle's collapse retarded completion of both the bridge and the trackage west to Osprey Lake.

Murdock McKay, a KVR locomotive engineer who had joined the company in 1911 as an assistant to Andrew McCulloch, related to the author in 1969 an episode he experienced during the construction of Trout Creek Bridge that, even after the passage of half a century, still filled him with admiration for the Kettle Valley Railway's brilliant chief engineer. McKay recalled that McCulloch had got into an argument with the Canada Foundry engineer handling the initial stages of the bridgework. The argument concerned the Canada Foundry engineer's computation of a certain bridge dimension, which McCulloch insisted was incorrect. After considerable debate, and the assertion of three KVR assistant engineers that the Canada Foundry figures were correct, McCulloch, with McKay assisting him, took a surveying transit and steel measuring tape and resurveyed the entire canyon terrain himself. McKay recalled climbing up and down the steep canyon nearly a dozen times that afternoon while assisting McCulloch. Even at his young age, McKay was barely able to keep pace with McCulloch, then a man nearly 50 year old. At the end of the day McKay returned to his tent and flopped onto his cot, dead weary from exhaustion. The following morning, when McKay stumbled into McCulloch's tent, he discovered McCulloch had not even gone to bed, but he had stayed up the entire night reducing his measurements and calculations from the day previous, and was now readying to put in another day's work. Using his authority as chief engineer, McCulloch overruled the four engineers with whom he had disagreed and took upon himself the responsibility for the accuracy of the bridge dimensions. McKay recalled the crowning moment four months later when he, McCulloch and the four engineers stood and watched the final section of the 250-foot-long main span being put into place—a piece that was only one-quarter of an inch short of being a perfect fit. They had merely to wait for the morning sun to warm the bridge and expand the steel to the exact position required. It was an amazing memory of an amazing man.

Across Okanagan Lake from Trout Creek, on the Penticton-Hydraulic Lake section, 1,200 men had worked through the winter. By spring the number had swelled to more than 2,000. The contractor on this section, Grant Smith & Company, had acquired several parcels of real estate in both Naramata and Kelowna for storing the large volume of construction supplies—principally explosives—needed for railway work. The demand for explosives was particularly acute not only because of the large volume of rockwork involved but because the density of the rock itself proved particularly troublesome. In fact the east side rock was found to be so hard that black powder, the traditional explosive of the early railroad builders, had to be abandoned completely. Not until a special explosive, consisting of 90% nitroglycerine and only just developed in 1913, was delivered could construction resume. A single blast could utilize as many as five boxcars of explosives.[3]

Handling such explosives was delicate work under the best of conditions and fatal accidents occurred with regularity. What was most tragic about the accidents was that many of them occurred, not because of improper drilling or premature explosion, but because of the almost unbelievable disregard shown by workmen for even the most basic safety rules. The handling of frozen dynamite was exemplary of this carelessness. During the winter months, when temperatures were often well below freezing for extended periods, the nitroglycerine in dynamite often froze, rendering the explosive ineffective. The proper technique for dealing with frozen dynamite was to place the dynamite sticks in a special hot water jacket designed to safely thaw the delicate chemical components. Too often the workmen spent their evenings at the local poker scene and awoke the next morning too late to carry out the thawing chore prior to the hour when work was scheduled to commence. Rather than face a chewing out from their foreman, or perhaps dismissal, the workmen often shortcut the thawing procedures by placing the dynamite sticks near an open fire or roasting the explosives in a frying pan. Needless to say, more than one workman misjudged the thermal capacity of a stick of dynamite and paid a most tragic price for his stupidity. Were it not for the extensive documentation of such incidents, they could almost be dismissed as fantasy.

Within the Okanagan Valley, Scandinavian and central European immigrants dominated the railway labour force. Skilled Italian stone-masons were used for the intricate job of constructing the mortarless retaining walls at selected points on the roadbed above Naramata, and the care with which they performed their work is evidenced by the fact the walls still stand today, even after the railway has been abandoned. For most of these workers, life in the construction camps consisted of long months of dreary manual toil broken only by the occasional visits of some inquisitive news reporter or friendly delegate bringing to the isolated camp the books and magazines local citizens had donated for their benefit. Visiting preachers were also among the camp callers. Ted Logie, whose father was one such gospel minister, wrote of the Sunday camp sermons: "Although I would like to think that our efforts were appreciated and the redemption of lost sheep was of magnificent proportions, in retrospect I have come to the conclusion that any attendance at the meetings was prompted by sheer boredom on the part of the construction workers, or perhaps by a financial drought which prevented them from sitting in at the perpetual poker game."[4]

Local citizens and the workers themselves frequently staged entertainment concerts, and the KVR construction workers boasted one of the best hockey teams in the Okanagan Valley. Several former construction workers related to the author that their fondest memory of the KVR construction days was sitting around the evening campfire listening to Andrew McCulloch recite Shakespearian poetry or plays, invariably without reference to text or notes. For many of these workers, it was their first introduction to English literature and the great heritage of the English language. Even as they had grown old in years, none with whom the author spoke had forgotten the gift of language first given to them by Andrew McCulloch.

The immigrant railway workers were the chosen target for the militant labour movement known as the Industrial Workers of the World. Following several violent clashes with law enforcement agencies in the Unites States, the IWW infiltrated British Columbia to spread the gospel of discontent among railway workers. In 1912, the IWW precipitated a major strike on the Canadian Northern system and early in 1913 it turned its attention to the Kettle Valley Railway. On March 26, 1913, the IWW infiltrators were able to convince a number of men at one subcontractor's camp to strike in an attempt to raise wages from $2.75 to $3.00 per day.

After five weeks of continued IWW agitation, more than 2,000 men, including virtually all the workers between Penticton and Hydraulic Lake, had been persuaded to lay down their tools. In reality, the strike was more the result of the workers seeking a respite from their otherwise ceaseless toil than sympathy with the IWW.[5] By the middle of May, less than two weeks after the full-scale strike had begun, the workers had spent the last of their wages and were returning to work in defiance of the IWW pickets. Although the Provincial Police came in to ensure preservation of the peace, their presence was unnecessary. Even in such a large workforce as the KVR it was an age when pride in one's work and the relationship with one's boss played an important role in labour relations. Concerning the IWW failure, one authority commented: "Friendly relations and mutual respect usually counted for more than a few additional dollars."[6]

In mid-October the great steel bridge at Trout Creek was completed, and on October 25, 1913 J.J. Warren had his private car attached to KVR locomotive 2 so Penticton's elite could ride over it on the first official train.[7] Naturally, some of the passengers had serious reservations about riding along the narrow ledge blasted out of the cliff edge above Okanagan Lake or riding over the high bridge. But Angus Gillis, one of the KVR's first and most colourful locomotive engineers, walked through Warren's car humorously assuring everyone that if he couldn't keep the train on the tracks, the least he would do was to stay within the right-of-way limits. Despite the misgivings, the trip was a definite success and Warren found it an appropriate occasion to announce that five additional locomotives would soon be delivered to the KVR.[8] He also announced that, now Trout Creek Bridge had been completed, crews completing tracklaying to Coquihalla Summit would be immediately transferred to the Okanagan Valley to lay track over the completed grade from the bridge to Osprey Lake. By the year's end, track reached west from Penticton to Osprey Lake station, a distance of 38.8 miles. Three additional crossings of Trout Creek were involved above West Summerland, with a ruling grade of 2.2% from Penticton to Kirton and 1.0% from Kirton to the summit.[9]

On August 26, 1913 work was started on extending track from "The Loop" southwest to Coquihalla Summit using two borrowed CPR locomotives.[10] Initially, a good rate of progress was achieved, primarily because of the small amount of bridgework on this section. During the night of September 28, 1913, a serious fire destroyed three bunk cars and much of the tracklaying equipment on the siding at "The Loop" and injected a month long delay in the advancement of railhead towards the coast.

A week later, on the same spot, another mishap occurred. Fifteen side dump cars, being loaded with ballast, broke loose and began running away down the grade for Merritt. Fortunately, locomotive engineer Jack Crosby, who was bringing a string of cars up from Merritt, alertly noticed the runaways. By reversing his train and backing downgrade at high speed until the runaway cars nudged into the pilot of his locomotive with minimal impact, he was able to bring them under control, thereby averting what could have been a serious accident. Crosby gained nationwide attention for his quick thinking and bravery, and this reputation stayed with him until he died tragically in the wreck of a passenger train near Beaverdell in 1924.[11]

In March 1913 work was started conducting soundings of the Fraser River in the Hope area to determine a suitable location for the bridge connecting the KVR with the CPR mainline. By mid-summer a decision had been made to locate the bridge half a mile upstream of the Hope townsite, despite the fact several of the test holes drilled at this site had passed the 150-foot mark without reaching bedrock. This location was not entirely satisfactory because it required more than two miles of difficult trackage to reach the CPR mainline from the north end of the bridge, but McCulloch decided it was more suitable than a crossing at Ruby Creek, the only alternative site suggested by the soundings. On November 7, 1913 the KVR awarded a contract for the bridge substructure, consisting of three main piers and two end abutments, to Armstrong, Morrison & Company, a prominent Vancouver engineering and contracting firm that had gained a reputation for building difficult bridge foundations throughout the province. Construction of the bridge piers began shortly after the contract award. A spectacular accident occurred on February 11, 1914 when an ice jam, formed on the upper Fraser River by a long cold spell, broke loose and smashed out 250 feet of falsework placed as bridge support. The mishap did not seriously disrupt the work, and the bridge piers were completed before the return of high water in the spring.

On the West Fork, 1913 was also a productive year. In January, regular train service was introduced between Midway and Carmi and, commencing May 1, 1913, track was laid northward of the latter point.[12] Tracklaying on this section was not vigorously pursued because supplies for work on the section west of Hydraulic Lake could be easily delivered by the lakeboats on Okanagan Lake, which meant progress westward was not dependent upon completion of track work. The KVR's chronic shortage of locomotives also precluded assignment of high priority to this task. Not until early December 1913 did track reach the summit at Hydraulic Lake.[13]

By the end of 1913, the Kettle Valley Railway had 83 miles of track from Midway to Hydraulic Lake, 39 miles from Penticton to Osprey Lake, 30 miles from Merritt to Otter Summit, and 11 miles partway to Coquihalla Summit. This trackage, together with trackage in Penticton and Merritt yards, totalled 163 miles, roughly double the track mileage at the end of 1912. On the remainder of the railway, approximately 50 miles of grade were ready for rails and 50 miles more under contract for construction. This was a considerable improvement over the state of affairs on the KVR a year previous.

As well as the construction advances made in 1913, the KVR progressed with a number of agreements to formalize the company's relationship with the Canadian Pacific Railway that, in reality if not in law, had existed since construction began in 1910. At the annual meeting of the Kettle Valley Railway on June 2, 1913, the board of directors approved an agreement granting a lease of the KVR to the CPR for a period of 999 years, effective July 1, 1913.[14] The board also approved an agreement, already signed by the CPR, giving the KVR authority to operate its trains over the CPR mainline from the proposed junction near Hope into Vancouver. This second agreement was of merely academic concern because under the same agreement the CPR committed itself to provide all the motive power and rolling stock required for the KVR's future operations, making the KVR physically indistinguishable from its parent corporation. That year the KVR and CPR also put into effect the terms of an agreement signed in 1912 for the joint use of rail facilities at Grand Forks. Under this agreement, KVR locomotives in use on the Grand Forks-Republic line and the North Fork line were permitted to use the CPR roundhouse in Grand Forks in exchange for the CPR being permitted to operate its passenger trains into the KVR depot in downtown Grand Forks. This latter move proved to be a superior arrangement to that existing since the CPR's arrival in 1899, which required CPR passengers to make the rough journey to the station at Columbia, a mile west of the city proper.[15]

With the start of 1914, McCulloch and Warren still faced a number of difficult challenges in completing the Kettle Valley Railway. The most pressing matter was the commencement of construction on the long overland section from Osprey Lake to Otter Summit. As of April 1912, when the KVR first announced that it would alter its mainline to pass through Princeton, it was planned that the railway would use a continuous grade of 1.0% westward from Osprey Lake down the valley of Five Mile Creek to the Similkameen River five miles east of Princeton and then along the north side of the Similkameen Valley into Princeton. This location would produce an ideal line from the standpoint of gradient, but in adhering to the 1.0% grade limitation set by Shaughnessy the line would be forced around the high cliff face of a rock bluff at the mouth of Five Mile Creek. Naturally, McCulloch sought to avoid this highly expensive proposition if he could. The only alternative was either to descend Five Mile Creek on a steeper grade, thus carrying the line around the base of the bluff rather than across its face, or to cross the intervening ridge to the valley of Summers Creek and make a rapid descent down Summers Creek into Princeton. Both these alternatives were of lower anticipated construction cost than the first plan but they involved grades in excess of the 1.0% limitation.

Facing such a dilemma would not have deterred McCulloch and Warren a few years earlier—a great deal of extra expense had been entailed in securing the 1.0% grade on the railway between Carmi and Hydraulic Lake and between Kingsvale and Otter Summit—but the rapidly deteriorating economic conditions in North America at the time caused McCulloch and Warren to consider relaxing the limitation on the section leading down into Princeton. In a letter dated January 19, 1914, McCulloch asked Shaughnessy for a directive on the matter.

Four days later, on January 23, Warren opened discussions in St. Paul with GN president Carl Gray concerning the KVR's option under the Coquihalla Agreement for trackage rights between Princeton and Otter Summit. In the first week of February 1914, Warren awarded a contract to Guthrie, McDougall & Company for construction of the first ten miles of line west of Osprey Lake, as this section of line was needed for any of the alternative routings down into Princeton.

On February 18, 1914 Warren conferred with Shaughnessy in Montreal. The CPR president indicated that in view of the rapidly deteriorating political and economic situation, he believed it advisable to complete the KVR as expeditiously as possible, without unduly compromising the quality of the railway, thereby giving the Kootenays a connection with the coast. Shaughnessy's choice for the railway route was to use 21 miles of 1.0% line down the valley of Five Mile Creek to a point about seven miles northwest of Princeton, cross the saddle of the hillside to Summers Creek and descend to Princeton on a 2.2% grade. He instructed Warren to utilize trackage rights over the VV&E between Princeton and Otter Summit.

Having secured Shaughnessy's direction, Warren returned to British Columbia and immediately approached Richard McBride. The route change announced by Warren in 1912 to put the KVR mainline through Princeton had never been followed by an official alteration of the terms of the 1910 agreement, which was based on the originally proposed route through the area south of Aspen Grove. Therefore, Warren sought to have the agreement modified to take into account the change endorsed by Shaughnessy. The request naturally brought protests from those with vested interests along the originally planned route, but McBride supported Shaughnessy's concerns that the railway should be completed with reasonable dispatch. The agreement permitting the change was signed on February 28, 1914.

Shortly after securing provincial approval for the route change, Warren awarded Guthrie, McDougall & Company a contract for the remaining section of the railway down into Princeton, and by the end of April the railway was being actively graded over almost its entire length. On July 10, 1914 the KVR completed the route change matter by signing an agreement with the VV&E to bind the terms for the KVR to utilize the VV&E line between Princeton and Otter Summit. An almost word-for-word copy of the celebrated Coquihalla Agreement, this second trackage rights agreement was made with ironic simplicity considering the long decades of conflict which had preceded the first agreement.[16]

At the end of 1913 the grading work on the 57-mile section between Penticton and Hydraulic Lake was completed, except for a few large cuts and the spiral tunnel below Chute Lake.[17] In mid-January 1914 tracklaying eastward from Penticton began. Owing to the necessity of having to build several large timber trestles, the tracklaying work on this section went slowly. Early in March track was laid through the 162-foot-long "Little Tunnel" directly above Naramata and reached the 1,604-foot-long spiral tunnel, or "Big Tunnel" as it became known, by month's end. To celebrate the progress of his tracklayers, Warren again invited a party of Penticton citizens for a ride in his private car, and on March 29 a capacity load of enthusiastic passengers was carried up to the end of track. The incredible view obtained from the vantage point high above Okanagan Lake made an obviously favourable impression upon the first-time visitors. Before the viewers lay Okanagan Lake, nestled like a giant sapphire in the spring sunshine, with the ribbon of the Okanagan River stretching all the way south to the United States boundary. Even more impressive was the view of Penticton itself. Despite the fact the travellers had journeyed more than 20 miles by rail, the great reverse curve on the mountainside east of Okanagan Lake had brought them back to a point where they were practically overlooking the town they had left.

Tracklaying continued through spring and by July steel had been extended well past Chute Lake, the top of the 2.2% climb out of Penticton. Tracklaying was also being carried out westward from Hydraulic Lake although the rate of progress on this section was much slower owing to the large number of trestles required. Through the innovative use of prefabricated trestle bents, prepared by carpenter crews in a large framing yard at Carmi and delivered by flatcar to the end of track for placement, McCulloch sped the work as best he could. Even so, the task was immense. Eighteen trestles—one of them 13 decks high and nearly 1,000 feet long—were built in the five-mile section through Myra Canyon. More than 200 carpenters were needed for the framing work at Carmi. Bridge bolts were consumed in incredible numbers, as many as a carload of bolts per day.

Nevertheless, the difficult task was eventually completed and on October 2, 1914 the final spike on the Hydraulic Lake-Penticton section was driven at the bridge over West Fork Canyon Creek, just west of the highest elevation point on the entire Kettle Valley Railway—4,178 feet. Four days later, the first train ran over the line. On October 16 the dominion government inspector approved it for regular operations. Part of the Kettle Valley Railway was thus completed. However, shortly afterwards Warren announced that because the line west of Penticton was not yet finished there would be little point in inaugurating regular service. With the exception of a few freight trains bringing in Penticton's winter supply of coal and a special train of CPR officials, only work trains used the line. On December 5, 1914 the line was closed completely for the winter.[18]

Warren's decision to postpone inauguration of regular service between Midway and Penticton was not made solely because of the lack of completion of the remaining sections of the KVR. In August 1914 war had broken out in Europe, and Canada's allegiance to Great Britain in the struggle resulted in widespread ramifications upon railway construction throughout the dominion. Thousands of railway labourers were laying aside their picks and scrapers to bear arms, and quickly instituted government regulations committing explosives and other strategic commodities to the war effort had a dramatic impact. Immigration and foreign investment stopped instantly.

Faced with this crisis, McCulloch and Warren decided to concentrate their rapidly diminishing resources on completing the section between Osprey Lake and Princeton, thereby giving the interior a connection with the coast via Spences Bridge. The short line through Coquihalla Pass, they deemed, could be left until after the completion of the line via Merritt. Since this strategy depended on the Great Northern completing its trackage between Coalmont and Otter Summit, McCulloch and Warren pressed upon the GN to finish the line, which was entirely graded and awaiting rails at the outbreak of the war. Despite such urgings the work went slowly. It took two and a half months for the railway to complete the same distance Hill's crews had routinely hammered off in three or four days some years before. Not until October 25, 1914 did GN tracklayers reach Otter Summit.

That same day, in a brief informal ceremony, Louis Hill drove the last spike at Otter Summit before a small number of GN officials. A special KVR train was sent from Merritt to deliver a large number of citizens who intended to witness the event, but the train was delayed by a small mudslide and they missed the ceremony. Despite this disappointment the outing was a success, as the KVR train was used to carry the onlookers, and many of the GN officials, to the end of track on the Coquihalla line so they could get a first look at the joint railway through Coquihalla Pass. The GN men expressed themselves well pleased with the quality of the Coquihalla work. They also expressed approval of the newly completed section of the VV&E between Coalmont and Otter Summit. Accustomed as they were to J.J. Hill's uncompromising standards of construction, they were impressed with the easy curves and nearly five-mile-long tangent at Manning, soon dubbed "The Race Track" by railway crews. The special trip also gave the GN men the opportunity to inspect the preliminary work being done in laying out a joint divisional point at Otter Summit. That same year, the site of the divisional point was renamed Brookmere, in honour of Harry Brooks, the pioneer who had homesteaded the summit land years earlier.[19]

The linking of the VV&E and KVR at Brookmere effectively gave the Kootenays an unbroken rail connection with the coast, albeit by a somewhat roundabout route. Train service was not inaugurated over the combined lines, largely owing to the fact the VV&E track was not yet ballasted.[20] To ensure the KVR would be ready when the ballasting was complete, McCulloch rushed work on the line from Osprey Lake down into Princeton. On March 16, 1915 tracklaying was started at Osprey Lake. Two weeks later track was across Siwash Creek trestle and another two weeks saw rails partway down the three giant loops laid out on the grassy slopes above Summers Creek to allow the rail line sufficient distance to maintain the 2.2% grade down into Princeton. The 2.2% section soon became known as "The Jura Hill" to train crews.

On April 21, 1915 rails reached Princeton, thus bringing tracklaying on the Midway-Merritt line to a close. Actually, work was not quite finished that day; the switch requisitioned for the junction with the VV&E at the east end of town had not been delivered so the tracks could not be joined. Tracklaying superintendent Charles Taylor figured enough time had already been spent on the railway's construction and he hammered down the last spike, saying, "Well, the big stunt is done!"[21] Taylor's speech, while rivalling Van Horne's famous oration at Craigellachie for brevity, lacked something of the same enduring commemoration, and two days later, on April 23, after the switch had been installed, a more dignified last spike ceremony was held, with Mrs. G.D. Griffiths, the wife of the local minister, tapping home the final piece of steel. Another month was still needed to ballast the newly laid track. As of April 23, 1915 the Kettle Valley Railway, with the exception of the line through Coquihalla Pass and some future branch lines, was complete.[22]

On May 31, 1915 the Kettle Valley Railway line between Midway and Merritt was formally opened for service. That same day, the first passenger trains operated over the line to Penticton, one from Merritt and another from Midway, marking the inauguration of regular train service and bringing prominent businessmen and government representatives from all over southern British Columbia to a celebration banquet. More than half of Penticton's 3,000 citizens were on hand at the lakeshore depot to greet the first train, which consisted of KVR locomotive 4 and three CPR passenger cars, when it arrived from Merritt late in the afternoon. Many of these people waited at the station on into the evening to greet the train from Midway. After its arrival, a banquet was held at the Incola Hotel.

Of course, a banquet would not be considered complete without a long repertoire of speeches, and close to a dozen were given that night. J.J. Warren, in a few brief and memorable sentences, presented the most complimentary address: "I was fortunate to have associated with me Andrew McCulloch as Chief Engineer, a man of great experience, industry and perseverance."[23] Warren assured the people present that without McCulloch the great dream of direct rail connections between the coast and the Kootenays would not have been realized. He added that the dominion government had accepted his recommendation to have the railway station at Hydraulic Lake named "McCulloch" as a permanent monument to honour the remarkable man who had built the remarkable railway.

The many other speeches that night offered similar praise for McCulloch, and also gave credit to Warren for his less visible work as KVR president. The favourable speeches continued, but at four a.m. the hotel's tiny electric light plant broke down, plunging the banquet room into darkness. By industriously scratching a few matches, the master of ceremonies was able to produce enough light to have the last of the speeches safely concluded. Not until after five o'clock did the delegates struggle off to bed, leaving the banquet room—and the newly-opened Kettle Valley Railway— to the awakening light of a new day.

Owing to the wartime restrictions in effect in Canada during 1915 and the difficulties in securing proper connections with the CPR on the west, the initial passenger operations on the Kettle Valley Railway were modest. Service consisted of a tri-weekly mixed train out of Merritt in the early morning on Mondays, Wednesdays and Fridays, reaching Penticton late in the afternoon where it met a similar mixed train from Midway. On Tuesdays, Thursdays and Saturdays both trains left Penticton in the morning for their respective destinations of Merritt and Midway. Handling both freight and passenger traffic on the same train made the service slow, the forced overnight stay at Penticton adding to the delay. As well, transfers had to be made to the CPR Nicola Branch train at Merritt and to a mainline train at Spences Bridge. The sum effect was to actually make the journey to the coast from Nelson via the KVR half a day longer than via either of the traditional routes, north to the CPR mainline or south to the GN mainline. This improved marginally on November 1, 1915 when the CPR turned over the Nicola Branch to the KVR, thus enabling KVR trains to run directly through to Spences Bridge. However, service remained relatively unattractive until the opening of the Coquihalla line the following year.

The trains themselves were handled almost exclusively by leased CPR M2 class 2-8-0s in the 3200 number series, with a few of the older 3100s left over from construction days assisting as needed.[24] Mixed train service between Merritt and Penticton utilized one coach, or more when demand warranted, with a noon meal stop in both directions at Princeton, where connections were made with the GN tri-weekly train from Oroville. East of Penticton, the mixed train service utilized a coach and cafe car during the initial days of operation, but the extra weight of the cafe car on the steep grade motivated the railway to temporarily abandon this service. As of January 1916, a restaurant was opened at McCulloch to serve lunch for eastbound passengers and supper to those going west who had left Nelson in the morning. Change of cars was not necessary at Midway because the entire train was run through to Nelson. However, train crews changed at Midway, as this was the change in railway jurisdiction between the KVR and CPR.

The completion of the Midway-Merritt line allowed Andrew McCulloch and his engineering staff to devote their complete attention to construction of the line through Coquihalla Pass. Actually, the Coquihalla line was surprisingly near completion at the time war broke out in August 1914, and if sufficient manpower and explosives had been available during 1914 the Coquihalla section quite possibly could have been opened along with the rest of the KVR in May 1915. As of August 1914, 21 of the 36 miles of line between Hope and Coquihalla Summit had been graded, all tunnels on the line had been started, contracts for construction of the many timber trestles had been awarded, and the foundations of the bridge over the Fraser River at Hope had been completed. Tracklaying on the grade leading from the CPR mainline to the bridge was given priority so that steel for the bridge superstructure could be delivered. As of September 15, 1914, track was laid from the junction eastward. A little over a month later, on October 25, the first piece of steel on the bridge was laid by the Canadian Bridge Company, which had been awarded the contract to build the superstructure. In keeping with the provincial agreement, trackage was laid on the lower deck of the bridge, with the upper deck reserved for a roadway for vehicular traffic, a function the bridge still serves today, many years after the tracks on the lower deck were removed.

A few hundred feet east of the bridge site at Hope, the railway began an abrupt 2.2% ascending grade. It crossed over the Canadian Northern Pacific line with a level crossing and continued climbing until a few miles above town where the line entered Coquihalla Canyon. As the grade slackened construction difficulties were not eased. On the contrary, only four miles above Hope the Coquihalla River, having assumed an aura of relative innocence after cutting the awesome canyon closer to the summit, suddenly rebelled against the railway builders by throwing up a straight-walled abyss rising vertically from the riverbed to a height of more than 300 feet. Even worse, the river had not made a straight cut through the narrow canyon. Instead it had executed an abrupt horseshoe turn, thus obviating the simple solution of constructing a trestle to straddle the river over this the short section. Several engineers said it would be impossible to build a railway through this canyon. One authority wrote: "The only available outlet was wholly occupied by the roaring stream, sunk between lofty walls of solid granite, absolutely bare of all signs of vegetation."[25] Even J.J. Hill, a man who rarely backed away from any challenge geography threw at him, had chosen to avoid the problem by swinging his survey across a hillside a mile to the north. Hill's engineers told him that maintaining a level line through the canyon would require a tunnel nearly a mile in length.

McCulloch was not as certain as Hill's engineers that a long tunnel was necessary. The section of canyon was actually very short—only a third of a mile long—and McCulloch was certain a shorter line, with better grades, could be achieved. He daringly lowered himself and several of his fellow engineers in a small woven basket, suspended by ropes, down from the cliff tops into the canyon. There they cut narrow footholds into the rock walls upon which they could set up their survey instruments. After several weeks of such perilous work, McCulloch confirmed his earlier suspicions. Instead of a single tunnel nearly a mile in length, he found that a line requiring barely a quarter as much tunnel work could be cut directly through the canyon. Moreover, by careful selection of the alignment, McCulloch's route permitted the railway to cut not one, but four tunnels, thus exposing a multiple of working faces, which reduced the drilling time. Two bridges were to be built between three of the tunnels, each of them flush with the adjacent tunnel portals because of the abrupt drop to the river abyss below. Amazingly, all four tunnels and two bridges were set on a tangent alignment. With this unique alignment—unequalled anywhere else in the world—McCulloch was able to push the tunnels, later known as the Quintette Tunnels, through the entire canyon with a scant third of a mile of trackage.[26] It was, reported one writer, literally "threading the canyon . . . (of this) awe-inspiring gorge."[27]

On March 4, 1915 the first work train crossed the bridge at Hope and tracklayers started for Coquihalla Canyon. The many bridges made tracklaying comparatively slow and it was not until early September that track reached Ladner Creek, 17.5 miles above Hope. Here, track would have to delay while crews assembled a large steel bridge, consisting of nine plate girder spans on four steel towers, totalling 560 feet in length. The bridge was set on a curve of 12 degrees and 36 minutes, the sharpest of the 234 curves on the Coquihalla line.

Track was also being pushed westward from Coquihalla Summit. During the first nine months of 1915 only five miles of track had been laid on this section. However, considering the necessity of building six tunnels and ten timber trestles, all of impressive dimensions, progress was far from unsatisfactory. A massive steel arch truss bridge leaping 430 feet across the avalanche-swept chasm of Slide Creek served as another major delay to tracklayers.

Warren and McCulloch pushed the crews throughout the latter part of 1915 in the hope of having the railway complete and open for operation before winter. The push mounted after September when, despite one of the wettest months in coastal history, the bridge at Slide Creek was completed and the remaining gap closed to less than five miles. By mid-October the rains had turned to snow, and later that month, to compound matters, a rockslide completely demolished the bridge camp at Ladner Creek. Luckily, the slide occurred in the middle of the day when all hands were at work and there were no injuries, but the damage forced a critical shutdown of bridgework while a new camp was constructed. The workmen responded to this catastrophe by exerting a more determined push than ever in trying to get the railway completed. As fast as they worked, the snow continued to fall. By mid-November the snow at the summit was more than three feet deep, too deep to be merely pushed aside by a locomotive pilot.

Warren brought in two snowplows he acquired from the CPR. One was a well-used wing plow left over from better days in Rogers Pass. The other was the sole rotary plow from the narrow-gauge Kaslo & Slocan Railway, refitted with a larger snout and mounted on standard-gauge trucks. With this equipment, Warren believed the lifeline to the railhead west of Coquihalla Summit could be maintained. But at Coquihalla Summit the three feet of snow on the ground had become ten feet by the beginning of December, and even with the two plows working around the clock the railway crews were losing the battle against winter. Within the first week of December the plow crews were no longer fighting merely to keep the line open for construction trains; they were locked in a life or death struggle to prevent being stranded in the isolated wilderness of the Coquihalla. Work on closing the gap in the railway—now only a scant mile—became a secondary consideration.

On December 8, 1915 the KVR rotary plow, being pushed by KVR 1 and KVR 4 in tandem, derailed in a heavy snowdrift two miles west of Coquihalla Summit. Before the plow could be rerailed, the rapidly falling snow had filled the tracks behind it to a depth of four feet, trapping the train in the Pass. The wing plow was promptly dispatched from Brookmere to rescue the stranded train, but it too found the snow had become too deep and three full days were required for the wing plow to cover the 18 miles from Brookmere to Coquihalla Summit. Late in the evening of December 11, shortly after the rotary train had been reached, a massive slide came down ten miles below the summit, covering the tracks to a depth of 50 feet and trapping 35 work cars and all of the construction workers between there and Ladner Creek.

On December 24 another storm struck Coquihalla Pass. More snow, accompanied by high winds and freezing temperatures, hit the besieged workers. All along the line, slides were crashing down upon the railway. Train crews, valiantly fighting to reopen the line despite the harshness of the winter storm, found their work futile. In some cases the water in their locomotive tenders froze solid. Finally, on December 27, with only two weeks of work remaining to be done on the railway, McCulloch decided to order all work abandoned. Workers were instructed to snowshoe to the railhead at Ladner Creek from where they would be taken by train to Hope. Coquihalla Pass had shown it would put up a tough fight against intruders.

No further attempt was made to return to Coquihalla Pass until March 1916, when McCulloch hiked through the pass on snowshoes to determine when crews could resume work on the railway. What he saw was hardly encouraging. At many points along the tracks the snow was 30 to 40 feet deep and several snowsheds had been scattered across the canyon floor like kindling. The bridge at Boston Bar Creek, which had

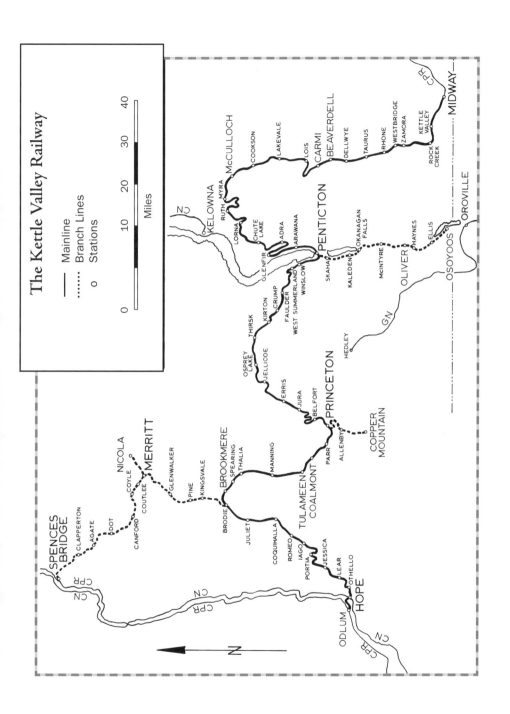

The Kettle Valley Railway

Legend:
— Mainline
...... Branch Lines
o Stations

Miles
0 10 20 30 40

been completed only a few weeks before work on the line was stopped in December, had met a similar fate. Records showed an incredible 67 feet of snow had fallen at Coquihalla Summit over the winter.[28] It was no longer a matter of two weeks work to open the line. McCulloch estimated four months would be needed to clear the line, repair the damage and complete the work on the bridge at Ladner Creek.

By early June, the massive bridge at Ladner Creek was essentially complete and on June 11, 1916 the first train made the crossing. Jim Fairley, for many years the telegraph operator at Brookmere, told the author that just before the first train crossed, Bill Collins, the bridge construction foreman, walked out to the centre span and jumped up and down on the ties several times to humorously test the strength of the bridge before waving the train ahead. Another seven weeks were needed to repair the damage of the previous winter. Even in mid-July the two KVR snowplows were at work helping clear away the last of the snow slides—a haunting premonition of what was in store for the Kettle Valley Railway in the years to come. When the repair work was completed, an informal last spike ceremony was held near the east end of Ladner Creek Bridge, and on July 31, 1916 the Coquihalla Pass rail line was opened for operation. That same day, daily through passenger train service was inaugurated between Vancouver and Nelson.

The completion of the Coquihalla Pass rail line marked the triumphant end to nearly a third of a century of struggle to achieve direct rail connections between the coast and the Kootenays. Unfortunately, the realization of the dream for which so much effort had been expended was overshadowed by the tragedy of a global war, and few British Columbians showed an interest in the railway's completion commensurate with the regard displayed in the preceding years. Only a handful of British Columbia newspapers rated the Kettle Valley Railway completion as front-page news, a dramatic alteration from the headline positions news of the Coast-to-Kootenay railway had commanded in the past. In numerous papers, the only coverage at all was the CPR's paid advertisement announcing the rail line's opening.

Canadians could be forgiven their disinterest in the KVR's completion. The news of loved-ones overseas, many of whom would not return, was dominant in their concern. Even Thomas Shaughnessy, the man to whom the Kettle Valley Railway owed so much, would lose a son in battle before the war ended. The country that Wilfrid Laurier had said ". . . was

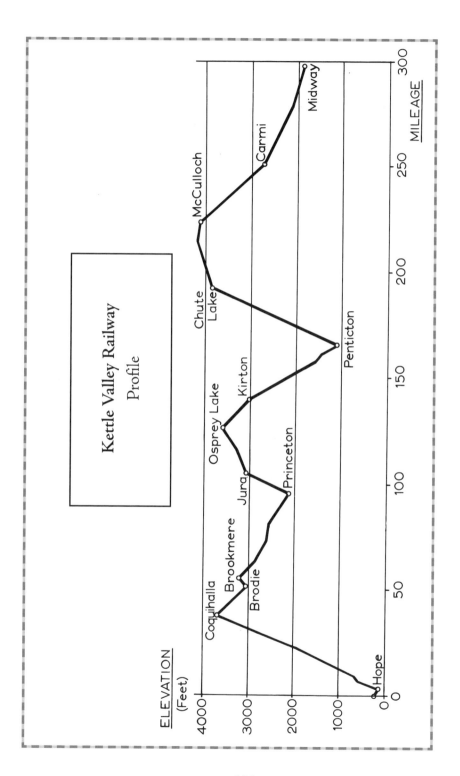

Kettle Valley Railway
Profile

ELEVATION (Feet)

4000

3000

2000

1000

0

MILEAGE

0   50   100   150   200   250   300

Hope

Coquihalla

Brookmere

Brodie

Jura

Osprey Lake

Kirton

Princeton

Penticton

Chute Lake

McCulloch

Carmi

Midway

more interested in boxcars than battleships" was just beginning to learn what global war meant.[29]

What interest there was in railways at the time was largely dominated by the completion of the Canadian Northern system and the opening of the Panama Canal, both of which served to greatly expand the hinterland of the port of Vancouver beyond the more limited scope the Coast-to-Kootenay railway dreamers had envisioned of it. The port's expansion in turn reduced the impact of the newly achieved connections with the Kootenays. Therefore, it was hardly surprising that the press and public completely overlooked the fact the opening of the rail line through Coquihalla Pass also served to link the VV&E's line on the coast with the network of GN subsidiary lines lacing the border country of the interior.

The defeat of the reciprocity issue in 1911 had dealt a severe blow to the Great Northern's empire in Canada, although J.J. Hill—still his crusty old self at age 77—appeared to lose little of his strong personal interest in southern British Columbia. Late in 1915, when it appeared the joint Coquihalla Pass line would soon be completed, Hill intended his trains soon to scorch the Coquihalla steel in competition with the KVR. The subsequent delay in the completion of the Coquihalla Pass line caused by the severe winter snows forced Hill to postpone inauguration of service over the line.

Throughout early 1916, as McCulloch's crews worked to close the narrow gap in Coquihalla Pass, Hill's own crews worked to complete the VV&E trackage between Kilgard and the Canadian Northern Pacific Railway at Sumas River. They were also readying to construct the quarter mile section of VV&E trackage linking the CNP with the KVR at Hope. On Vancouver's False Creek, a magnificent brick station was rising to handle GN trains operating south to Seattle and east to the Kootenays, and at Hope a three-stall roundhouse, turntable and fuel tanks were being built.[30] At Brookmere, the meeting point of the joint track sections and a divisional point for both railways, the GN was laying out similar facilities.

Indeed, it was the presence of the GN that accounted for the unusual nature of the railway yard at Brookmere. Under the terms of the Coquihalla Agreement, the KVR and GN were to share the station and locomotive watering facilities. Fuel and locomotive servicing facilities were the sole responsibility of each railway. Thus, instead of placing the station to one side of the rail yard, as would normally have been done to permit public access from one side without crossing the tracks, the two railways placed the Brookmere station squarely in the middle of the yard so that it would equally serve the two sets of tracks on the north side of the station, designated for the KVR, and the two on the south side, reserved for the GN. Similarly, the water tank at the west end of the yard was equipped with a spout on each side to permit use by either railway. North of the station the KVR built a crew bunkhouse, coal tower, turntable and three-stall roundhouse.[31] To the east of the station a plot of land on the south side of the tracks was set aside for use by the Great Northern.

Unfortunately, on May 29, 1916—just two months before the rail line through Coquihalla pass was to open—James J. Hill died unexpectedly, and with him died any serious interest in British Columbia within the Great Northern management. The work at Sumas River and at Hope was allowed to lag and it was not until the end of September, two months after the KVR had begun using the Coquihalla line, that the GN was in a position to begin operation. Even then, the service the GN introduced was hardly reflective of Hill's earlier ambitions. A tri-weekly mixed train service between Vancouver and Hope was all the GN inaugurated, and even this would be discontinued within three years.

Probably not even this service would have been introduced had Louis Hill not felt a moral obligation to carry out at least some of his father's wishes. Louis Hill's influence within the Great Northern was not enough to convince others in the company management to introduce the daily through Vancouver-Spokane passenger service his father had earlier planned to operate over the VV&E. As a token tribute to his father, on September 27, 1916 Louis Hill headed a small party of GN officials who rode over the line from Vancouver to Princeton on board a special Great Northern train. The following day the party continued through to Spokane, thus, technically at least, fulfilling J.J. Hill's dream. Louis Hill's trip was to be the only GN train to run through Coquihalla Pass. No other GN trains were ever operated. The railway some said was the most expensive in the world, paid for in part by the Great Northern Railway, was to be all but abandoned by that corporation after passage of a single train.[32]

In the years following the completion of the Kettle Valley Railway, the line through Coquihalla Pass gained a considerable reputation in engineering circles around the world as a masterpiece of mountain railroad engineering. Interestingly, the rail line gained even wider renown as a cultural curiosity because of its unusual station names. Each station on the Coquihalla line—with the exception of Coquihalla Summit, which in 1916 was renamed simply Coquihalla—was given the name of a character from the plays of Shakespeare.[33] Over the years, thousands of tourists would venture from around the world to see and photograph the stationboards of Othello, Lear, Jessica, Portia, Iago, Romeo and Juliet or to mail off letters or postcards to secure postmarks from those stations with post offices as a souvenir of a unique journey. Of course each visitor had his own version of the Shakespearian railway fable to tell his friends, and in time many colourful but erroneous stories concerning the origin of the Shakespearian names were generated. In actuality, the names of the stations in Coquihalla Pass, as the names for all the stations on the Kettle Valley Railway, were chosen by McCulloch and Warren. The Coquihalla stations were named at the suggestion of Andrew McCulloch to honour the Bard whose works he had always loved, an ironic touch of gentility considering the railway traversed one of the most rugged regions on the face of the earth.[34]

Thomas Shaughnessy, as he rode over the line for the first time on a special inspection train on September 15, 1916 in the company of McCulloch and Warren, expressed himself "greatly impressed" by McCulloch's novel idea for the station names and by the high quality of the line's construction.[35] Shaughnessy said the railway's opening was the realization not only of the dream long held by the people of British Columbia but also of a great personal dream. He prophesied the years ahead would reveal the wisdom of the railway's construction.[36]

Perhaps Shaughnessy appeared to be boasting. If he was, he had justifiable right to do so. With the assistance of Warren and McCulloch he had just built one of the most difficult and expensive railways in the world. It was also a railway that, without these three men, almost certainly would not have been completed. Hill's sudden withdrawal from British Columbia, and a world war that drastically altered the evolutionary pattern of Canadian railways, had ended forever further railway expansion of consequence in southern British Columbia.

It is unlikely there were three men more proud that day than Thomas Shaughnessy, James Warren and Andrew McCulloch as they sat on the open platform of Shaughnessy's brass-railed private car leaning to the graceful curves of the railway and clattering across great bridges spanning the conquered chasms of the Coquihalla. Thanks to these three men, the dream of an entire generation of British Columbians had come true. Coast and Kootenay were now directly connected by rail. Nelson had become only a day's travel away from Vancouver. Penticton was a scant ten hours away. The Kootenays, once the sole preserve of the city of Spokane, were now firmly in British Columbia's control. In fact, the trade of southern British Columbia had all but ceased to flow across the border to the United States. Instead, the trade was coming west across the backbone of the mountains of British Columbia. West over the railway less believing men had vowed could not be built. West on the steel trail the poet Bliss Carmen would later say an eagle needed wings to ride. West to the ports of coastal British Columbia. The dream had been fulfilled.

12: Steel Rails and Iron Men

The Kettle Valley Railway 1916 to 1930

In July 1916, immediately following the opening of the Kettle Valley Railway line through Coquihalla Pass, the massive force of engineers, surveyors and labourers employed in the construction of the railway during the previous six years began to disband. Andrew McCulloch was not to be among them. Even though the Coquihalla line had nominally been opened, the shortage of labour caused by the war had prevented completion of snowshed work. Considerable construction supervision remained. Moreover, McCulloch had been given additional responsibilities for the railway's operations. The previous winter in Coquihalla Pass had convinced Thomas Shaughnessy that the operation of the Kettle Valley Railway would demand a man at least the equal of the one who had built the incredible railway. And in the mind of Thomas Shaughnessy at least, only Andrew McCulloch could be that equal. Thus, McCulloch was to stay with the Kettle Valley Railway.[1]

Within a month of Shaughnessy's September 1916 tour, Coquihalla Pass experienced its first snowfall of the coming winter. Two feet of snow fell in a single night on the final day of October. The following day, November 1, 1916, a rockslide just west of Coquihalla smashed into a plow train, fatally injuring the train's conductor—the first of many KVR operating employees who were to lose their lives at the hands of a harsh and unforgiving Coquihalla.[2] The next day more rocks came down, followed by more snow. On November 8, three slides blocked the line at Iago and a hundred feet of track washed out near Jessica, forcing trains to detour via the Fraser Canyon and Spences Bridge. No sooner was the track repaired than more snow fell, closing the line again a week later. On February 18, 1917, after great effort, the KVR line was reopened. However, winter quickly struck again. Another six feet of snow fell upon the pass and trapped a passenger train at Iago. So deep was the snow that plow trains, trying to rescue the stranded passengers, became entombed themselves, requiring two full days to reach the besieged passengers and a whole month to reopen the line. Then it took winter seven hours to close it again. In fact, not until late May was there anything approaching uninterrupted service. Just as Shaughnessy had feared, the tenuous link between coast and Kootenay was to be as difficult to maintain as it had been to achieve.

Notwithstanding the severe operational problems the KVR faced in Coquihalla Pass during the winter of 1916-17, the Kettle Valley Railway quickly proved its value. Even when passenger trains had to be detoured over the longer route via Spences Bridge, travel time between coastal points and the southern interior was greatly reduced. This reduction, coupled with the elimination of any layovers, made the KVR extremely popular, especially after the restrictive war years. Eastbound, the daily passenger train left Vancouver in the early evening, reached Penticton the next morning and got to Nelson by nightfall of the second day. Westbound, the passenger train left Nelson in the morning, passed through Penticton late that evening and arrived at Vancouver early the next morning.

This was the basic schedule KVR passenger trains were to follow for much of the railway's history. With this timing, passenger trains in both directions normally passed through Coquihalla Pass in the middle of the night, generating the colourful story that the railway had adopted the schedule solely to keep passengers from seeing the rocky cliff edges and spidery-footed trestles over which the railway operated. The rationale for the revised schedule, however, was based more on practicality than legend. Since Coquihalla Pass was virtually uninhabited, it seemed logical to run trains through there at night so residents of all the major communities west of Nelson, except for Princeton, could board the train at a convenient daytime hour and reach Vancouver the following morning in time for a day's business. They could then leave Vancouver at the end of the day and arrive back home during daylight hours the following day.

Passenger trains normally consisted of a single baggage car, a mail-express car, one or more standard coaches, one first class coach and one sleeper. In the early days of operation, a cafe-observation car was used on the daylight portion of the trip east of Penticton and a full dining car was added between Vancouver and Hope. This latter arrangement allowed eastbound passengers to enjoy a leisurely dinner after leaving Vancouver while freeing the railway from hauling the extra weight of the diner up the steep grade through Coquihalla Pass during the night when it was not needed. The westbound train in the morning would pick up the dining car at Hope so that passengers could have breakfast on board before reaching Vancouver. In later years the dining car was allowed to remain with the train all the way between Vancouver and Nelson.

Even when the dining car was allowed to run through, it was still necessary for passenger trains to stop at Hope because the KVR, for reasons not apparent, never exercised the option of the agreement with its parent Canadian Pacific permitting the KVR to run its trains over the CPR mainline into and out of Vancouver. Instead, CPR crews handled passenger trains from Vancouver to Hope where they were turned over to KVR crews. Locomotives were also changed at Hope. CPR locomotives used on the 90-mile dead level run from Vancouver to Hope were replaced at Hope by the KVR's leased CPR M1 and M2 2-8-0 steam locomotives in the 3200 number series and D9 4-6-0s in the 500 number series, which were more suitable for the mountain-climbing role east of Hope. The crew change procedure was repeated at Midway. Because of the similarity of motive power used on the KVR and the CPR line between Midway and Nelson, an arrangement was soon made to allow passenger trains to keep the same engine from Penticton through to Nelson and return. The people of Merritt and the Nicola Valley were provided with a daily-except-Sunday mixed train from Brookmere to Spences Bridge and back that made connections with through passenger trains at both ends of the line.

Leased CPR 2-8-0s also formed the backbone of freight motive power. Through freight traffic from the Kootenays generally provided sufficient business for at least one train per day, with passenger trains, way freights, work trains and "helper" service keeping the remainder of the KVR's fleet of some 20 locomotives actively employed. The majority of the locomotives were assigned to Penticton, the location of the KVR's headquarters and principal maintenance facilities. It was also where "helper" engines were based for assisting trains up the 2.2% grades out of the Okanagan Valley. The other locomotives were assigned to Brookmere or Hope, with an additional one based at Merritt for handling log trains.

A turntable and three-stall roundhouse for servicing locomotives had already been built at Brookmere before the Coquihalla line opened, and in 1917 a three-stall enginehouse was built at Hope, at the tail of the wye opposite the station. At the same time a two-stall enginehouse was built at

Coquihalla. However, the KVR found it was more practical to base "helper" engines at Hope or Brookmere than Coquihalla, so the Coquihalla enginehouse was closed not long after it was built. "Helper" engines were also used occasionally on the short 2.2% grade east from Princeton to Jura although it was more common for freight trains to "double" this section of grade. This meant the train was broken into two parts at Princeton, with the crew taking the first half up to the siding at Jura and then returning to Princeton for the second half before continuing on from Jura with the entire train. Engines were not regularly assigned to Princeton except for handling ore trains on the Copper Mountain branch constructed a few years later.

For operating and administrative purposes, the Kettle Valley Railway divided its line into four sections, or what railroaders called subdivisions. The line from Midway to Penticton yard and the extension to the waterfront station became known as the Carmi Subdivision. The line from Penticton to Brookmere, including the section of the VV&E used between Princeton and Brookmere, became known as the Princeton Subdivision. The line from Brookmere to the junction with the CPR mainline just west of Hope became known as the Coquihalla Subdivision. The line from Brodie, just west of Brookmere, to Merritt and Spences Bridge, with the spur from Merritt to Nicola, became known as the Merritt Subdivision. There was a fifth subdivision, the North Fork Subdivision, for the short line from Grand Forks northward, but this line was geographically disconnected from the others and was soon assigned to the CPR even though its ownership remained vested in the Kettle Valley Railway.

Kettle Valley Railway train crews, like the KVR's locomotives, were primarily based at Penticton, with lesser numbers assigned to Hope, Brookmere and Merritt. Hope did not last long as a terminal point. The crew change point was soon moved from Hope to Ruby Creek, on the CPR mainline 10 miles west, largely because of the major disruption to crew assignments whenever the Coquihalla line was closed, which proved to be much more frequently than originally expected. The relocation was unpopular with train crews because Ruby Creek offered few amenities, such as stores and schools, whereas Hope had better facilities. When the CPR formally took over the KVR in 1931, former KVR employees became employees of the CPR and passenger runs were extended through to Vancouver, but freight crews continued to work only as far west as Ruby Creek.

The KVR decided not to base any train crews at Midway. Crews based at Penticton worked all trains on the Carmi Subdivision. Since there was considerably greater tonnage of traffic moving westbound than eastbound, westbound freight trains frequently had to "double" the grade from Midway to McCulloch in a manner that became known to crews as a "McCulloch Turn." This consisted of a through run from Penticton to Midway, where the return train would be made up. The crew would then take half the train up the long grade to McCulloch, set the cars on the siding and run back with just the engine and caboose to Midway. They would then return to McCulloch with the second half of the train and reassemble the cars for the run over easier track through to Penticton. The grade from Midway to McCulloch was limited to 1.0%, largely due to the ingenuity of the man for whom the latter point was named. But the run was still an arduous one, owing to the considerably greater tonnage of traffic moving westbound than eastbound. While the employment of McCulloch Turns spared the KVR from having to base locomotives or crews at Midway, the assignments were never well liked by the train crews.[3]

In more recent times, railroaders of that early period have been much romanticized in poetry and song. However, the life of most such railroaders, on the KVR in particular, was far from romantic. Through runs were long, with crews often absent from home for several days at a time. Crews based at Hope, if assigned to "helper" service, could expect to do two or sometimes three round trips between Hope and Coquihalla in the course of a day's work. Crews in "helper" service based at Penticton would also typically do two or three round trips up to Chute Lake or Kirton, the top of the 2.2% grades climbing east and west from the Okanagan Valley. During such a shift the fireman of a steam locomotive could expect to shovel as much as 24 tons of coal. Such work was hardly romantic. It was simply unglamorous, man-killing toil.

Danger was also ever present on the Kettle Valley Railway, waiting to snuff out the life of even the most careful crewman. Regrettably, over the years numerous KVR employees were killed or seriously injured, principally by rockslides along the railway. Others lived long into retirement. One such employee, Joe Collett, earned the distinction of being the only KVR employee to receive a CPR gold pass, the symbol of 50 years continuous employment with the company. Among other employees were such men as William "Smoky" Clapperton, Angus Gillis, Murdock McKay, Jack Fletcher, Jim Meldrum and his son George, Fred Deater, Oscar

Cummings, Bob MacBeth, Guy Beasom, Harry Percival and F.P. "Perley" McPherson. While their names may mean nothing to a new generation, to these men, and others like them, remains owing a great debt for their dedication in keeping alive the Coast-to-Kootenay railway dream. An unforgiving Coquihalla made it more and more apparent just how fragile that dream would remain.

On September 12, 1917 a rockslide two miles west of Coquihalla sealed off a tunnel mouth, forcing trains via Spences Bridge for a week. On October 3 another slide knocked out a 360-foot trestle at Jessica. Then, on December 13 a fierce snowstorm hit Coquihalla Pass. That same day, a slide struck the rear of a plow train at Iago and knocked the caboose 700 feet down into the canyon, killing one crew member and seriously injuring two others. Even Andrew McCulloch, who rarely left Coquihalla Pass that winter, narrowly escaped being killed by a slide; despite an injured leg he walked the 25 miles to Hope inspecting the repair work underway on the remaining section of the line.

On December 21, long before the first snowfall had been cleared away, another storm hit Coquihalla Pass. So heavy was this new snowfall an entire week was consumed just clearing the 18-mile stretch from Brookmere to Coquihalla. Compounding the troubles, a two-engine plow train working west from Coquihalla on December 19 stalled in a snowdrift at the lower end of the Bridalveil Falls Creek trestle near Romeo, and while crews were trying to dig themselves out another snowslide whistled down the canyon behind them, sweeping away all but the few trestle bents upon which the end of their train was standing. Unable to move forward or backward, and with the snow continuing to fall, the plow crews could do little but drain the locomotive boilers and abandon their train to winter.

After the crews had hiked out of Coquihalla Pass, snow continued to fall for another week. However, on January 8, 1918 a quick thaw brought a rapid reversal of conditions and crews came back into the pass on snowshoes in the hope of freeing their locomotives and reopening the line. Although the men were able to fire up their locomotives again and free them, the thaw brought with it dozens of snowslides. Not until an incredible 20 days later did the train reach clear track at Portia, 13 miles away. For most of that distance, broken trestle and snowshed timbers were used to fire the locomotives. Despite even these heroic efforts, the tracks behind them were quickly blocked by new slides and no attempt could be made to rebuild the Bridalveil Falls Creek trestle. The line was simply abandoned until May. The Kettle Valley Railway's troubles during the winter of 1917-18 didn't end there either. On April 30, 1918 a log jam piled up against the main pier of the bridge over the Kettle River at mile 15.5 Carmi Subdivision just north of Rock Creek, causing the bridge to be severely damaged, with a resulting closure of the line to through traffic for nearly two weeks.

Perhaps of greater discouragement was the volume of freight traffic on the railway. As the war in Europe dragged on, the Kootenays and Boundary smelters directed more and more of their output to eastern Canadian industrial centres, thus depriving the KVR of the principal traffic it had been built to carry. Coal mines and sawmills along the railway experienced great difficulty in maintaining their prewar production as a result of the wholesale loss of labour to the higher-paying shipbuilding and related war industries.

The military also took many workers. One of the casualties of such shortages was the KVR passenger service. Owing to government restrictions and shortages of manpower and equipment, the daily passenger service inaugurated in 1916 was cut back to three times per week early in 1918. Similar shortages forced suspension of routine maintenance on the railway and caused mishaps, such as the bridge log jam at Rock Creek, to tie up the railway unduly for want of men to speedily repair the damage. Thus, the war made a difficult time for the fledgling KVR. However, it also provided the motivation for the construction of the KVR's first major branch line: the line to Copper Mountain.

When put forth early in World War I, the suggestion of building a railway to Copper Mountain was not new. Indeed, such plans were practically as old as the knowledge that this low-crested mountain on the east side of the Similkameen River, ten miles south of Princeton, contained sizeable volumes of copper ore. In the years following the first copper claim on the mountain—the Sunset made by R.A. "Volcanic" Brown in 1888—dozens of formal proposals were put forth to provide the mountain with rail connections.[4] Brown boasted the Sunset would make him so rich he would solve all the world's problems by giving away oceans of money. No doubt he was overly optimistic on several counts, but the claim did possess genuine merit and Brown was later able to sell it to the Sunset Copper Company for $45,000. The claim was sold twice more, finally passing into the hands of the Canada Copper Company, which began extensive exploration work on the property in 1914. The wartime labour shortage initially retarded progress, but by 1916 the demand for copper by the war industries had become so great the company was allocated the manpower necessary to undertake comprehensive development.

In April 1917, Canada Copper formally approached the KVR to have the railway company build a spur line from Princeton to Copper Mountain. It was planned that ore would be hauled from Copper Mountain to a concentrator mill to be built partway between the two communities, with the copper concentrates taken to the smelter at Trail. The KVR agreed, and by November McCulloch had completed all survey work. The planned spur would cut off from the edge of the GN loop track west of the Princeton townsite, cross the Similkameen River on a low bridge and loop up the hillside opposite the town in a stiff 2.2% climb. Along the eight miles of track from the top of the grade through to the mine at Copper Mountain the grade would be much more moderate. The sacrifice to achieve good operating conditions would produce some impressive construction statistics for what was only a branch line. The line required 24 trestles, 17 of them in the four miles immediately before reaching Copper Mountain, four tunnels and the movement of 360,000 cubic yards of solid rock. A secondary spur—dubbed the "High Line" by train crews—would run to the top of the concentrator mill, a site called Allenby.[5]

In March 1918, the construction contract for the entire line was awarded to W.P. Tierney & Company, and by the middle of April work was started next to the GN enginehouse in Princeton. Tierney was plagued by setbacks. First, wartime labour shortages slowed progress. Then the nationwide influenza epidemic in the fall devastated his workforce. A labour strike from April to July 1919 further aggravated the delays. Not until October 7, 1920 was the railway finally completed and approved by the federal government for operation. To climax the line's frustrating beginning, shortly after the first train of ore had been loaded on October 27, Canada Copper announced that owing to the drastic drop in copper prices following termination of the war the mine and concentrator mill would be closed. On December 9, 1920 the Copper Mountain mine ceased operation and two days later the Allenby mill closed. Later that week the railway branch line, now having no purpose, shut down.

The drop in copper prices brought about by the end of the war had a broader impact upon the Kettle Valley Railway than just the closure of the Copper Mountain branch line. Between late 1918 and 1920, every copper smelter in the Boundary District closed down, effectively destroying Warren and McCulloch's hopes that Boundary copper traffic would be redirected to Vancouver following the war. The lessened demand for copper also sealed the fate of the KVR's affiliate, the Spokane & British Columbia Railway, which ceased operation on September 27, 1919 and ended its colourful history shortly afterwards when the rails between Grand Forks and Republic were removed.[6] The CPR and GN also soon abandoned their branch lines into Phoenix and their spurs to the Grand Forks smelter. Considering the aggressiveness with which both companies had built their copper camp trackage, it was like a Gilbert and Sullivan opera seeing them now engage in a race to pull up trackage, each wanting to be first because of a fear the Board of Railway Commissioners might order the remaining line to continue operations.

This drop in metal prices and the ensuing financial crisis required J.J. Warren to devote increasing amounts of his time to the management of the Trail smelter, with which he had become associated some years previously. As a consequence, he resigned as president of the Kettle Valley Railway in April 1920. That same month, D'Alton Coleman, an Ontario native who later rose to the ranks of CPR president, took over Warren's former position. Andrew McCulloch, now general superintendent, remained in charge of the railway's operations.

Despite the loss of through traffic following World War I, there were a number of success stories in the Kettle Valley Railway's operations. On June 1, 1919 the KVR resumed daily passenger service with the inauguration of the *Kootenay Express* westbound and the *Kettle Valley Express* eastbound. They were numbered Train 11 and Train 12 respectively, numbers they were to keep throughout most of the KVR's history. The KVR that year also operated a number of highly popular picnic trains carrying Penticton citizens up to Chute and Osprey Lakes for day long outings, and in September of 1919 the Prince of Wales, Edward VIII, made a highly enjoyed tour of the line. The KVR's biggest success during the immediate postwar years was the healthy amount of local freight traffic the railway enjoyed, a surprise considering the KVR had been built primarily to give Kootenay freight a direct route to the coast. The KVR's three biggest local traffic commodities—coal, lumber and fruit—experienced substantial postwar growth and continued to provide the railway with traffic for many years afterwards.

Traffic in lumber and related forest products tended to concentrate west of Princeton where the wet coastal climate produced larger trees than the drier climates in the mountain lees. Sawmills at Canford, Merritt, Brookmere and Princeton, plus a few smaller locations, generated finished lumber traffic. The sawmill at Canford owned by the Nicola Pine Mills Limited, the successor of the older Nicola Valley Lumber Company, also provided the KVR with a log supply operation that was to grow to be one of the railway's most important operations. In fact, the volume of log traffic was so great that the KVR regularly assigned a locomotive to Merritt exclusively for handling cars from the many logging spurs in the Coldwater Valley above Merritt down to the mill at Canford.

Len Smuin, a locomotive engineer with the KVR for many years, laughingly looked back as he told the author of his introduction to both the KVR and some of its more colourful employees on the Merritt Branch log train. Being too young to go off to war, Len was taken on by the KVR in 1917 as a fireman, and his first assignment was on the Brookmere-Spences Bridge mixed train run with Oscar Cummings, an engineer notorious among KVR employees for his outgoing personality and unabashed voracity at pulling pranks. Len related that Oscar took a liking to him right from the start and thus Len was luckily never made the victim of Oscar's fun-loving tricks. It didn't take long for him to see how Oscar operated.

The Merritt Subdivision mixed train to which both Len and Oscar were assigned regularly met the log train partway along its journey. About once per month, the crews of the two trains would swap locomotives when they met so the Merritt-based log train locomotive could work through to Penticton for its routine boiler washing and inspection. Len recalled that on one such occasion the locomotive change had been made, but Gordon Sutherland, the log train engineer, forgot to take with him the canvas bag containing his good clothes for his later night life in Merritt. Of course, Oscar could not allow Gordon to go without his good clothes and as Oscar highballed out of the siding he tossed the canvas bag down to Gordon. Gordon beamed with thanks at Oscar's consideration. It need hardly be stated that Gordon's appreciation ended very abruptly when he came out of the bath at Merritt later that night to discover that Oscar had snipped all the buttons from the front of his good pants!

Oscar's reputation was soon well established around the KVR. One of his favourite tricks on steep upgrades was to get down on the tender footplate, with the assistance of his not unwilling fireman, and pour the contents of their locomotive oilcans onto the rails over which their engine had just passed. By the time the exasperated crew of the next train made it through to the terminal, Oscar had thumbed through his ample mental thesaurus to select the most appropriate adjectives describing his superior ability at moving trains up a heavy grade.

Even the editor of the *Princeton Star* found Oscar's pranks a little severe. On one occasion the paper published a sharp editorial warning Oscar of the dire actions the citizens of Princeton might take if he did not cease his practise of leaning on the locomotive whistle cord when he roared into town with the 4 a.m. passenger train from Vancouver. The unappreciated entrance, the editor stated, "would wake up the dead, or even the *Merritt Herald*."[7] On another occasion the editor, who happened to eat in the same Princeton hash house as most of the railroaders, wrote of his latest meeting with Oscar: "He was in tow of Perley McPherson, therefore he could not repeat the story of how he put wings on an engine and flew over a three mile snowslide, as Perley's early Presbyterian training might make O.C.'s veracity look like thirty cents with the three off."[8]

Len and Oscar were working the Merritt Branch on May 27, 1919, the day a fire, fanned by a high wind, destroyed the Nicola Pine Mills sawmill at Canford. Unfortunately, they arrived at Canford too late to save the 13 boxcars of lumber also destroyed for want of a locomotive to pull them out of danger. Almost immediately after the fire the mill's owner, Henry Meeker, announced that a replacement mill would be built at Merritt on the west side of the Coldwater River, just below the Middlesboro mine spur. Construction of the new mill was promised immediately. Early in January 1920, as the new mill neared completion, Meeker announced that his company would build a private logging railway to supply the new mill with sufficient timber. The railway was to branch off the KVR at a point 11.8 miles southwest of Merritt, a point later called Pine by the KVR, and follow the valley of Midday Creek to the west of the Coldwater River. The railway was to be only a few miles in length initially, but it would be extended, Meeker promised, as logging moved further back into the bush.

On March 30, 1920 construction began, and by late spring four miles of the logging railway had been built. The KVR operated the logging spur for several months until Nicola Pine Mills acquired a Shay locomotive to operate the line itself. In January 1922 the company added a second-hand Climax type geared locomotive to its roster, which it utilized exclusively for switching at the Merritt mill, and later that year it added a third locomotive, another Climax, to assist the Shay in the bush west of Pine.

Railcars loaded with logs were hauled from the bush to Pine by the Nicola Pine Mills locomotives and taken by the KVR log train to the Merritt mill. For a time, Nicola Pine Mills engines even hauled the logs directly to the mill. During 1923 and 1924, trackage was extended 15 miles westward. The company also constructed several bush spurs near Juliet, although these were operated exclusively by the KVR. Through the 1920s and part-way into the 1930s, before the depression bankrupted Nicola Pine Mills, these spurs all provided log traffic for the KVR. Other log and lumber traffic, while never as substantial as that from Nicola Pine Mills, would continue to provide freight business for the KVR.

The growth of coal traffic on the KVR experienced a history similar to the log and lumber trade. The coal mines at Merritt, having started when the CPR branch from Spences Bridge was opened in 1907, were the first to operate along the KVR. After reaching their peak production in 1912, they suffered a severe decline when the CPR commenced a wholesale changeover from coal to oil locomotive fuel in British Columbia that year. Fortunately for the coal mines, the war two years later caused an oil shortage, and by 1917 virtually all CPR locomotives had been reconverted to burn coal. The Princeton area coal mines were not as severely affected because they produced predominately lignite coal, used mostly as domestic fuel and never utilized to any extent by the CPR, KVR or GN. Indeed, the one trial run made on the KVR using Princeton coal resulted in so many bush fires along the right-of-way it took the railway two days to extinguish them all. In spite of this negative verdict on Princeton coal for locomotive fuel, it was a strong competitor on the Vancouver domestic market starting in 1912, when the Princeton Coal & Land Company daringly shipped coal to Vancouver via the GN, then a 700-mile haul over the mountains to Spokane and back over the mountains to the coast. Princeton coal also proved popular throughout the interior. In all, nine major coal companies would operate in the Princeton area between 1909 and the mid-1940s. Five of those mines had railway spurs leading directly to the mine tipples.[9]

The biggest and most important coal producer on the Kettle Valley Railway was Coalmont Collieries. Taking over from the Columbia Coal & Coke Company in 1913, Coalmont Collieries began extensive development work that year in an outcropping four miles southwest of the Coalmont townsite, where the coal seam quickly proved to be of equal quality and considerably greater quantity than the original seam close to town. The wartime labour shortage forced the company to discontinue work temporarily, and it was not until 1917, when Blake Wilson of Vancouver and Patrick Burns of Calgary bought out Coalmont Collieries, that sufficient manpower was available for work to resume. The new minesite quickly acquired a name appropriate to its new owners—Blakeburn—but because the mine was both a considerable distance from, and elevation above, the railway, trucks had to be used to carry the coal down to the loading tipple at the railway siding.

Unfortunately trucks of that period were not sufficiently robust for the demands of the mine and Coalmont Collieries subsequently approached McCulloch with a request that the KVR build a spur to the mine. McCulloch and his staff did considerable survey work in 1917 and 1918, discovering that a spur could not be built to the mine with grades of less than 3.1%. After lengthy consideration, including the proposal to use Shay geared locomotives, thoughts of building a rail line were dropped. Instead, work began on the construction of an aerial cable tramway. In June of 1921, the tramway was completed and with the start of its operation, Coalmont Collieries quickly became one of the major coal producers in the province.

Coalmont Collieries coal was generally regarded as one of the best steam coals in western North America. Just how highly the railways rated the coal was visibly evident from the number of GN and CPR official cars that seemed to be almost permanent fixtures on the Coalmont siding in the early 1920s while high-ranking officials of both companies bartered for the mine's output. Even the Canadian National tried to secure a share of the mine's production, which from 1921 onward exceeded 160,000 tons annually.

The Kettle Valley Railway used mostly Coalmont Collieries coal for its locomotives after the mine's effective opening in 1921. The KVR also transported a sizable amount of coal through to Ruby Creek for use on the CPR mainline. The volume of coal being transported was sufficient to justify the KVR regularly assigning Brookmere train crews to a "Coalmont Turn." An engine and crew would run from Brookmere to Coalmont, usually with just a caboose. At Coalmont the crew would remove loaded cars from the tipple track and replace them with empty cars left on the siding from an earlier eastbound freight. They would then take the loaded cars through to Coquihalla and leave them there, at the top of the grade to the coast, for the next westbound train. Their work now done, they would return with their caboose to Brookmere.

This assignment ended rather abruptly in the late 1920s when the CPR began a boycott of Coalmont Collieries because the company raised its price 25 cents per ton above the going price of other collieries. The KVR continued to use Coalmont coal, at least until the CPR formally took over operations in 1931 and switched the KVR from Coalmont to Merritt coal. This move earned the CPR the nickname "Cheapie-R" by locomotive crews because Merritt coal, while a hot coal suitable for the light trains of the Merritt line, or the mainline west of Kamloops where grades were moderate, tended to clinker badly, making it difficult for the fireman to keep a good base of coals on the firebox grate when the locomotive was working hard. Clinkering was especially prevalent in coal from the Inland Coke & Coal Company mine, which earned the company a derogatory nickname of its own, the Inland Slate & Rock Company. This drawback added to the almost overwhelming task a fireman faced working the Coquihalla line in the days before mechanical stokers or oil-fired steam locomotives. Freight crews taking on coal Brookmere for the trip west tried to load only as much Merritt coal as they figured they needed to get through Ruby Creek, hoping to arrive with an empty tender that they could fill with better quality Vancouver Island coal for the tough fight back up the Coquihalla. Sometimes they underestimated, and more than one freight train stalled on the short grade up to the CPR mainline west of Hope because the engine had run out of coal. Later the CPR resumed buying some coal from Coalmont Collieries but never the amount taken in the early 1920s. An explosion in the Blakeburn mine on August 13, 1930, which killed 45 workers, combined with the CPR's boycott and the GN's total switchover to oil fuel, resulted in a steady decline in the mine's production until it closed in 1940.

As well as the sizeable coal trade the Kettle Valley Railway and the Great Northern carried out of the Tulameen Valley in the early 1920s, the GN maintained a fascinating yet practically unknown ice harvesting operation at Otter Lake, just beyond Tulameen. In the age before mechanical refrigeration became widespread, railways needed reliable sources of natural ice for cooling their passenger and fruit cars during the summer. The ice was cut during winter months and stored in sawdust in large ice-houses at strategic points until needed during warmer weather. The CPR obtained most of its ice from a location near Banff and the KVR extensively used Osprey Lake ice for packing Okanagan fruit. Therefore neither of these companies utilized Otter Lake, other than a brief trial cut by the KVR one winter. For the GN Otter Lake was perfect. Its ice had a reputation of being unusually clear and hard and it was at the end of an all downhill run from the lakeshore at Tulameen to the fruit packinghouses of Wenatchee, 200 miles away.

Starting in the winter of 1915-16, the GN cut ice at Otter Lake for every one of its icehouses west of Spokane. Ice cutting normally began late in January when the ice was at its maximum thickness, the prime cutting season generally being limited to about two weeks. Despite the short time interval, an incredible amount of ice would be cut. Statistics alone cannot adequately convey the magnitude of the operation but in early 1919—the record year—3,000 cars of ice were loaded and shipped in the span of only 15 days. All of the work had to be done by human and animal muscle. Several hundred men, aided by dozens of teams of horses, were employed cutting and sliding the ice to the awaiting boxcars. Thanks to J.J. Hill's insistent foresight, the grades to the GN mainline permitted trains in excess of 75 cars to be operated in an age when 20 cars was considered long for a freight train. The author talked with numerous Princeton residents who remembered that the highlight of the winter season in the early 1920s was to gather with friends at the local station to watch the great ice trains pass through from Tulameen, often one train right after the other. As artificial ice production became more common in the 1920s, the volume of ice cut at Tulameen dropped rapidly and in early 1925 only 450 cars were loaded. On January 20, 1925, the last such train left Tulameen, ending forever this fascinating operation.

Another significant traffic for the Kettle Valley Railway during its first decade of operation was the transportation of automobiles. Until 1926, when a highway was completed through the Fraser Canyon, there was no direct road connection between the coast and the interior of British Columbia. Motorists wanting to get from Vancouver to the interior had to make a long diversion through the United States and return to Canada at Osoyoos, or ship their automobile by rail. The KVR offered an automobile transfer service between Hope and Princeton, with service also to Merritt. Motorists could drive their automobiles onto flatcars at Hope and wait for the next passenger train or, if they signed a release of liability, ride the freight train.

John Hall, a travelling salesman in the 1920s, related to the author his less than satisfactory experience with the automobile transfer service. One day in the spring of 1922 he loaded his automobile onto a railway flatcar at Hope for transfer to Princeton, and since it was a beautiful spring day, he and another motorist decided to remain with their cars rather than wait for the evening passenger. The ride up through the Coquihalla was spectacular. However, at Iago the freight train pulled into the passing track. Hall thought the stop was only to meet an opposing train, but to his horror he saw the engine uncouple from the train and roll back down the main track past him headed for Hope. A nearby sectionman advised him there was a big rockslide at Romeo and the line would be closed until the slide could be cleared. Four days later Hall and the other motorist reached Princeton. He said the conductor of the work train clearing the slide gave them steak dinners in a cook car but that was small consolation for their forced confinement on the Kettle Valley Railway. Little did they appreciate that nearly a century later many people would eagerly endure such hardships if only they could make a ride on the Coquihalla railway.

During its earlier construction period, the Kettle Valley Railway had secured federal authority to build a number of branch lines, but only the line to Copper Mountain had actually been built, owing in large part to the restrictions of World War I. When the war ended and economic conditions began to improve, the KVR turned its attention once more to the construction of what was to become its second major branch line—from Penticton to Osoyoos. The prime motivation for first proposing construction of the line in 1911 was to discourage Jim Hill from building a branch of the Great Northern along the valley of the Okanagan River. However, when provincial premier John Oliver in 1919 announced a major government plan for irrigation and land settlement of returning war veterans in the South Okanagan, the necessary financial justification for the line's construction was provided.

McCulloch's preliminary surveys found that, despite the easy appearance of the Okanagan Valley, the cost of construction would be relatively high owing to the boggy nature of much of the valley lowlands. Because of this expense, the government and the KVR signed an agreement on March 3, 1920 permitting the KVR to initially construct only the 16 miles of line from Okanagan Falls, at the south end of Skaha Lake, southward to a point just beyond the new town of Oliver, named after the premier who had initiated the development plan. A spur would be built from Penticton yard to the north end of Skaha Lake, a distance of about two miles, and a barge service would be provided on Skaha Lake, forestalling the expense of constructing trackage along the lakeshore. It was agreed the lakeshore track-age, and the continuation of the line through to Osoyoos, would be under-taken when conditions warranted. No public subsidy was granted for the railway work.

In July 1920 the KVR awarded a contract to P.J. Salvus for the grading of the spur from the Penticton yard to Skaha Lake. That same month, the CPR screw tug *York* steamed down the Okanagan River from Okanagan Lake to provide the motive power for the planned Skaha Lake barge serv-ice. The tug's arrival was marred somewhat by an embarrassing indignity shortly afterwards when a crew member accidentally left a valve open and the tug sank up to her hips in eight feet of water. However, after being pumped out she was none the worse for the experience. In October 1920 grading of the Skaha Lake spur was completed, but land settlement in the South Okanagan fell well below expected levels and it was not until September a year later that the contract for the work from Okanagan Falls southward was awarded. It took nearly a year to complete grading of the railway and not until July 31, 1922 did tracklaying begin. That too went slowly. On March 20, 1923 the Board of Railway Commissioners inspector finally approved the line for operation.[10]

The principal traffic for the line was expected to be fruit from the orchards of the new land development. Since it took time for the newly planted fruit trees to mature and produce crops, many farmers planted cantaloupe between the rows of growing fruit trees to generate an early income. This resulted in the train on the line being dubbed the "Cantaloupe Express," although the normal twice-weekly romp from Penticton to Oliver and back with the Penticton yard switcher hardly qual-ified as an express service. No formal passenger service was ever operated on the line; while the KVR tariff did permit passengers to ride in the freight train's caboose if they wished, the infrequency of service, the neces-sity of shunting the train on and off the barge at each end of the lake and the added vagaries of service in winter, when Skaha Lake often froze over, effectively discouraged any extensive use of this service. By the time the lake's rail link was completed some years later, the automobile had become the dominant form of passenger transportation within the valley.

The increase in fruit and other traffic experienced in the early years after World War I prompted the Kettle Valley Railway, in July 1920, to sup-plement its fleet of leased CPR M2 class 3200 series 2-8-0 locomotives with three M4 class 3400s of the same wheel arrangement—3405, 3454 and 3481. Unfortunately, the first run of an M4 class locomotive west of Penticton was marred by a mishap, and while no one was killed or injured, the accident proved costly to the railway.

The episode began early in the morning of July 20, 1920. Engine 3454 left Penticton shortly after midnight that day with a freight train of ten cars destined for Hope. The train proceeded without difficulties to Princeton, where five cars of livestock were added. On the climb up the Tulameen Valley, the engine crew experienced problems with the 3454 and immediately upon arrival at Brookmere just after sunrise the locomotive crew cut the engine off the train and took it over to the roundhouse for repairs. Knowing that there would probably be a delay before their train continued onward to Hope, the tail-end crew left their caboose and hustled over to the Brookmere Hotel for breakfast.

The engine troubles were repaired in short order and the 3454 returned to couple up with the train. When the 3454 nudged into the cars standing on the mainline, the coupling three cars back of the engine broke loose, for reasons never determined. The headend brakeman, attending to his chores of coupling up the 3454, did not notice the break in the train until the 12 remaining cars and caboose were almost out of sight, rolling back down the 1.2% grade towards Princeton. Upon realizing what had happened, the engine crew quickly shunted the three remaining cars onto the siding and set off with the 3454 after the runaway cars. The cars had a generous head start, and the locomotive crew didn't dare attempt too rapid a pursuit of the cars in a bid to couple onto them and bring them to a stop, lest they round a curve at high speed and find the runaway cars smashed across the tracks, in which case they would add their own engine and themselves to the wreckage. The crew decided all they could do was drift downgrade looking for the wreck they expected to soon encounter.

Left to run freely down the grade, the runaway cars did not take long to accelerate to high speed. The cattle on board, terrified by the careening motion of the cars, stampeded within their quarters, causing the cars to sway even more violently. A mile and a half west of Thalia, five miles from where they had started their runaway, the cattle cars flipped off the tracks and crashed into a gully alongside the railway, killing most of the cattle on board. Two boxcars dragged over the embankment with the cattle cars were also reduced to kindling. By some miracle, the caboose and the five other freight cars managed to stay on the track, coming safely to rest a stone's throw from Otter Lake, some 19 miles from the point where they had broken loose. Even so, the accident was costly to the railway. It was also a sobering reminder to train crews what fate awaited them should they ever lose control of their trains on the steep grades of the KVR.

Three years later, almost to the day, the KVR experienced another spectacular accident. On July 18, 1923, a boxcar in the middle of an eastbound freight train from Penticton derailed on the giant wooden trestle over West Fork Canyon Creek and, along with several other cars, plunged to the canyon floor, smashing into a thousand pieces. After the crash, it was discovered that among the contents of the car were eight cases of dynamite bound for the Highland Bell mine at Beaverdell. Luckily none had exploded; if they had, the 180-foot high trestle, tenuously linking the coast with the Kootenays, would likely have been destroyed.

The KVR's most difficult and recurring problems were in Coquihalla Pass, where trouble proved to be the norm rather than the exception. In fact, from the time the line opened in July 1916 until July 1923, the rail line was closed through most of the winter season for five of those seven years. Even during the two winters when the line had remained "open," disruptions to train service of up to a month had occurred. Because of the difficulties of keeping the line operational, McCulloch and Coleman decided early in 1922 to upgrade the older Spences Bridge-Merritt line to a standard equal to the sections of the railway the KVR had constructed itself. The necessity of so doing was obvious. The older wooden Howe truss bridges, built in 1906 and 1907, were at the end of their useful life and the light 56-pound rails on the line, satisfactory for its original branch line purpose, were inadequate for the high volume of heavy Kootenay freight and passenger traffic the line was required to accept at discouragingly frequent intervals. Starting that summer, all the wooden bridges on the line between Spences Bridge and Merritt were replaced with steel bridges, many of them salvaged from other parts of the CPR system. New 80-pound rails were also laid and a number of minor track relocations constructed.

The wisdom of the decision to upgrade the Merritt Subdivision quickly proved itself. On September 23, 1924—just one month after all the improvement work was completed—a slide two miles east of Romeo plugged the west end of a tunnel, forcing trains to be diverted via Spences Bridge. Four days later, another slide came down upon the crews who were trying to clear the first slide, seriously injuring a number of workers. More rockslide occurred in October and in November deep snow blocked the line. On December 11, after the line had just been reopened, a chinook wind hit Coquihalla Pass, melting much of the snow that had fallen during the previous month and causing even more havoc. A bridge at Portia washed out, the bridge over Boston Bar Creek was severely damaged and dozens of minor slides and washouts hit other sections of the line, trapping two freight trains partway through the pass. Four days later, on December 15, the weather changed radically again. In a matter of hours, temperatures plunged from well above freezing to 25 degrees below. The stalled trains were literally frozen to the rails, as the wet snow of the day before turned as solid as Cordilleran stone. Three days passed with temperatures at 34 degrees below, accompanied by a stiff wind. There appeared to be no letup. Ten days later the line was abandoned—train and all—until spring. Once more, the Kettle Valley Railway was forced to concede the battle for Coquihalla Pass. Through the remainder of that winter, the rail line through the Coquihalla remained closed. Not until early April was the line reopened. Less than a week later, on April 12, 1925, locomotive 3217 piled into a rockslide near Lakevale, once again severing connections with the Kootenays.

Despite the difficulties, April 1925 was a happy month for the KVR, as it was announced that month the Copper Mountain mine would be reopened. Following closure of the Copper Mountain mine in 1920, Canada Copper Company had sold the property to Granby Consolidated Mining & Smelting Company. At that time, Granby had just closed its Boundary operations and thus showed little immediate interest in its new property. In 1923 a subsidiary company, Allenby Copper Company, was formed to reopen the mine, and the entire railway to the mine was repaired late that year. But at the last minute the company had a change of heart, and after only a handful of trains had run over the repaired railway it was again closed down. In April 1925, Allenby Copper once more proposed reopening the mine and the KVR again obliged the company by beginning work that month to reopen the rail line. The railway repair work was completed in August, and on August 24, 1925 the Allenby concentrator began processing ore at the rate of 500 tons per day. Shortly after the mine reopening Allenby Copper was dissolved, thereafter Granby running the operation under its own name. Production quickly jumped to an impressive 2,000 tons of ore per day.

To handle this volume of ore the KVR assigned a 15-car ore train to the line, which generally made three round trips per day between the mine and the concentrator. Train crews for the line were initially based at Brookmere but this was soon changed to Princeton. A day crew made two round trips between Copper Mountain and Allenby with the ore train, while a night crew made one round trip with the ore train and handled all the switching, including transferring the cars of concentrates from Allenby down to Princeton. The Copper Mountain run was generally popular with crews because of the minimal grades on the line and the premium pay. The concentrates from Allenby initially went to the Consolidated Mining & Smelting Company smelter at Trail. However, American-controlled Granby and Canadian-controlled Consolidated never saw eye to eye on smelting charges, so later most of the mine's output went to a smelter at Tacoma in Washington State. In either case, the KVR received a healthy business from the mine. In 1927, an average year, the KVR handled 13,696 cars of ore and 861 cars of concentrates on its Copper Mountain line.

The year 1925 also witnessed the retirement of Andrew McCulloch as general superintendent of the Kettle Valley Railway, and the appointment of Tom Crump, father of a later CPR president, to that position. The exact date of succession was June 16, 1925, McCulloch's 61st birthday, or as McCulloch preferred to refer to it "the 20th anniversary of my 41st birthday."[11] Even with this shedding of a major responsibility, McCulloch had no thoughts of retiring. He retained his position as chief engineer of the Kettle Valley Railway and would hold that position for another eight years. The task of climbing up canyon slopes along the railway right-of-way to inspect every bridge, tunnel and structure on the KVR system at least once every year was a responsibility he accepted with the energy and enthusiasm of a man 40 years his junior. Crump too demonstrated an abundance of energy, which he soon discovered he needed to capacity as general superintendent. Managing the Kettle Valley Railway turned out not to be the "slack haul" many of his colleagues reported it would be when he left the CPR to join its corporate subsidiary. Coquihalla Pass in particular gave Crump a good introduction to the KVR.

On September 23, 1925 a rockslide at Romeo sealed off the line. Two days later, before clearing of the slide was finished, another slide hit. Then another. All through October, slides continued to occur as fast as they could be cleared. On November 9 the line was finally reopened but it was closed the next day by another slide. When that slide was cleared away, a bridge at Iago was smashed out on November 26 by yet another rockslide. These frustrating difficulties continued to plague the KVR all through

December. Finally, just before Christmas a prominent CPR official publicly stated that, as a result of these great difficulties, the corporation was considering abandoning the Coquihalla line. Pending a decision, all maintenance work on the railway was to be suspended. The threat of abandonment—a threat that hung over Coquihalla line throughout most of its remaining years—revealed itself less than a decade after the line had been completed.

As it turned out, the early part of 1926 moderated considerably and went on record as the easiest winter season for the KVR. In fact, the railway's snowplows, usually in service from November through to March or April, hardly moved out of the yard at Brookmere all through early 1926. Given this respite, the CPR seemed to forget the difficulties of the previous fall and thoughts of abandoning the Coquihalla line were dismissed, at least for a time.

In other areas of the KVR's operation during 1926, additional encouraging signs were in evidence. The reopening of the Copper Mountain mine the year before had substantially boosted the tonnage of originating freight over the 1925 level, and the Consolidated Mining & Smelting Company smelter at Trail—under J.J. Warren's command—was shipping increasing quantities of lead and zinc ingots over the railway. For the first year in its history, the KVR went well into the black financially. The KVR also found 1926 a good year for passenger business. Despite intense competition from the Canadian National, which had inaugurated Okanagan Lake boat service with the vessel *Pentowna* in July to entice Penticton passengers to ride the CNR system to the coast, the vast majority of passengers preferred to use the KVR. Capping the records of 1926, the KVR chalked up several months during which not a single passenger train was late.

Labour Day Sunday—September 5, 1926—was also a record day for the Kettle Valley Railway. There were no indications it would be such to engineer Bob Marks and fireman Ray Letts as they walked out of the Brookmere Hotel and headed across to the roundhouse to begin work that morning. In fact, as Letts related to the author, it was one of those beautiful fall mornings that seem so unique to the Otter and Tulameen Valleys. The sun had just come up, brightening the gold on the aspen trees dotting the valley and chasing away the thin veil of mist hanging over the east end of the railway yard. A light dusting of snow whitened Brodie Mountain to the west. "Winter's coming," Marks said to Letts as they climbed aboard locomotive 3401 next to the roundhouse for what they expected to be a routine run to Hope.

Marks allowed Letts to water the engine and hook it up to its train for the coast—18 cars, consisting mainly of lead and zinc ingots from Trail and a few flats loaded with automobiles for Hope, trailed by a caboose. The headend brakeman, Charles "Charlie" Johnston, soon had the engine coupled up. As he stepped on board to join Marks and Letts in the engine cab, a slight jolt indicated "pusher" locomotive 578, which had been assigned to help their heavy train up the grade to Coquihalla, had coupled on. Bill Osborne, the engineer of 578, and Bob Barwick, the fireman, watched as the rearend brakeman, Francis "Mickey" Stringer, fastened the front coupler of their locomotive to the rear of the caboose. Ten more freight cars and a second caboose trailed the 578.

Moments later, John "Jack" Quinn, the freight train's conductor, came out of the station, his face buried in a handful of train orders. He walked up to the cab of the 3401 and passed up a set of orders to Letts, who relayed them across to Marks. "Our helper is going with us through to Hope," Quinn said. "They need her to bring a drag up the Pass this afternoon." Quinn promptly left and, after reaching the caboose, waved the highball. Marks whistled twice to let the crew of the 578 know he was leaving, released the brakes and inched back on the throttle. Within seconds, the rhythmic beat of the wheels rapping on rail joints was drowning out the sound of the exhaust as the train eased downgrade to Brodie.

From Brodie to Coquihalla it was all upgrade and Letts was kept busy bailing coal onto the grates as fast as Marks could strip it away. However, Letts knew that west of the summit he would have an easy time. He also knew he would have time to relax at Coquihalla while 12 cars of coal from Coalmont, set out by an engine and crew working a Coalmont Turn the night before, were added to his train. After the cars were cut into the train, the brakes were tested and the two brakeman flipped the retainers on each car to help hold in the air so necessary for the control of their heavy train on the steep grade ahead. As Marks eased back on the throttle he once more instinctively looked back to make sure all was clear. It was then he noticed on top of the train a number of youths, perhaps a dozen or more. "It's always bad at this time of year," he said to Letts as he turned forward again. "Tuesday morning those kids will be back in school in Vancouver and within a week they will have spent all the money they have earned picking fruit." Little did Marks realize he and his "passengers" had just bought a ticket on a train ride to eternity.

After leaving Coquihalla, the train slowly worked its way down the steep 2.2% grade through Coquihalla Pass. However, near Iago something went wrong. The train started to accelerate unexpectedly. Marks detected the sudden increase in speed and calmly reached for the brake lever. He moved the valve to let out some air and activate the brakes, but it wasn't enough. Moments later he pushed the brake lever to full emergency, letting out all the air from the brake line. Still the train accelerated. Marks grabbed the whistle cord, screaming out a signal for the train crew to man the hand brakes. Johnston grabbed a club and was over the back of the tender, furiously turning the handbrakes as he ran along the top of the train. Stringer and Quinn had left the caboose the second they heard the whistle. Marks turned to Letts and said, "You're gone here boy! Save your life and jump!" Letts ignored the order, grabbed a club and followed Johnston. Every second was now precious. If enough hand brakes could be set before the train's speed became excessive, there was a good chance Marks could recharge the air brakes and bring the runaway under control. But the steep grade would not give them that chance. As rapidly as the crewmen turned the handbrakes the train accelerated. Faster and faster it plunged through the blackened tunnels and pounded across the high trestles of the Coquihalla in unquestioning obedience to the law of gravity.

Realizing the train's fate was now sealed, young Bob Barwick, the 23-year old fireman on the helper engine, courageously scampered out on the catwalk of the wildly swaying 578 and pulled the coupler lever, freeing the "pusher" engine from the forward caboose. Barwick reasoned that with only ten cars behind, Osborne would be able to bring his part of the train under control. He was right. Moments after Barwick had released the couplers, there was a secure tug on the train. Its speed was checked. After travelling half a mile it was able to stop. However, Barwick could do nothing for the front portion of the train. Barwick stood on the pilot and watched as the runaway rounded a curve ahead, every member of the crew except Marks on top of the train manning the hand brakes. He offered them a silent prayer. He knew that this would be their last trip down the Coquihalla.

Down the line at Jessica, Tony Rascalla, the section foreman, had just stepped out into the still Sunday morning air to sit on the sectionhouse porch for a leisurely after-breakfast smoke, when he heard a faint noise up the canyon. At first Rascalla thought it was a rockslide. But the noise did not stop. Instead it grew louder and louder. Within a minute it became a continuous thunder. Then the runaway train rounded a curve to the east of Jessica siding. With flames pouring from the brakeshoes the train hurtled down upon Rascalla. Three coal cars and the caboose broke off the end of the train and plowed into the water tower, demolishing it and sending cascades of water upon the wreckage. Before the splinters of that crash had settled the rest of the train had disappeared from sight. After another few seconds there was a horrifying crash that seemed to echo in the canyon for an eternity. Then all was silent.

Immediately after notifying the dispatcher, Rascalla ran down the tracks. Just to the west of the passing track, he found three more coal cars smashed against the face of the mountainside. Not far beyond them, on a sharp curve between two trestles, a few slightly dislocated rails were the only visible indication anything had happened. Far down in the canyon the shattered remains of a locomotive and 25 freight cars lay in a flaming heap. The hot ashes from the locomotive firebox had scattered over the wreckage, setting it on fire. Fed by the remaining six cars of coal, the fire soon reduced the wreckage to little more than a dozen ribbons of molten lead running down over the rocks.[12]

Marks, Quinn, Johnston and Stringer were killed. By an amazing miracle, Ray Letts had been thrown from the train on a sharp curve, and although badly injured he ultimately recovered and returned to work for the KVR for many years afterwards. The testimony of Letts and the "pusher" crew that a dozen or more young boys were "riding the rods" was discounted by the Board of Railway Commissioners, which set the official death toll at four. However, the inquest jury set the death toll at four crew and six or seven others. Even this latter figure was considered by some to be conservative.[13] The cause of the wreck was never conclusively established, every scrap of evidence having been destroyed in the fire. In fact, the only clear evidence about the wreck—the worst in Kettle Valley Railway history—was that four brave railroaders had died in an attempt to prevent it.[14]

Later that same year, Bob Barwick, the young fireman "whose heroism stirred the railroad world of Canada," was promoted to engineer.[15] Unfortunately, he too was killed when engine 3478 on which he was working slammed into a rockslide and rolled over on March 28, 1930, not far from the spot where four years earlier he had saved his train.

Despite the tragic accident in 1926, and a number of other accidents the railway suffered, the Kettle Valley Railway managed to chalk up one of the best railroad safety records on the continent. In fact, the KVR's passenger safety record was flawless. From the day regular passenger service began in 1915 until its termination 49 years later not a single passenger was killed and only a handful ever received injuries. This record was achieved despite the fact, as a CPR president stated: "Much greater hazard is involved in keeping that route open than any other in our experience."[16]

Constant vigilance and a sober respect for the forces of nature were behind the KVR's excellent record. A trackcar checking for slides and washouts preceded every train through Coquihalla Pass. In winter a plow train would run ahead of the track car. Foot patrols checked every inch of track at least once per day. From the earliest days of KVR service, air operated swivel headlights were standard equipment on all locomotives to ensure engine crews would be able to spot a track obstruction as early as possible. Every train religiously tested its brakes before descending the steep grades on the railway and stops to cool train wheels were made unfailingly. Snowsheds and bridges were kept in faultless repair, with every joint and timber checked at least once per year.

Although the careful regard for safety was unquestionably the principal reason for the KVR's remarkable safety record, one cannot discount the generous good luck it also seemed to enjoy. An example of this uncanny luck is apparent in the story of James Porteous—more commonly known among the railway crews as "Coquihalla Red"—who for the first two decades of the railway's operation was the sectionman at Iago. Red had an unexplained ability to predict when slides would hit the railway during the winter, based on his careful observation of a pair of eagles that nested in a tree just back of the sectionhouse. If the eagles left their nest and flew along the railway, Red knew that all would be well. If the eagles flew across the canyon, he would immediately phone the dispatcher to send out a crew to clear the line. Within an hour, somewhere nearby, a slide would come down upon the railway. How the eagles predicted the slides no one could explain, but the recurring phenomenon seemed too frequent to be merely coincidental. Certainly the dispatchers and the railwaymen were never doubtful about Red's predictions. More than once, they knew, serious accidents had been averted because of his timely predictions.

Other railroaders recalled lucky moments of their own. Len Smuin remembered getting his trousers splashed with mud when a rockslide came down on the tracks right behind his track car in Myra Canyon just after he had passed over the spot where the slide hit. Art Lowe awoke in the middle of the night in a bunk car on a siding in Coquihalla Pass and felt a need to go to the bathroom. While he was away, a ten-ton boulder crashed through the bunk car roof and landed on the bed he had just vacated. "Perley" McPherson recalled watching a cougar atop the west portal of "Big Tunnel" at Adra try to scamper away after being frightened by the noise of the locomotive of an eastbound train blasting up the grade for Chute Lake. The cougar slipped on ice and fell from the tunnel portal onto the coal pile in the locomotive tender just as the locomotive—with its startled engine crew—plunged into the blackness. The train emerged at the other end of the tunnel with the cougar nowhere to be seen. Perhaps luckiest of all was John Peebles, a 19-year old trackwalker who was buried in a snowslide near Iago and dug out a day and a half later; he recovered in hospital to tell his tale to disbelieving press reporters.

On January 28, 1929, the CPR suffered a serious accident on its mainline between Revelstoke and Golden when an engine crashed through the bridge over Surprise Creek while the bridge was being reconstructed. The serious damage to the bridge was expected to require six weeks to repair, forcing the railway to find alternative routing for the heavy volume of mainline traffic while the repair work was undertaken. Within hours, the Kettle Valley Railway and the other CPR lines forming the rail link across southern British Columbia were starting to feel the crush of what was to be the longest sustained diversion of mainline traffic in the CPR's history. On the KVR, 21 extra crews were immediately assigned to Penticton and nine to Brookmere. Mainline locomotives, sometimes eight to a train, were soon moving heavy freights up Coquihalla Pass and over the grades east and west of Penticton. Temporary operator shacks were thrown up at several points along the line to aid in expediting the movement of the extra traffic.

Fortunately, the CPR was able to get the Surprise Creek Bridge repaired more quickly than originally anticipated and the diversion lasted only three weeks, not the six expected. Even so, the forced closure of its mainline caused CPR management to recognize the value of the Kootenay-Kettle Valley route as a valuable bypass route for the mainline. One week after the mainline had been reopened, the CPR announced that work would immediately begin on upgrading the line across southern British Columbia to minimize the effects of future mainline disruptions.

The principal component of the CPR's improvement plan was the construction of a rail line from Procter to Kootenay Landing, closing the gap in trackage along Kootenay Lake that had remained since the Crows Nest line's original construction in 1898. The CPR also planned to replace all major wooden trestles on the KVR with permanent steel structures or fills, and replace the original KVR rail (much of it laid under the restricted conditions of World War I) with heavier rail. New and more powerful locomotives would be introduced. The CPR also stated that operations of the Kettle Valley Railway—one of the few CPR lines ever permitted a reasonable degree of operational independence—would be integrated into the rest of the CPR system. Clearly, the CPR wanted its southern British Columbia line ready to accept mainline traffic at any time it might be called upon to do so again.

The planned work included replacing the large wooden trestles at East Fork Canyon Creek and West Fork Canyon Creek in Myra Canyon, and at Dry Creek between Penticton and Princeton. Much of the improvement work was completed or well advanced by the end of 1930 and at midnight December 31, 1930, with the Kootenay Lake rail line set to open the following morning, the CPR formally took over operations of the Kettle Valley Railway. Legally, the trackage would remain owned by the Kettle Valley Railway until 1956, when for the simplicity of bookkeeping the CPR abolished its corporate subsidiary. However, for all practical purposes the Kettle Valley Railway ceased to exist as of December 31, 1930 when it became the CPR's Kettle Valley Division. CPR timetables and train orders quickly replaced those of the KVR. The change of passenger crews at Hope and Midway was eliminated, as former KVR passenger crews were permitted to work from Penticton to Vancouver westbound and from Penticton to Nelson eastbound, with a corresponding number of CPR employees on other divisions being allowed to work runs covering portions of the former KVR. Passenger trains 11 and 12, which until then had operated only between Vancouver and Nelson, were soon extended east through Crows Nest Pass to a mainline connection at Medicine Hat in eastern Alberta. Only the locomotive paint schemes did not change, CPR engines having worked the KVR ever since opening.

Despite the formal change, for most people the railway was still the Kettle Valley Railway, not the CPR's Kettle Valley Division. And to them it would always remain the Kettle Valley Railway, or simply "The KV" as it had become affectionately known. The spirit of independence that had developed in KVR employees during their decade and a half of handling trains over what was arguably the most difficult rail line in Canada could not be erased by merely absorbing the KVR into the Canadian Pacific empire. The memories and habits of the early days would take a long time to die.

13: Coming of Age

The Kettle Valley Railway 1931 to 1958

The CPR's takeover of the Kettle Valley Railway at the start of 1931 gave Canadian Pacific a truly integrated rail network in British Columbia. Unfortunately, the unification was coincident with the beginning of a long period of economic depression in Canada that more than offset any gains made by the amalgamation. On November 15, 1930, just six weeks prior to the CPR takeover of the KVR, the Copper Mountain mine closed down, in one day slicing off about 25% of the KVR's traffic. The Trail smelter, the KVR's other significant traffic generator, also faced serious difficulties. Although it managed to remain in operation throughout the depression, its production was severely reduced. Coal and lumber traffic slumped badly as well.

Compounding the KVR's plight of sharply reduced mineral and lumber traffic was the almost total loss of fruit traffic in 1931. The summer of 1931 was the hottest and driest summer in southern British Columbia since records started being kept well before the turn of the century. The Okanagan fruit crop that year was a disaster. Refrigerator cars sat idle in the railway yard at Penticton for want of any cargo to carry. Grasshoppers swept the barren fruit trees by the millions. Legions of the locusts died along the right-of-way, so greasing the rails with their broken carcasses that trains could sometimes hardly move. On the Jura Hill out of Princeton, freight trains were briefly were restricted to night operation, so difficult was it to ascend the slippery rails.

Throughout the province that long, hot summer, forest fires ravaged the countryside. On July 6, 1931, a bad fire near Portia came dangerously close to wiping out a score of railway bridges. A month later, on August 3, another fire sprang up near Juliet and swept across the mountain crest towards Brookmere; the fire came so near to the townsite that the railway set out a dozen boxcars on the main track in front of the station for residents to load their possessions, ready for a quick evacuation. Only a last minute change in wind direction saved the townsite. At Jura, the railway was not so fortunate; here the railway buildings were destroyed in a fire that month. Yet another fire damaged a section of the rail line near Carmi on August 18. A week later a forest fire ran up Myra Canyon south of Kelowna, threatening the many huge wooden trestles in the canyon between Ruth and Myra; a special train of tank cars loaded with water was rushed to the bridge sites from Penticton, and only by the heroic efforts of a KVR train crew, who battled thick smoke to keep the trestles well wetted down, was the fire prevented from rendering the railway out of service for many weeks. In all, it was a discouraging year.

These discouragements no doubt tested the CPR, which had announced the year before that the majority of the improvement programs it had begun, including the upgrading of the Kettle Valley Railway, would continue despite the depression. That announcement had been coupled with a press release stating the CPR would also undertake construction of several new rail lines in an effort to spur the economy and provide railway connections to new sources of revenue. Although forced to suspend dividends on what was once blue chip stock to carry out the programs, the CPR's decision was a bold reaffirmation of its faith in Canada's future.

Foremost in the CPR's plans for expansion in British Columbia was the construction of an eight-mile-long rail line along the west side of Skaha Lake, linking Penticton with Okanagan Falls, thereby eliminating barge service on Skaha Lake. Appropriations for the line were authorized early in the fall of 1930, and on October 27 survey work began. The surveys indicated that, with the exception of one or two spots of rockwork, construction would be relatively easy, especially because much of the line could be built over the existing road along the lakeshore and a new road built higher up the hillside. Construction began on January 19, 1931. Tracklaying was completed on August 26 of that same year, and late in October the line was opened for operation.[1] The use of the new line rendered the barge service obsolete; following its 11 years of faithful service, the tug *York* unceremoniously steamed away to Okanagan Landing to be pulled onto the ways, never again to sail on Okanagan or Skaha Lake.

The completion of the Skaha Lake line marked the last engineering work on the Kettle Valley Railway done by Andrew McCulloch. He formally retired on January 31, 1933 after 23 years of association with the KVR and the CPR's Kettle Valley Division. Naturally McCulloch received the usual retirement blessings from the CPR when he finished work that day. A much greater tribute to him—and the true measure of the respect that he had earned from his subordinates—came a month later at a retirement banquet held in his honour by the railwaymen of the KVR. In addition to sponsoring the banquet—in itself no minor sacrifice on the part of the railwaymen during those times of economic adversity—the men who had built the railway under him and those who had served under him in operations presented him with a chair-and-desk set bearing a gold presentation plate. They said their gift was a token of their great esteem for Andrew McCulloch. His retirement meant they were losing both a superb leader and a close friend. The editor of the *Penticton Herald* commented: "Never to a greater degree in Penticton has the affection of fellow workers and friends been displayed towards a man than in the case of Andrew McCulloch, retired chief engineer, K.V. Division of the CPR."[2]

Despite his official retirement at age 69, McCulloch was not finished with his railroad career. He continued to do consulting engineering for the CPR, the Pacific Great Eastern Railway and a number of other railways. He was also asked to locate several new rail lines, including a 500-mile-long mountain railway in Mexico for which task he was invited to specify his own salary. McCulloch declined this and many other offers, including one to run as a candidate for his provincial riding.

Although he travelled extensively following his retirement, McCulloch preferred to spend his time hunting and fishing in the countryside around Penticton or travelling on the KVR. He especially enjoyed walking with J.J. Warren along sections of the railway while they reminisced about their earlier days during the line's construction. In 1937, after one of their walks through Coquihalla Pass together, Warren wrote to McCulloch: "It is not often that men of mature age become such friends as we did—and are. Those journeys together and the unexpected occurrences will never be forgotten and unfortunately cannot be repeated. I think our first trip down the Coquihalla as far as Boston Bar [Creek] made the most lasting impression. Then, we used to speculate as to what in H— would be carried by the railway, and now see the loads go by."[3]

Many other friends McCulloch had made during his railway career also loved to renew their association with him. Rarely would a CPR official pass through Penticton and not invite McCulloch down to his private car to talk about the KVR or the CPR. Friendship was a commodity Andrew McCulloch never exhausted, and when he died on December 13, 1945, the common engineers and trainmen of the KVR were the most saddened of the mourners.[4]

Despite the initial optimism the CPR had expressed in 1930, the economic depression did not abate; rather it continued to linger well into the decade. To the CPR's credit, it continued much of its bridge replacement program, and in 1932 introduced the first two of numerous P1 class 2-8-2 locomotives in the 5100 series that were to rule on the Kettle Valley Division until diesel locomotives took over in the early 1950s.[5] Numerous employees noted the irony that larger, more powerful locomotives were arriving coincident with a considerable reduction in freight and passenger traffic and layoffs of train crews. Bob Barwick, the young fireman who had acted so heroically in the great runaway of 1926 and was promoted to engineman as a result, found himself bumped back to fireman. On March 28, 1930, on one of his first runs back as a fireman, engine 3478 ran into a rockslide at Brodie and turned over onto its left side, fatally injuring him. The engineer, on the right side of the engine cab where Barwick had sat only a short time before, escaped without serious injury. Such were the misfortunes of time and circumstance.

As the depression continued, even as large a corporation as Canadian Pacific could not continue major capital expenditures on improving its rail lines in the face of protracted low revenues, and many of the improvement programs were halted. Severe cuts in operational expenses were also made. During the three winters following the CPR takeover of the KVR, the rail line through Coquihalla Pass was deliberately closed as a result of CPR policy to accept the inevitable Coquihalla winters. Rather than struggle to keep the line open, trains were diverted over the longer line via the Fraser Canyon and Spences Bridge beginning in the late autumn.

The depression also caused abandonment of poorly utilized rail lines in southern British Columbia. On April 26, 1931, the Great Northern discontinued service on the steeply graded line between Oroville and Molson and shortly thereafter pulled up the rails.[6] Soon to follow were the GN line through the Fraser Valley and the section of trackage whose construction had generated the greatest battle of the gang-war history of the CPR and Great Northern, the line from Curlew via Midway to Molson.[7] In 1935, the KVR abandoned its 17.4-mile long North Fork line.[8]

Next to follow was the Great Northern line in the Similkameen Valley. On April 23, 1934, high waters in the Similkameen River washed out a long section of the Great Northern line a few miles southeast of Princeton and damaged the bridge at the east end of the Princeton yard, forcing the GN to suspend service into Princeton. After close inspection of the damage, GN management declined to effect immediate repairs and instead sought permission from the Board of Railway Commissioners to abandon the line from the border north. At first the BRC ruled that the Great Northern had to resume service to Princeton. However, business conditions remained depressed and on September 30, 1937, after numerous time extensions of the earlier order, the BRC granted the GN permission to abandon trackage between Princeton and Hedley, subject to the understanding that GN would operate the remainder of the line between Oroville and Hedley with a reasonable frequency of service. Despite the line's official abandonment in 1937, the GN did not remove the rails until after September 1939, when they were salvaged for needed wartime scrap. Later the roadbed was graded over to form part of the Southern Transprovincial Highway, so now only the long tangents and easy curves of the highway bear testimony to the fact the route was once part of J.J. Hill's dream of a line from Spokane to the Pacific Coast.[9]

Although the GN ceased to possess any physical connection with Princeton following abandonment of the western portion of its line up the Similkameen Valley, it continued to own the rail line between Princeton and Brookmere. It also continued to possess trackage rights over the KVR line through Coquihalla Pass and over the Canadian National line between Hope and Sumas River. In fact the GN continued to hold these trackage rights until 1944, when the GN finally terminated the original agreements. Because of the long-term nature of the agreements, the Great Northern was forced to pay a veritable fortune for release of its contractual obligations. The price finally settled upon was $950,000 to the CNR and $4,500,000 to the CPR. Added to these substantial amounts were the annual rental fees the GN had paid, roughly $50,000 and $150,000, respectively, to the two corporations every year since 1916. Early in 1945 the Great Northern sold the Princeton-Brookmere rail line to the CPR for $1,500,000, but even subtracting this payment, the amount lost by the GN was colossal.[10] These figures suggest the one trip made by Louis Hill through Coquihalla Pass in September 1916 could well have been the most expensive train ride in history!

The heavy spring rains of early 1934 that damaged the GN line into Princeton also caused slides and washouts along the Kettle Valley Railway, creating major disruptions in service. The following year the KVR suffered another interruption that proved to be the worst single tie-up in the railway's history, discounting the closures of Coquihalla Pass. The KVR's troubles began late in the afternoon of January 20, 1935. Temperatures had been well below freezing since the previous week. At Princeton the thermometer hovered at 38 degrees below zero and at McCulloch it was 42 below (Fahrenheit). In the morning Vancouver had reported a light snowfall. That afternoon Coquihalla reported the same. By nightfall the full force of a fierce storm blowing in from the Pacific Ocean hit the coast. In Vancouver, the snow mounted swiftly during the evening—a foot by eight o'clock, two feet by midnight. A record three feet had fallen by morning. In the mountains to the east, the effects were greatly magnified. At Coquihalla, 12 feet of fresh snow lay on the ground and buildings were completely out of sight. The snow was more than six feet deep all the way south to Princeton and north to Merritt. At Coalmont, Train 11, which had left Penticton the night before with 150 people on board, was stalled in a snowdrift. A freight and plow train were buried in Coquihalla Pass.

By late afternoon that day, a plow train that had left Brookmere at dawn reached Coalmont, and after a long delay in turning the plow train on the snow clogged wye, it returned to Brookmere followed by the belated passenger train. The plow immediately continued on down to Merritt, any thoughts of attempting to route through Coquihalla Pass having been abandoned. The passenger train delayed for a short time to refuel the locomotive, then followed. During this short interval between trains, a massive snowslide came down upon the tracks three miles west of Brookmere, blocking the line behind the plow train. Upon encountering the slide, the passenger train crew wisely backed the train to the relative safety of the yard at Brookmere. But even that move posed serious problems. The snow in Brookmere was shoulder depth and the coal needed to fire the locomotive and keep the train warm was not sufficient to withstand a prolonged delay. Food was also running low. When word arrived that the plow train had become trapped in a snowdrift at Kingsvale, the passengers and townspeople alike were immediately rationed to one meal per day in anticipation of a long delay before rescue.

Luckily crews were able to open the line to Merritt two days later.[11] At two o'clock in the morning on January 24, the passenger train finally reached Merritt, where the hospitable businessmen promptly declared the town shops open for business in the middle of the night. Little did the passengers know this delay was just the beginning of their long journey to the coast. The CPR and CNR mainlines were both blocked east and west of Spences Bridge so passengers would have to wait in Merritt indefinitely.

The problems created by the unusually heavy snowfall were compounded when temperatures suddenly jumped to well above freezing and heavy rains hit the coast in the wake of the original storm. The deep snowdrifts suddenly melted, causing nearby streams and rivers to swell into torrents. Massive avalanches, set loose by the rising temperatures and heavy rains, roared down the mountain slopes and swept away everything in their path. A slide at Iago completely buried a snowshed under more than 50 feet of snow, trapping members of a plow train that had sought sanctuary there. Charlie Johnson, an extra gang foreman on board the plow train, said the slide blocked not only the ends of the snowshed but the front face, stopping all air supply. The engineer was just about to douse the fire in the locomotive firebox to keep everyone from suffocating when some of the snow broke away from the front face of the snowshed and the men were able to crawl out of their potential tomb. Johnson said the last remains of the avalanche did not melt until the second summer afterwards.

On January 25, an ice jam set free by the warm weather swept down the Tulameen River and struck the double-span Howe truss bridge five miles west of Princeton, crushing the centre supporting pier and destroying one of the trusses. The second truss escaped damage but was carried so far downstream by the current that recovery was impractical. Thus the line was severed once more. Fortunately, the bridge was located just downstream of a second bridge the Great Northern had put in 23 years earlier to carry the line across to the west bank briefly to avoid a rock bluff and bad slide area on the east bank. By building a short piece of trackage down the east bank and having passengers walk between trains, the KVR was able to restore at least temporary passenger service around the missing bridge as soon as the remainder of the line had been cleared. Freight service would remain severed.

The stranded passenger train at Merritt was finally able to leave on January 26. West of Spences Bridge, the Fraser Canyon was stilled blocked by snowslides, so the train went eastward on the mainline to Sicamous, then south to Kelowna where passengers were transferred by lakeboat back to Penticton. For passengers still wishing to travel to the coast, a special train was waiting at Penticton to take them eastward to Nelson and Yahk, south over the Spokane International to Spokane, and finally west over the Great Northern to Seattle, from where a CPR boat took them to Vancouver. On the evening of January 29, 1935, the passengers ended their journey of nine days—a journey that would normally take nine hours. That same day, service on the CPR mainline was restored. A day later, passenger service on the KVR resumed, with the foot transfer west of Princeton. Not until February 12 did KVR freight service resume, using a temporary pile trestle at the site of the bridge washout. The Coquihalla line—with the trapped freight and plow train—remained blocked until the middle of May.

Late in 1936, the civil war in Spain boosted the price of copper, prompting Granby to reopen the mine at Copper Mountain. For the third time the rail line was repaired, and in June 1937, the mine once again began operations. As well as reopening the mine, Granby constructed a coal-fired electrical power plant just across the Similkameen River from the Princeton loop track; a tussle with West Kootenay Power & Light Company over rates had resulted in Granby refusing to renew its former contract for supply of power to the mine and concentrator mill. Thus the KVR also secured a reasonable amount of coal traffic, mainly from Coalmont Collieries, for the power plant.

Even with the mine's reopening, overall business on the KVR remained poor. For reasons of economy, especially after the trying experience of January 1935, the CPR deliberately closed the line through Coquihalla Pass each winter for the rest of the decade. In fact, from late 1937 until May 1939, the Coquihalla line was in service for only a few weeks. In 1938, not long after the line was reopened following a hard winter, a disastrous forest fire on July 21 destroyed three major wooden trestles near Romeo, and by the time the trestles were rebuilt, winter was approaching. Following the long closure in 1938, the CPR announced early in 1939 that the Coquihalla line would be permanently closed. C.A. Cotterell, assistant general manager of CPR Western Lines, expressed the corporation's reluctance to abandon the line, but stated that the continuing heavy expenditures required to keep it open were not justifiable. The Coquihalla Subdivision, he said, had been the most difficult line on the entire CPR system to operate, more difficult even than the original CPR line through Rogers Pass, which had prompted the construction of the five-mile long Connaught Tunnel. W.M. Neal, another CPR official, added: "Our records show that ever since we took over the line in 1916, the Coquihalla has been closed each year for varying periods."[12] The alternate Merritt line could be kept open year-round without difficulty, a fact supporting permanent closure of the Coquihalla line. Neal said that application for authorization to abandon the line would be made to the Board of Railway Commissioners in the spring.

In spite of these statements, in March 1939, the CPR changed its mind and, for reasons never publicly revealed, reopened the Coquihalla line for regular service. The wisdom of the decision was quickly proven. Four months after service resumed on the Coquihalla line, Canada became embroiled in another world war; almost overnight the depression-shrouded 1930s gave way to a new decade dominated by the industry and commerce of war. Traffic on the KVR increased dramatically. Demand for copper, lead, coal and lumber skyrocketed and, since the Canadian west coast had become a significant industrial centre, the bulk of Kootenay mineral traffic was now directed to Vancouver, not eastward as in the previous conflict. Okanagan fruit production was also pushed to record limits by the demand for food in war-torn Great Britain; in the latter years of the war, more than 14,000 railcars of fruit left the Okanagan annually, straining the KVR's ability to handle its share.

Early in the war, the CPR realized this sudden increase in freight traffic would force it to end its depression-era policy of relinquishing the Coquihalla line to the ravages of winter after the first few snowfalls. The single track mainline through the Fraser Canyon west of Spences Bridge was jammed with wartime traffic of its own and locomotives, freight cars and operating personnel were all in short supply because of the war. Moreover, fears the Fraser Canyon mainlines of the CPR and CNR could be crippled by natural disasters or saboteurs blowing up key bridges justified the maintenance of the Coquihalla line as a potential bypass route. Coquihalla Pass proved to be far from willing to oblige the CPR. Death waited around every twist and curve of that rail line and, while fighting to keep open the lifeline of the west coast war industries, more than one denim-clad soldier of the KVR was required to pay a price equal to that of his khaki-clad comrades in Europe.

Cliff Inkster, a former KVR "hogger," as locomotive engineers were called, was one of many who remember the difficulties in keeping the railway open during those wartime winters. He especially remembers his own glimpse of the hereafter provided by the unrelenting Coquihalla early one winter morning. Cliff had spent the evening working a "helper" engine assisting a freight train up the grade east from Hope to Coquihalla. There, he turned his engine on the wye and waited to couple onto the front of Train 11, the late coast-bound passenger train, just before daybreak. (Coupling returning "helper" engines to other trains was standard practice during those busy times to ease the dispatcher's workload and conserve track capacity.) On the way back down the Coquihalla, Cliff spotted a fresh snowslide across the tracks just below Romeo, and brought the train to a stop. A cursory inspection of the slide indicated it was only small, so rather than cause further delay to the already late passenger train, Cliff and the hogger of the train's regular locomotive decided to cut their locomotives off the train and buck their way through the slide with the pilot of the lead locomotive.

Their first run into the slide succeeded only in piling up the snow somewhat. A second run proved no more successful. Just as Cliff was about to try again, the hogger of the trailing locomotive climbed over the tender into Cliff's cab and muttered that, as a "junior," Cliff should stand back and watch "how the real railroaders do it." The senior engineer promptly whistled to his own fireman, who had assumed temporary command of the other locomotive. The two engines in tandem backed up the grade several hundred feet and then came crashing into the snowdrift like a piledriver. This run was no more successful than the others, and was accompanied by the disheartening crunch of the locomotive headlight on the lead locomotive being broken by the snowdrift. Cliff crawled out on the catwalk to inspect the damage but recalls he never even looked at the broken headlight. His knees turned to rubber as he peered over the snowdrift and discovered that, hidden by the innocent white of the snowslide, a massive boulder had smashed the tracks completely out of alignment, twisting them straight over the edge of the narrow rock shelf that constituted the railway right-of-way. The thin veneer of snow remaining was all that stood between the locomotive and the canyon-floor several hundred feet below.

Len Smuin, another KVR engineer, also experienced death's icy breath in Coquihalla Pass during one of those wartime winters. A snowslide thundered down upon his train near Iago and sent a huge block of ice crashing through the locomotive cab window. The ice block pinned him and his fireman to the side of the cab and wedged the locomotive throttle wide open. Only because a second slide a few hundred feet away trapped the wildly running locomotive, was the crew spared from death or serous injury.

The passage of years added colour to railroaders' memories of their narrow escapes, and dulled their memories of buddies who rode over the canyon walls, never to return. However, their sacrifices were still very real, and were certainly not in vain. Between 1940 and 1945, the aggregate time the Coquihalla line was closed was less than the time lost in any single winter season of the previous decade.

The pressures of traffic demands on the KVR, along with the wartime shortage of men and materials, resulted in a great deal of deferred maintenance work. Nevertheless, the KVR was permitted to replace its lakeshore station in Penticton—rendered obsolete by the withdrawal of the last passenger vessel on Okanagan Lake—with a new station at the railway yard on Fairview Road, which opened on December 15, 1941. By eliminating the run to and from the lakeshore, the KVR was able to shorten the running time of Trains 11 and 12 by half an hour in each direction. Many of the tunnels in Coquihalla Pass were concrete lined or had concrete portals constructed during the war to eliminate the danger of cave-ins that would tie up the rail line and delay important war traffic. Jim Cherrington, division engineer on the Kettle Valley Division from 1941 to 1948, said he spent so much time in Coquihalla Pass during the war that his wife once quipped to him, as he was walking out the door, "Off to see Jessica again, I suppose."

Cherrington also said the demands of war brought great ingenuity out of people responsible for keeping the railway running. For years, the railway had routine problems with its trestle over Honeysuckle Creek on the Copper Mountain line, where the line crossed a bad bentonite outbreak that caused the trestle to progressively slide downward towards the Similkameen River. Frequently, the rail line, and its important copper ore traffic, had to be shut down while new piles were driven for the trestle. One day, while the piledriver was at work, a suggestion was made to have the piledriver set several extra rows of piles above the trestle, ready for the trestle deck to be moved onto them the next time the ground shifted. That way the number of times the piledriver had to be brought out would be cut in half or more. The idea was tested and worked splendidly. Cherrington said the idea came, not from himself or fellow civil engineers, but from an uneducated track worker who could barely speak English.

The pressures of war also resulted in the CPR introducing bulldozers for snow fighting. In handling the snows of Coquihalla Pass, the power and flexibility of these machines proved superior to the previous method of combining rotary and wing plows with bull gangs using hand shovels. The close proximity of Coquihalla Pass to the Pacific Coast meant Coquihalla snow was usually wet and sticky, thus hard to handle. Moreover, avalanches usually brought down trees and rocks as well as snow. These intrusions damaged the blades of rotary plows and frequently derailed wing plows. Bulldozers, however, were able to handle anything that fell on the tracks and were not subject to derailment. The availability of these versatile machines resulted in the CPR deciding partway through the war not to rebuild many of the Coquihalla snowsheds requiring replacement of the timber structures. During the war, most of the snowsheds were removed, and within two years after the war only five of the original 15 snowsheds remained. Some people maintained the introduction of bulldozers took the romance out of railroad snow fighting. Nevertheless it took the same bravery to drive a "cat" across the snow-covered deck of the high trestles of Coquihalla Pass that it took in the days of the snowplow.

Harry Percival, a fireman promoted to engineman during the war, recalled his good fortune that one of his first trips as an engineer never got recorded in the CPR files. He was preparing a westbound freight in Brookmere yard after dark one winter evening. Switching was nearly complete when he looked back through the inky darkness and saw what looked like the lantern of the rearend brakeman waving a "highball" signal, meaning the connection with the caboose had been made and the train could depart. He called his fireman across the cab saying, "Does that look like a highball signal to you?" The fireman replied, "Sure does to me." Harry promptly pulled away for Hope, his train orders indicating a clear run. However, when he arrived at Coquihalla, the station train order board was in the stop position. The station operator, waiting on the station platform with a grim look on his face, said to Harry, "You left Brookmere without your caboose!" Sure enough, the caboose was nowhere to be seen. The operators at Coquihalla and Brookmere covertly agreed to hold any trains while Harry made an unauthorized run back to Brookmere to get the forgotten caboose. There the engine crew discovered that some maintenance workers had left a large pile of ties alongside the tracks, and the pile had partially obscured the lantern signal in the dark. The brakeman had actually signalled to back up, not go ahead. While serous enough at the time, it was one of those events railroaders laughed about from the safety of retirement.

One significant consequence of the war was the completion of the Osoyoos line. In order to increase fruit shipments to war-torn Great Britain, the CPR was granted special government permission in 1944 to extend the line in the South Okanagan Valley from the end of track just south of Oliver to Osoyoos. The significance of the permission can be gained from the fact this was the only railway construction of consequence undertaken in all of Canada during World War II. Grading work for the extension began in July 1944, and the entire 10 miles of line was graded in a few weeks by only 15 men using bulldozers, a sharp contrast with the thousands of labourers who were needed for the construction of the KVR mainline a generation earlier. When the work was completed, George Fraser, a prominent Osoyoos businessman, drove the last spike on the extension in an elaborate ceremony at Osoyoos on December 28, 1944. Assisting him was Frank Latimer, who as a young man had helped survey the CPR's Shuswap & Okanagan Railway branch line southward into the Okanagan Valley from Sicamous in the early 1890s. With the exception of a few minor industrial spurs, this was to be the last piece of trackage constructed on the Kettle Valley Railway.[13]

Not long after the completion of the Osoyoos line World War II ended, relieving Canadian railways of much of the great demand placed upon them by the war. Nevertheless, the heavy traffic volume of the war years convinced the CPR its Kettle Valley Division would remain one of its most important divisions in western Canada. In January 1946, with wartime rationing and restrictions winding down, the CPR announced it would immediately undertake an ambitious program to bring the KVR up to a standard equivalent to the Canadian Pacific Railway mainline. The stations at Penticton and West Summerland would be enlarged, all ties and small wooden bridges would be renewed, and those large wooden trestles originally slated for replacement with steel structures or fills in the cancelled 1929 program would now be replaced. This included construction of a 780-foot-long steel bridge across Bellevue Creek between Ruth and Lorna on the Carmi Subdivision and a huge earth fill over Siwash Creek near Jellicoe on the Princeton Subdivision. The latter project alone cost $368,000.

Major upgrading was also started on the line between Princeton and

Brookmere, acquired from the Great Northern only a few months previous. Three of the original wooden Howe truss span bridges on this section, built by the GN more than 30 years earlier, were replaced by steel structures. Two other bridges, where the line had jumped from the east bank of the Tulameen River to the west bank for half a mile to avoid a large rock bluff, were eliminated by a new section of line entirely on the east bank. Under the CPR's new commitment to improvements, a tunnel 484 feet long was drilled through the bluff to avoid crossing the river. The tunnel, lined with reinforced concrete throughout, was not completed until 1950 because of the complexity of the work.[14]

Improvement work was also delayed by the massive floods of the spring of 1948, when the Fraser River overflowed its banks in the Fraser Valley and washed out both the CPR and CNR mainlines and the Trans-Canada Highway, as well as flooding large areas of farmland and many communities. While the KVR line between Hope and Midway was not seriously damaged, the raging Nicola River caused several major breaks along the Merritt Subdivision, and the line remained out of service for nearly three months that summer. The heavy demands on railway maintenance crews and contractors to repair the CPR mainline meant repairs to the Merritt Subdivision and planned improvement work on the KVR had to be deferred.

The CPR's large capital investment in the Kettle Valley Railway after World War II was rationalized by the heavy volume of freight continuing to come over the railway despite the end of hostilities. The Trail smelter in particular continued to ship a large portion of its output over the KVR for export either from Vancouver or the CPR's affiliate Pacific Coast Terminals, in New Westminster. Lumber traffic also remained significant. And fruit traffic grew so much that on April 27, 1947, the CPR introduced a new daily express train service between Penticton and Vancouver, numbered Train 45 westbound from Penticton and Train 46 eastbound from Vancouver. The train left Penticton in the early evening, after the fruit cars had been loaded during the day, and returned the next evening from Vancouver with empty cars. Although the transport of fruit was the prime purpose for the train, an express car, passenger coach and one or more sleepers were added for the convenience of passengers and express users.

To handle both the new express service and the steady growth in other freight traffic, the CPR supplemented the P1 class 2-8-2 steam locomotives in the 5100 series in use on the KVR with P1n class locomotives of the same wheel arrangement in 5200s series. Interestingly, some of these latter locomotives had seen previous service on the KVR, having been rebuilt and renumbered from older 2-8-0 locomotives in the 3600 number series. A few 5700 series 2-10-0s were also moved down from the mainline to help the ever-lengthening trains on the tough grades east and west of Penticton.[15] Early in 1949 oil tanks were erected at Penticton, Princeton, Midway and Brookmere to allow KVR steam locomotives to burn oil fuel.

Throughout the late 1940s and early 1950s, the CPR also continued its wartime policy of keeping the line through Coquihalla Pass open for as much of the year as possible. Damage wrought by the heavy rains or snows of winter was quickly repaired and continuing permanent improvements were made to the line. In March 1950, 14 bulldozers worked 24 hours per day for an entire month to permanently fill the site of a damaged trestle at Jessica. On January 25, 1951, a massive snowslide destroyed the centre section of a wooden snowshed near Iago and when it was reconstructed it was built entirely of concrete to minimize the possibility of being destroyed again. Telegraph and other communication lines were all buried underground, away from winter slides. Earth fills replaced many of the wooden trestles in the lower Coquihalla. The rail line, built under the restricted conditions of World War I, and starved for improvements by a shortage of money during the depression and a shortage of manpower and materials during World War II, was steadily approaching the CPR's objective of becoming the second mainline.

On September 2, 1951, the CPR introduced the Kettle Valley Railway to its first diesel-electric locomotive. This new form of motive power was then rapidly taking over from steam locomotives on American railroads, and on that day the Canadian Locomotive Company twin-unit demonstrator diesel locomotive *City of Kingston* hauled a freight train from Midway to Penticton, the first occasion on which diesel power was used on the KVR. The following day the two units continued through to Vancouver with the same train. During October three of four more test runs were made with the locomotives. Impressed with the results, the CPR expanded the test to include one trial passenger train run early in January 1952 and afterwards announced it would convert the mainline between Calgary and Revelstoke entirely to diesel power later that year, and the Kootenay and Kettle Valley Divisions the year following, as rapidly as the locomotives could be delivered by manufacturers. The CPR stated the two divisions in southern British Columbia were being given priority over the rest of the mainline because of the many heavy grades on the route, for which the diesel locomotive, with its smooth traction and multiple unit operation capabilities, was deemed superior to the steam locomotive. Construction was begun almost immediately on a diesel locomotive servicing facility at Nelson to handle the new type of motive power on both divisions. The plan called for delivery of 73 diesel units during 1953. Work was soon begun lengthening numerous passing tracks from typically 35 cars to 75 cars so the longer freight trains expected to be made possible with diesel locomotives could be accommodated.

In addition to its plans to convert from steam to diesel locomotives, the CPR announced that, effective April 27, 1952, substantial improvements would be made to KVR passenger service in an attempt to reverse the serious loss of passenger traffic following the November 1949 opening of the Hope-Princeton Highway. Prior to that date, the KVR enjoyed a significantly shorter and faster route than its automobile competition, which was routed through the Fraser Canyon to Spences Bridge. Indeed, for many years the transportation of automobiles across the Hope Mountains was an important source of revenue for the KVR, but with the opening of the Hope-Princeton Highway the KVR lost its distance and time advantage and passenger traffic seriously declined. The average number of passengers per trip on the Vancouver-Penticton run plunged by more than 60% between 1949 and 1950, and dropped again in 1951.

Attempting to recoup these losses, the CPR stated it would make a major schedule revision to Train 11, the *Kootenay Express*, and Train 12, the *Kettle Valley Express*. With the April 1952 change, Train 12 would be scheduled out of Vancouver in the morning instead of the evening and Train 11 would leave Nelson in the evening, effectively 12 hours different than previously. This change resulted in passengers in both directions having the previously rare opportunity to view Coquihalla Pass in the daylight hours. However, the CPR's prime motive for the change was to allow the two through passenger trains to better coordinate with the Vancouver-Penticton fruit and passenger express, Trains 45 and 46. The new schedule offered passengers going from Vancouver to Penticton a choice of a morning departure on Train 12 or an evening departure on Train 46. Similarly, passengers from Penticton destined to Vancouver could leave in the morning on Train 11 or in the evening on Train 45. Some other improvements were offered as well. Altogether, the changes represented a sincere effort on the part of the CPR to halt the declining use of its railway passenger services in southern British Columbia.

Early in 1953, the CPR introduced diesel locomotives for regular service on the KVR. At first the diesels were confined to freight service, a handful of General Motors GP7R road-switchers in the 8400 series being allocated for through freight service, and Montreal Locomotive Works S-4 yard switchers in the 7100 series handling switching and way freights. Then, in May a large number of Canadian Locomotive Company diesel units of Fairbanks-Morse design, affectionately dubbed "F-Ms" by engine crews and railway fans alike, arrived on the Kettle Valley and Kootenay Divisions where they were to spend most of their working lives. These units took over Trains 11 and 12 immediately and by summer most freight service as well.[16]

In the early days of operation the diesels had their share of problems. Ironically, the worst was the large number of brush fires the "F-M" units started along the KVR right-of-way that summer, something rarely encountered with the KVR's oil-fired steam locomotives. Then, in January 1954 diesel unit 4083 on the head of passenger Train 12 hit a slide at Iago and tumbled 300 feet to the canyon bottom. Nearly a month was required to extricate it. Despite such problems, the diesels quickly proved their overall advantages and soon had almost exclusive dominion on "The Kettle." Only Trains 45 and 46, operated from the Coquitlam locomotive pool, which was still dominated by steam locomotives, remained staunchly defended by the 5200 series 2-8-2s originally assigned to handle them.

Unfortunately, the CPR's attempt to improve passenger service was to no avail in stemming the public drift away from the KVR. In the face of ever-diminishing passenger patronage and the almost total loss of Penticton-Vancouver fruit traffic to truck competition over the new highway, the CPR announced in the summer of 1954 that Trains 45 and 46 would be discontinued and through passenger Trains 11 and 12 would revert to their pre-1952 schedule. On Saturday morning, September 25, 1954, locomotive 5212 pulled into Penticton with the final run of Train 46. The following morning it returned to Vancouver with the remnants of the previous day's Train 11 on what was reported in the newspapers as the last occasion when a steam locomotive operated on the Kettle Valley Railway.[17]

Compounding the loss of passenger traffic on the KVR was a serious blow to freight traffic on April 30, 1957 when Granby operated the last shift at its Copper Mountain mine, bringing to an end 20 years of continuous ore traffic business. Of course, it was not the first time the mine had shut down and Granby admitted that a great deal of ore remained in the mine, but this time the closure would be permanent. While the CPR continued to operate trains over the line after the closure to assist Granby in removing equipment, this function was short-lived, and soon after engine 8714 towed away the last trainload of equipment on July 19, 1957, work was begun in dismantling the spur. By summer's end all track between Copper Mountain and Allenby had been removed. Trackage between Princeton and Allenby was left in place for a time because the Allenby concentrator mill was converted into a manufacturing plant, but the enterprise proved unsuccessful and trackage on the remainder of the line was torn up, with the exception of a few hundred feet of track immediately south of the loop track at Princeton. Curiously, only the rails were removed. All ties, trestles and structures on the line were left intact. For many years after the line's abandonment, the water tower at Copper Mountain stood with its spout hanging forlornly downward over the rotting ties, as if it were waiting to fill the tender of some long-departed steam locomotive.

Passenger traffic on the KVR continued to drop through the mid-1950s and the CPR announced that effective October 27, 1957, passenger service on the company's line across southern British Columbia would be put on a revised and greatly accelerated schedule in a further attempt to stem the loss of patronage. A faster running time—an 11-hour reduction each way on the 962-mile run between Vancouver and the mainline connection at Medicine Hat—would be achieved by replacing conventional passenger trains with faster self-propelled rail diesel cars, or Budd Cars as they are more commonly known in the railroad industry. Simultaneously, all express, sleeping car and dining car service would be discontinued. Mixed trains 805 and 806, which had been running in one form or other between Spences Bridge and Brookmere since 1916, were also to be discontinued, as would most of the other connecting rail services feeding into the southern British Columbia line. The revised trains were to be given the numbers of the fruit and passenger express cancelled three years earlier, Train 45 westbound and Train 46 eastbound.[18] Throughout the southern interior there was criticism of the CPR for the removal of sleeping and dining car service. However, the new Vancouver-Medicine Hat train service represented an honest attempt by the CPR to seek the best compromise in the pattern of rising costs and diminishing revenues being experienced all North American railways.

Trains 45 and 46 began operation on October 27, 1957 as planned, but the rail diesel cars slated to provide the service were delayed in their delivery from the Budd manufacturer and service was introduced that day using a conventional diesel unit pulling a single baggage car and day coach. Despite the accelerated schedule, passenger traffic continued to drop and effective February 4, 1958 the CPR, on very short public notice, cut passenger service on the sparsely populated Midway-Nelson section of the southern route from daily to twice weekly.[19] Dwindling patronage was only part of the reason for the curtailment of service between Penticton and Nelson. During the 1950s, the CPR had suffered numerous bombings of its line near Castlegar by the militant Sons of Freedom Doukhobor sect, and restricting the operation of passenger train service on this section of line to daylight-only hours was believed to be a safety precaution, or so the CPR claimed. Between Vancouver and Penticton, service continued on a daily basis.

On March 3, 1958 the CPR introduced the promised Budd Cars to the Kettle Valley Railway.[20] Unfortunately, the cutback in service frequency and the introduction of overnight layovers at Penticton and Nelson more than offset any gains made by the new equipment. Patronage continued to decline. Numerous complaints about the reduction in service were forwarded to the Board of Railway Commissioners and a public hearing was held. H.H. Griffin, the assistant chief commissioner, sided with the railway. His lengthy report was summed up in a single short sentence that outlined the familiar conclusion the Board had been so often forced to make: "In my opinion the Company has made every reasonable endeavour to attract passenger traffic to its trains, but nonetheless the patronage given the trains by the travelling public has declined."[21] The Board refused to order the railway either to restore daily service between Penticton and Nelson or to adjust its schedules.

The decline in Kettle Valley Railway passenger traffic during the late 1950s, while undoubtedly disappointing to the CPR, did not provide an accurate measure of the railway's general status. Rail passenger travel was on the wane all over North America throughout the decade, so the loss of this traffic was not unique to the KVR. Even with this loss, and the loss of significant local freight traffic to trucking competition on the Hope-Princeton Highway, the KVR remained a busy railway. Freight trains leaving Penticton for the coast with four headend diesels and a sling of "pushers" were common in the late 1950s as the output of the Kootenay mines rolled westward in increasing tonnages. Lumber traffic was also growing substantially, and the transportation of wood chips, a newly introduced traffic for the railway, was soon to equal lumber in volume, if not in revenue. A new copper mine near Merritt offset much of the loss of the Copper Mountain ore trade. Similarly, coal traffic from the mines of the Tulameen and Nicola was replaced by petroleum deliveries from distant refineries. The oil companies provided indirect business for the KVR too, as the railway hauled large volumes of equipment, pipe and supplies into Coquihalla Pass for the construction of the Trans Mountain Oil Pipeline Company oil pipeline. Later, the railway helped construct the Westcoast Transmission gas pipeline through Coquihalla Pass as well. Major improvements continued to be made on the railway, especially on the Coquihalla Subdivision. In 1959 alone, the CPR spent more than half a million dollars on the Coquihalla line, and similar amounts on other parts of its Kettle Valley Division.[22]

The many improvements to the railway's fixed plant and the growing importance of through traffic reflected the gradual but steady change that had taken place in the character of the Kettle Valley Railway over the years following its completion. Built primarily to offer a coastal outlet for the products of the Boundary and Kootenay mines, the KVR had initially fallen short of the great dreams envisioned during its formative years at the turn of the century. First, a world war diverted much of the mining trade the railway had been built to serve. Then came a decade of disappointingly slow traffic growth, followed by a severe depression that cut traffic to barely subsistence levels. Not until the Second World War did the sizeable volumes of through traffic originally projected for the railway actually materialize, and yet another decade had to pass before the railway's physical condition reflected its final maturity.

By 1959 the Kettle Valley Railway was no longer merely a branch line feeding traffic to the Canadian Pacific mainline. With the improvements of the late 1940s and 1950s, the KVR had become equal in physical standard to any of the single-track portions of the CPR mainline in the province and second only to the mainline in traffic volume. Indeed, the KVR had become a mainline in its own right—the Coast-to-Kootenay mainline first envisioned in the late 1880s. What was then a daring dream was now a key artery of trade and commerce carrying the resources of southern British Columbia to the west coast ports and returning manufactured goods and products to the southern interior. The sacrifices of one generation had given prosperity to another, and as trains of growing length rolled down Coquihalla Pass for Vancouver there seemed little doubt the generation to follow was destined to prosper even more. The Kettle Valley Railway, in finally coming of age, had proven Thomas Shaughnessy's prophesy true.

14: Curtain Call for Coquihalla

The Kettle Valley Railway 1959 to 1964

At one thirty-five in the morning on Monday, November 23, 1959, the CPR dispatcher in Penticton received a telephone call from the Brookmere operator informing him freight train Extra 4079 East had just pulled into Brookmere following the three hour climb up the steep grade from Hope. The dispatcher had been waiting for this call. It meant the last train on the Kettle Valley Railway had "tied up" for the night, and with no trains due to move on the railway until daybreak the dispatcher could relax. In all probability he would have no further work to do during his shift. Little did the dispatcher realize he had just noted on his dispatch sheet the final freight train to operate over the Coquihalla Subdivision.

The dispatcher rested a moment, then began preparing a cup of coffee for himself. No sooner was he back at his desk than the silence of the dispatch office was broken by the telephone. The call was from the section foreman at Lear who explained that, while returning from his inspection trip up the line after Extra 4079 East had passed, he had discovered a section of track washed out near mile 43, to the east of Lear station. The sectionman asked the dispatcher to arrange for immediate assistance in repairing the damage. The dispatcher obliged and help was soon on the way. The washout meant the dispatcher would not have quite as relaxing a night as he had expected; still he wasn't overly concerned. A washout was hardly an unusual occurrence on the Coquihalla line, especially after the record heavy rain the coastal areas had experienced that weekend. With luck, the work train crew would have the line reopened for Train 46 out of Vancouver in the morning. What was actually transpiring in Coquihalla Pass that night was the prelude to an episode that would alter the course of railway history in all of southern British Columbia.

By daybreak, it had been discovered that the washout near Lear was not the only damage to the Coquihalla line; there were four additional washouts, plus two rockslides. Shortly after noon, engine 8606 departed from Brookmere with a ditcher and outfit to assist the five bulldozers and 50 men already dispatched to the scene. It took the train the next 11 hours to make Jessica, where the train and crew tied up for the night. At dawn the next day—November 24—the ditcher left Jessica and continued on down to the washout near mile 43, where it went to work trying to make at least a temporary passage around the washout. Engine 8606 remained behind at Jessica ready to remove the outfit cars when the repairs were completed.

Later that same day, more washouts were reported in the upper canyon. Then, close to midnight, a fill constructed across Tangent Creek at mile 38.3, five miles to the east of the first washout, was swept away leaving the tracks suspended in the air for some 200 feet. There was now no way for the engine to return to Brookmere; even a temporary bridge over the gap at mile 38.3 was out of the question. What followed was an epic four-day struggle while the 8606 and work train inched across spongy temporary fills and eroded trestles to reach Hope. So many were the disruptions that on November 28, the CPR announced the line would be closed temporarily until the unseasonably wet weather had abated and the damage could be repaired. As was customary when the Coquihalla line was closed for extended periods, the CPR evacuated all staff from the stations and sectionhouses in Coquihalla Pass. Trains 45 and 46 were re-routed via Spences Bridge, as were freight trains between the coast and Kootenays.[1]

The closure of the Coquihalla Pass rail line for a temporary period was hardly unusual news. The first hint that this time might be different came in March 1960 when the CPR quietly discontinued running Trains 45 and 46 between Spences Bridge and Vancouver. Ever since the diversion via Spences Bridge, Train 45 had been arriving into Vancouver at a decidedly inconvenient 2 a.m. Eastbound trains likewise had become inconvenient for passengers reaching Penticton, even if not so extreme as in the westbound direction. Effective March 7, 1960 Train 45 was scheduled to leave Penticton in the early evening and arrive at Spences Bridge at midnight, where passengers transferred to westbound mainline Train 7, *The Dominion*. The Budd Car then waited at Spences Bridge for the arrival of Train 8 from Vancouver at 2:35 a.m. bringing passengers from Vancouver for Okanagan and Kootenay points. After the transfer, the Budd Car, running as Train 46, operated through to Penticton, with a scheduled 8:00 a.m. arrival. On Tuesdays and Fridays the train continued from Penticton to Nelson. On Mondays and Thursdays Train 45 from Nelson continued west from Penticton to Spences Bridge. On the other days of the week Train 45 originated in Penticton, so that daily service remained between Penticton and Vancouver even with the inconvenience of a middle-of-the-night transfer. There was nothing in the CPR announcement concerning this schedule revision that stated whether the change was permanent or only temporary. In reality, Trains 46 and 46 never again operated to or from Vancouver.

The quiet stance of the CPR towards its Coquihalla Subdivision was also evidenced in Coquihalla Pass itself. While the CPR had earlier stated the line would be temporarily closed until the unseasonably wet weather had abated, when better conditions returned in the spring of 1960 the line remained silent. In fact, throughout all of 1960, Coquihalla Pass was devoid of the customary sounds of railroading. Finally, on January 9, 1961 the CPR issued a brief and stoic press announcement officially stating what many people had already come to suspect: the CPR did not intend to reopen its rail line through Coquihalla Pass. The press release stated that because of the cost of repairing the damage of November 1959, estimated at $251,000, the CPR had decided to abandon the line. The release said nothing more and no further explanation would ever be given by the corporation. There was no accounting of the years of struggle previous generations had devoted to the construction of the railway. Nor was there mention of the many railroaders who had died during the near half-century battle with the elements to keep the rail line operating. It was simply the end of the line for the Coquihalla.[2]

Although the CPR's announcement was not a total surprise, there seemed a certain unexplainable peculiarity about the decision. An outlay of $251,000 was hardly a large expenditure for the Coquihalla line. Indeed, considering the heavy investment the company had made in improving the Coquihalla line—including the expenditure of more than half a million dollars in 1959 alone—the CPR's refusal to allocate $251,000 for repairs seemed contradictory to the long-term program established in the early postwar years.[3] What the CPR press release did not say, and perhaps should have said, was that the decision to abandon the Coquihalla line was really a manifestation of a much larger decision. Owing to considerations other than merely the damage wrought to the Coquihalla line, the CPR had made a sudden and fundamental change in management philosophy towards the operation of its rail network in southern British Columbia. Rather than continue to haul coast-bound Kootenay freight over the Kettle Valley Railway, the CPR had decided that it would be more economical to divert this traffic north from the Kootenays over the Windermere Subdivision to the mainline at Golden then west over the mainline to the coast, even though lead and zinc from the Trail smelter would now face a 330-mile-longer journey. With this plan it was unnecessary to reopen the Coquihalla; the limited amount of local traffic generated by the Boundary District and Okanagan could easily be sent to the coast via the Merritt line to Spences Bridge. The Coquihalla railway was no longer an integral link in the rail line of southern British Columbia.

The CPR could not carry out its plan to abandon the Coquihalla Subdivision without the approval of the Board of Railway Commissioners, and a public hearing was called for early in the summer of 1961. However, even before the hearing began, CPR work crews were busily upgrading the Windermere Subdivision—work costing far more than $251,000—to accept traffic from the Kettle Valley Railway. Thus, the brief hearing did little more than put the rubber stamp of legal formality on the bitter truth of physical reality. On July 18, 1961, a year and a half after the last train had operated over the rail line and two weeks shy of the railway's 45th birthday, the Board of Railway Commissioners granted approval for the removal of the rails. A decision at Windsor Station, rather than a washout in the mountains of British Columbia, had destroyed the Coquihalla railway.

The end of the Coquihalla railway, like its opening in the harsh days of World War I, met with subdued reaction in the press. Many newspapers did not even carry the standard press releases about the railway and few expressed editorial comment. But some did. The *Similkameen Spotlight* wrote nostalgically: "It is with deep regret that we say good-bye to the Coquihalla train ride. As a child the Coquihalla train ride was just about the greatest delight there was. To ride down through the pass by train, looking down with awe at the gaping canyons, peering in the dark as the train passed through the tunnels and sheds, or just thinking what would happen if the train left the track at a certain point, was an adventure in itself. For a young lad to say that he had travelled over Coquihalla pass, was better than showing off a new pocket knife. All that is gone now. It is history. But for many Princeton people the closing of the Coquihalla pass will cause a tug at the heart. For over this pass was once the fastest means of transportation to the coast, and the nicest."[4]

Within a few weeks of receiving permission to abandon the railway, the CPR started its crews to work pulling up the rails westward from the mile 38.3 washout to Hope, and in September and October they removed rails from the washout east to Boston Bar Creek.[5] During 1962 rails on the balance of the line from Boston Bar Creek to Brodie were removed. The work ended with a brief and informal ceremony at Brodie on the afternoon of October 24, 1962 when a small group of railroaders, almost all of whom had spent their entire working lives on the Coquihalla line, watched as their most senior member pulled up the last spike.[6] Forty-six years earlier, as a young boy just beginning his career with the Kettle Valley Railway, this same man had been in Coquihalla Pass when the last spike had been driven to complete the railway. Now, when asked to give a speech, this man said nothing. The tears in his eyes told all he had to say.

With the exception of a few smaller steel bridges, the ties and rails were the only materials salvaged from the railway. All the wooden trestles and snowsheds and the major steel bridges at Ladner Creek and Slide Creek were left intact.[7] Some of these structures fell victim to demolition exercises of the Canadian Army. However, the Coquihalla itself was far harsher. Left to the ravages of the normal Coquihalla winters and the coastal rain-forest vegetation, much of the right-of-way quickly became unrecognizable as a railway. And what nature didn't destroy was blasted away by the construction of the four-lane superhighway through the lower reaches of Coquihalla Pass during the 1980s so that now only small sections of the line in the upper part of the canyon, carved from the mountainside by human sweat, remain as evidence the railway ever even existed.

The Shakespearian-named stations along the railway also quickly disappeared. Although the provincial government has placed small marker signs bearing Shakespearian names at selected points along the new highway through Coquihalla Pass, the markers give no clue as to the origin of the names or the fascinating man whose Shakespearian legacy has outlived his railway.[8]

The abandonment of the Coquihalla rail line would not, in itself, have radically changed the character of the remainder of the Kettle Valley Railway. After all, the KVR had endured many long closures of the line. However, the CPR decision to divert all coast-bound Kootenay freight traffic via the mainline had a devastating effect on the KVR. The opening of the Hope-Princeton Highway a decade earlier began a process that had stripped the KVR of most of its local traffic, so that when, effective September 1, 1961, the CPR discontinued operation of through freight trains, more than 80% of the KVR's freight traffic vanished in a single day. The 22 train crews based at Penticton were suddenly reduced to five, and the once-large mechanical and maintenance-of-way staff assigned to that point was almost entirely transferred to other parts of the CPR system. The following spring, on May 16, 1962, the dispatch office at Penticton was closed. Later that year, the Kettle Valley Division was abolished, with the remnants of the former KVR trackage being assigned to the Kootenay, Canyon and Revelstoke Divisions. Almost overnight, the Kettle Valley Railway had been transformed from the second mainline status it had enjoyed in the 1950s to little more than a minor branch line.

The closure of the Coquihalla line also caused an irreparable blow to KVR passenger service. While through passenger patronage between the coast and Kootenays had suffered badly as a result of the introduction of forced layovers at Penticton and Nelson, passenger traffic between Vancouver and Penticton had shown encouraging signs of stabilizing by 1959. The one Budd Car assigned to the run was normally nearly full and extra cars were customarily added on weekends and holidays. A group was even arranging to operate ski train specials from Vancouver to Princeton, with the service scheduled to begin in early December 1959, tragically only three weeks before the line was put out of commission. However, when passenger trains had to be diverted via Spences Bridge, patronage plunged dramatically. The diversion added more than three hours to travel time between Vancouver and Penticton, making train service decidedly less appealing than bus or private automobile. The necessity for passengers to change trains at Spences Bridge in the middle of the night made the train service even less appealing.

Faced with the almost complete desertion of its passenger trains, the CPR filed application with the Board of Transport Commissioners in June 1962 for permission to discontinue Trains 45 and 46. Because the trains served not only communities along the former Kettle Valley Railway, but east of Midway to Medicine Hat, the subsequent hearings took many months to complete. Ultimately the Board granted Canadian Pacific sanction to discontinue the trains. On January 17, 1964—one year short of half a century of operation—the last passenger train operated over the Kettle

Valley Railway. Among the passengers who made the final run were Alex Swift, the KVR's chief clerk; R.E. Gammon, a survey assistant under Andrew McCulloch during the construction of the railway; and "Charlie" Yule, a brakeman on the first regular passenger train to arrive in Penticton in May 1915.[9]

In many respects, that date marked the end of the Kettle Valley Railway. With through freight train service having been discontinued two and a half years earlier, the termination of passenger operations brought to an end all direct rail service between the coast and the Kootenays. In effect, the railway had ceased to serve the function for which it had been built. Curtain call for Coquihalla was really curtain call for Kettle Valley.

15: Gone But Not Forgotten

The legacy of the Kettle Valley Railway

In the quarter century following the last run of a Kettle Valley Railway passenger train in January 1964, the railway underwent an inexorable decline into operational oblivion. In August 1966, Brookmere was dropped as a terminal point and the crew layover point for the tri-weekly way freight west from Penticton was transferred to Merritt.[1] At the end of May 1972, the CPR discontinued operation of its tug and barge service on Okanagan Lake, which ended any significant transport of fruit by rail from the South Okanagan. The following year, in May 1973, train service between Midway and Penticton was discontinued and during 1979 and 1980 rails on the Carmi Subdivision were removed.[2] The Osoyoos Subdivision from Okanagan Falls south to Osoyoos saw its last train in 1977, with the rails being removed in 1979. In 1980, the spur from Merritt to Nicola was deleted. In September 1986, the roundhouse at Penticton was levelled and the yard removed, with subsequent total redevelopment of the land. By then, the former Kettle Valley Railway consisted of only a single subdivision, the Princeton Subdivision, stretching 178 miles from Spences Bridge to Penticton with a short spur line from Penticton south to Okanagan Falls.

More significantly, the line was down to only five regular customers— three sawmills at Merritt, the Weyerhaeuser sawmill at Princeton and a second mill owned by the same company at Okanagan Falls. Through the late 1980s three GP38 diesels, the class of motive power that had largely taken over from "first generation" diesels in 1976, were assigned to Merritt. One diesel handled local switching and a Monday-to-Friday run to Spences Bridge and back with all outbound traffic. The other two diesels made a twice-weekly run over the lonely 140 miles east to Penticton and returned the following day with lumber from the two Weyerhaeuser mills. All involved with the railway—and all whose passion was to watch it— knew the operation was untenable. Operating revenues from the line did not even cover wages, fuel and fixed expenses such as property taxes, let alone pay the cost of maintenance on what was still a difficult mountain railway. Between March and May 1989, service on the line was discontinued section by section and on May 12, 1989 the final train arrived at Spences Bridge. Just over a year later, on June 21, 1990, the National Transportation Agency authorized Canadian Pacific to abandon the railway, and during 1991 all track, with the exception of seven miles of track near Summerland saved for a tourist railway operation, was removed.[3] The Kettle Valley Railway became part of history.

To some people, the demise of the Kettle Valley Railway was all too predictable considering the significant changes in technology and economics that transpired in the years following the railway's construction. The KVR had been built in an age when railroads faced little competition except from each other. All travel and commodity traffic was then directed via the rails, and the relatively light trains of that era could tolerate the heavy grades encountered in crossing the mountains of southern British Columbia. The travel time and hauling distance saved between Vancouver and the southern interior made possible by the use of the KVR justified the railway's tortuous routing at the time of its construction. When the highways and airlines of a more modern age stripped the KVR of its passenger and mail trade and most lucrative freight traffic, the railway's steep grades took on new significance. The remaining bulk commodities traffic required longer and heavier trains to remain remunerative at the low tariffs these commodities commanded. Consequently, the CPR chose to divert this freight movement away from the KVR to the less arduous mainline. In the eyes of CPR management, the Kettle Valley Railway had been rendered redundant and, ultimately, dispensable.

John G. Sullivan, a former CPR chief engineer, was even more blunt in his assessment: "Of all the blunders in railway building history the CPR's southern British Columbia rail line is the greatest."[4] Certainly the KVR's financial ledgers would have supported this position. Although it managed to generate an operating profit for most of its years up to the closure of the Coquihalla line, the railway never came close to paying off the massive capital investment of its difficult construction. Several more recent writers have echoed Sullivan's viewpoint or argued that construction of the Kettle Valley Railway was a strategic mistake. The fact the railway has not survived is certainly one piece of evidence to support such a viewpoint.

In fairness to the people involved, any honest critique of the Kettle Valley Railway must take into account the circumstances under which the railway was built. John Sullivan and Andrew McCulloch had both spent time in the CPR engineering department in Montreal, where the feasibility of a railway from Midway to Hope was a frequent topic of conversation in the years leading up to the 1910 decision by Thomas Shaughnessy to build the Kettle Valley Railway. It is probably fair to say senior engineers within the CPR at the time were of a consensus a rail line from the Columbia River across southern British Columbia to Hope was not a viable economic proposition as a through railway. Heavy through traffic could only be economically transported on a direct railway with low grades, and low grades through the rugged mountains along any of the routes available to the CPR entirely north of the border could only be achieved with a massive investment in tunnels and bridges. Such investment could not be justified using any conventional economic analysis, especially when J.J. Hill's Great Northern already had a rail line from the Columbia River to Princeton with remarkably good operating characteristics. As far as the CPR engineering department was concerned, the battle for through trade in southern British Columbia was doomed to be lost to Hill. The CPR engineers were more ambivalent about the viability of a rail line built for purely local traffic. A rail line built to lower engineering standards over an indirect routing could be constructed at much lower cost than a direct route on easy grades, so a rail line meandering around hills and from mine to mine could potentially be viable on the basis of traffic picked up en route, especially because southern British Columbia at the time had many attractive mining prospects.

Perhaps the most legitimate criticism of the KVR's construction is that Thomas Shaughnessy seemed unable to clearly direct which of these two options the KVR was to be—a railway for through or local traffic. While his instruction to McCulloch that the railway must be "first class in every way" seems clear, there was in fact much room for interpretation within that directive. Certainly, McCulloch recognized the lack of clear direction almost immediately upon being given the assignment to build the KVR. The CPR's standard construction policy at the time was to build new rail lines relatively inexpensively and then undertake improvements as traffic proved to justify. So Shaughnessy's dictate "first class" appears to have meant "the best possible under our usual construction policy" rather than a railway of radically higher engineering standards at commensurate higher cost. Large wooden trestles needing renewal every 15 or 20 years were quite acceptable with the low labour wages prevailing at the time, even on a "first class" railway. Not until years later did the maintenance and renewal costs of such structures become an important consideration of railway economics. The fact that Shaughnessy virtually specified the KVR's route—a routing more suggestive of a local traffic than a through railway—added to the confusion since it seemed to contradict statements he was making to the public at the time that the KVR would be a direct route to the Kootenays. Had Shaughnessy clearly specified the KVR was to be built as a local traffic railway, McCulloch could have made many economies in construction. Had Shaughnessy clearly specified the KVR was to be built as a through railway—and given McCulloch complete freedom of route selection with a budget appropriate to such a directive—the railway might have been built very differently. In reality, the KVR cost the CPR a great deal of money without any realistic possibility of being later upgraded to a true "first class" railway.

Shaughnessy's vision of the Coquihalla line—undoubtedly the most expensive and controversial component of the Kettle Valley Railway's construction—seems even more cloaked in mystery. Comments made by Shaughnessy to McBride and the media clearly state he held the line to be vital, yet having committed the CPR to pay for its difficult construction, Shaughnessy rarely mentions the line again in either public statements or internal company documents. His few references to the Coquihalla line almost exclusively focus on the value of the line for handling diverted traffic from the CPR mainline while the company proceeded with planned upgrading and double tracking of its mainline through the Fraser Canyon, not on the importance of the line as a link to the Kootenays. World War I of course put an abrupt end to the plans to double track the CPR mainline through the Fraser Canyon. Indeed, the years from 1910 to 1916 were probably the most dramatic six years in world history in terms of altered outlook. So much changed so quickly. The ocean liner *Titanic* sank tragically and unexpectedly, shaking people's faith that rapidly advancing technology would solve all human problems. The subsequent war brought enormous economic upheaval, foreign investment disappeared, immigration abruptly halted and millions of men were slaughtered on the battlefields of Europe. The unexpected disappearance of the Great Northern Railway as a competitive force, despite the superiority of its rail line for through traffic, compounded the rapid adjustment. Indeed, the failure of the Great Northern Railway to seriously exploit its superior rail routing meant the Kettle Valley Railway escaped the acid test of Shaughnessy's ambivalent commitment.

Had Shaughnessy known how radically different the world of 1916 would be from 1910 he might well have not committed construction of the Kettle Valley Railway. Had he known how inflation and wartime short-ages would drive up construction costs for the KVR he likely would have at least hesitated. Had he also known reconciliation with the CPR's long-time corporate rival, the Great Northern Railway, would occur only three years later he might have decided upon a less ambitious construction pro-gram.

In retrospect, probably the most viable option open to Shaughnessy in 1910 would have been for the CPR to upgrade its line from Spences Bridge to Merritt to mainline standard, build a line of similar standard from Merritt to Princeton and make connections there with the completed tracks of the GN. By granting the GN trackage rights to run over the CPR from Princeton via Spences Bridge to Vancouver in return for the CPR being allowed to run over the GN from Grand Forks or Midway via Oroville to Princeton, and by building a line from Oroville north up the Okanagan Valley to Penticton, a workable rail network in southern British Columbia could have been completed at very modest cost. The extra dis-tance required to operate from the Kootenays to Vancouver via Spences Bridge instead of the Coquihalla line would have been virtually offset by the more direct routing between Grand Forks and Princeton offered by the GN line. This cooperative linkage would have produced a rail line across southern British Columbia no longer than the KVR as constructed, but with much better grades, few large trestles and without the heavy expense and troublesome disruptions of the Coquihalla line. After paying for this modest construction program, the CPR could have used the money saved from not building the Midway-Penticton-Princeton section and the Coquihalla line to upgrade the CPR mainline through the Thompson Canyon and Fraser Canyon west of Spences Bridge. An upgraded mainline would have not only reduced the time differential created by the longer routing via Spences Bridge but offered operational cost savings for the many trains to and from eastern Canada via the mainline. Such a cooperative proposal was not beyond conception at the time. Indeed, it was suggested to Shaughnessy even before he authorized construction of the Kettle Valley Railway, but he appears to have rejected it on the basis that an agreement with Hill was improbable. In the highly charged atmosphere of 1910 Shaughnessy was probably right, but had he and Hill the benefit of our hindsight as to the conditions that would exist only a few years later, it is likely a proposal such as this would have come to pass.

Besides being modest in both initial capital outlay and operating costs, the suggested network would have offered genuine potential for meaningful improvement—should later circumstances have warranted—by the construction of several long tunnels at strategic points. For example, a rail line directly from Keremeos to Oliver would have required a tunnel of only approximately six miles in length, thereby eliminating the diversion through the United States in travelling the GN route from Princeton to the Okanagan Valley. If the main tunnel had been drilled using a smaller "pioneer" tunnel alongside—a technique being introduced to speed up the drilling of long tunnels since it permitted multiple cutting faces—the leftover "pioneer" tunnel could have been used as a water tunnel for carrying water from the Similkameen River for irrigation in the Oliver land development scheme. A dam on the Similkameen River in the canyon immediately above Princeton could have provided both power for electrification of the railway and water for irrigation of the Okanagan orchards. In contrast, the route actually chosen by the Kettle Valley Railway offered little opportunity for meaningful upgrading without wholesale abandonment of large sections of the constructed railway.

Ultimately, Shaughnessy was responsible for the strategic decisions made concerning the Kettle Valley Railway. Had Shaughnessy and Hill been able to forge an earlier compromise along the lines suggested above, a working rail network might still survive in southern British Columbia. But that does not mean Shaughnessy's commitment to the construction of the Kettle Valley Railway was a mistake. The KVR halted the flow of Kootenay trade going to the United States at a critical time in British Columbia's history, and for more than three decades afterwards the railway was the lifeline of the region. Furthermore, the KVR formed the foundation on which all the later progress was based. Even Sullivan might have tempered his harsh statement had his assessment been made, not in the depths of the 1930s economic depression, but a few years later when the

KVR was carrying a flood of lead, zinc, copper and other war necessities for Canada's contribution to the Allied victory in World War II. In that regard, the KVR's value cannot be discounted merely because the newer modes of transport have relegated it oblivion.

Government policies also cannot be discounted. Provincially-owned BC Rail follows a route as geographically adverse as the Kettle Valley Railway yet remains in operation, largely because it enjoys an exemption from property taxes, corporate income taxes and numerous other financial burdens imposed upon private companies like the Canadian Pacific Railway. In the final year of operation of the Princeton Subdivision—1989—the CPR paid more than $5,000 per mile annually in property taxes for the Princeton Subdivision and further large assessments for its valuable land holdings within the City of Penticton. This meant a burden of more than a million dollars annually before the first carload of freight moved over the railway. Small wonder the CPR saw the futility of maintaining a rail line at its own expense when traffic could be trucked to its mainline on a highway paid for by the government. Lack of a comprehensive national transportation policy linking the various modes of transportation into a cohesive network capitalizing on the strengths of each mode must share the blame for the loss of the Kettle Valley Railway. Certainly the highway system cannot approach the KVR's unblemished safety record. Deaths by highway accident now seem so common as to be without news value or concern. Perhaps that fact alone is more tragic than the loss of any railway.

Trucks and automobiles now speed over the Coquihalla and Southern Transprovincial Highways carrying the freight and passengers once handled by the KVR. Jet planes have brought the cities of the southern interior as near to Vancouver in minutes as the wonder of 1916 had brought them in hours. But the trucks, automobiles and jet planes have not erased the great debt the people of British Columbia owe to those who conceived and built the railway upon which all this later progress was vitally dependent. Evolution may have destroyed the Kettle Valley Railway, but it cannot wipe out the fact that for an entire generation in southern British Columbia the railway was the lifeline of their existence. Nor can evolution wipe out the fact the Kettle Valley Railway, though it never made a penny profit for the CPR that built it, paid the people of British Columbia handsomely in the development of their province.

Ironically, the Kettle Valley Railway, in death, has gained a renown exceeding any it enjoyed during its life as an operating railway. Much of its roadbed has been turned into a hiking route, the Trans-Canada Trail. In spectacular Myra Canyon above Kelowna more people now walk the railway roadbed on any summer afternoon than likely rode through the canyon on trains during any day of the railway's existence. At the Quintette Tunnels near Hope, now the Coquihalla Canyon Provincial Park, busloads of Japanese tourists marvel at the roaring canyons of the Coquihalla River and the tunnels created by Andrew McCulloch and the labourers he commanded. A tourist train, powered by a steam locomotive, regularly carries enthralled passengers over the remaining tracks of the railway at Summerland. More than a dozen publications and five videos celebrate the railway. Although it has evolved, and probably would not be recognized by the pioneers who built it, the railway called McCulloch's Wonder remains a vibrant part of southern British Columbia.

Notes

Chapter 1: Coast-to-Kootenay: A Dream

1. James Douglas, "James Douglas Papers" *British Columbia Historical Quarterly*, Volume 2, page 81.
2. John Fahey, *Inland Empire: D.C. Corbin and Spokane* (Seattle, University of Washington Press, 1965), page 92.
3. *Vancouver News-Advertiser*, 1891-02-18.
4. Baker's railway was originally chartered as the Crow's Nest & Kootenay Lake Railway but in 1891 the name was changed to the British Columbia Southern Railway.
5. The Columbia & Kootenay Railway & Navigation Company was incorporated under British Columbia Statutes 1890, Chapter 62.
6. Fahey, page 126.
7. John Abraham Coryell (1861-1912). A station on the CPR line near Christina Lake was later named Coryell in his honour.
8. Walter Vaughan, *The Life and Works of Sir William Van Horne* (New York, The Century Company, 1920), page 229.
9. Vaughan, page 175.

Chapter 2: Empire Building

1. *Nelson Miner*, 1898-12-21.
2. Vaughan, page 223.
3. *The Province*, 1896-05-09.
4. *Vancouver Province*, 1927-04-10. Quoted in an article titled "B.C. Railways which did not Materialize: Dreams of Early Promoters."
5. Patricia Roy, Unpublished thesis: "Railways, Politicians and the Development of the City of Vancouver as a Metropolitan Centre." (University of Toronto, 1963), page 39.
6. J.L. McDougall, *Canadian Pacific: A Brief History* (Montreal, McGill University Press, 1966), page 76.

7. The CPR voluntarily reduced its rates on goods shipped between coastal points and the Kootenays in keeping with Shaughnessy's promise to the provincial government. Nothing in the terms of the Crows Nest Agreement required them to do so.

8. *The Province*, 1896-10-10.

9. The proposed VV&E route was identical to that of the Dewdney Trail. One might suspect that the VV&E engineer had not even inspected it as it was obviously unsuitable for a railway route.

10. For a brief time there was a rival railway scheme to the VV&E called the "People's Railway" promoted by T.E. Julian, who promised to build the railway and give it to the government. Initially the idea was popular but it quickly died because of its lack of economic viability.

11. *Vancouver News-Advertiser*, 1898-03-23.

12. *Vancouver News-Advertiser*, 1898-04-19.

13. *Nelson Miner*, 1898-12-10.

14. The CPR completed the Crows Nest line only as far west as Kootenay Landing, at the south end of Kootenay Lake, in 1898. Between that point and Nelson the CPR relied on boat service for passengers and rail barge service for freight to connect with the Columbia & Kootenay Railway. The gap was partially closed in 1902 by construction of a 20-mile-long rail line from Nelson to Procter, which was used almost exclusively for freight traffic. Passenger boats continued to operate to Nelson except when ice in the west arm of the lake forced boats to stop at Procter. Not until 1931 was a rail line opened to bridge the remaining 30-mile gap between Procter and Kootenay Landing.

15. *Vancouver News-Advertiser*, 1898-05-20.

16. *Vancouver News-Advertiser*, 1898-11-06.

17. The author devoted considerable effort in an attempt to determine the exact location of the VV&E grade through Penticton, but he was not entirely successful. It is known the grade began at the government wharf on Okanagan Lake at what is now the north end of Front Street and ran in a general southwest direction. Front Street was later constructed over the early roadbed, which accounts for the street's awkward intersection with Main Street. From that point the grade ran southward, parallel to and somewhat west of Main Street, although some evidence suggests the grade was not continuous. Further south, the grade intersected what is now South Main Street near Green Avenue. The grade continued for a half-mile under what is now South Main Street between that point and Skaha Lake. Penticton's growth into a major city appears to have destroyed any other evidence of the VV&E's contribution to its history. The Okanagan Historical Society mentions the grade in several of its publications, but has erroneously attributed the work to the

Columbia & Western Railway, probably because much of the land adjacent to Skaha Lake was in the C&W land grant reserve.

18. *Vancouver News-Advertiser*, 1899-10-29.

19. Vaughan, page 23.

20. *Vancouver News-Advertiser*, 1898-11-27. This comment was actually written about the commencement of CPR surveys west of Midway in 1898, which accounts for the discrepancy in dates from when the surveyors reached Hope.

Chapter 3: Mountains, Men and Paper Railroads

1. The CPR survey followed the Kettle River westward from Midway to Rock Creek, where it divided into two routes. One survey proceeded directly west through Meadow Lake Pass to the Okanagan. The other went north to Carmi, then via Dale's Pass to Penticton, and joined the first survey near Vaseux Lake. West from the Okanagan Valley the survey followed the Similkameen River to Princeton, followed Summers Creek and Quilchena Creek to Nicola Lake and followed the Nicola River to the CPR mainline at Spences Bridge, 180 miles east of Vancouver. An alternate route branched off this survey and cut through Coquihalla Pass to Hope. Maps of these routes are included in Chapter 8.

2. *Victoria Colonist*, 1900-12-13.

3. *Vancouver Province*, 1900-12-24.

4. Official Great Northern records indicate the GN began negotiating to secure control of the VV&E in December 1900 but it is likely that Hill had been involved with the VV&E somewhat earlier.

5. *The Golden Era*, as quoted in a political pamphlet titled *CPR vs the People of British Columbia: the Coast-Kootenay Railway*, printed in Victoria, 1901.

6. *Victoria Colonist*, 1901-03-20.

7. *Victoria Times*, as quoted in pamphlet noted in note 5.

8. Note the error in the title of the Vancouver, Victoria & Eastern Railway. Although the railway rarely appeared in papers except by its initials VV&E, when it did appear in full Victoria papers put the name Victoria first and Vancouver papers put their city's name first. Old jealousies died hard!

9. *Victoria Colonist*, 1901-03-22.

10. *Vancouver Province*, 1901-03-29.

11. The numerous railways proposed from Vancouver to the Kootenays were popularly called the Coast-to-Kootenay railway. The company proposed by Hunter & Oliver had the specific corporate name Coast-Kootenay Railway.

12. GN records show the company had gained control of 9,800 of the 10,000 outstanding shares of the VV&E. The remaining shares were listed as being held by "nominees of the Great Northern."

13. *Victoria Colonist*, 1901-07-16.

14. Henry Edward Cranmer Carry (1854-1928). Carry Creek, a tributary of the Coquihalla River, was named in honour of Carry's contribution to the expedition.

15. *Victoria Colonist*, 1902-01-21.

16. *Vancouver Province*, 1902-05-07.

17. The first of the three survey routes, 101 miles long with a summit elevation of 4,400 feet, followed the Nicolum, Sumallo and Skagit Rivers from Hope to Allison Pass, then down the Similkameen River to Princeton. This is essentially the same route now followed by the Hope-Princeton Highway. The second route, 87 miles long with a summit elevation of 3,650 feet, followed the Coquihalla and Coldwater Rivers to Pass Creek then crossed to Spearing Creek and descended Spearing Creek, Otter Creek and the Tulameen River to Princeton. This is the same route eventually chosen by the Kettle Valley Railway. The third route, 79 miles long with a summit elevation of 4,500 feet, followed the second route for 27 miles, then crossed over Railroad Pass, appropriately named by the Dewdney Expedition, and followed Railroad Creek and the Tulameen River to Princeton.

18. *Vancouver Province*, 1902-04-11.

19. Dewdney's report was more pessimistic than it need have been because of the limited scope of the assignment set by Dunsmuir. Dunsmuir instructed Dewdney only to determine if a railway route was feasible through the sparse and rugged territory between Hope and Princeton. Dewdney was not instructed to assess the proposed railway's value as a link to the Boundary and Kootenay Districts, regions known to be rich in potential through freight traffic. Several years later Dewdney expressed the viewpoint a railway line between Hope and Princeton would be quite feasible if the existing CPR mainline between the coast and Spences Bridge was used and a new line built from Spences Bridge via the Nicola and Similkameen Rivers, effectively going around the Hope Mountains rather than across them.

20. British Columbia Statutes 1902, Chapter 9.

21. *Victoria Colonist*, 1902-11-26.

22. *Kaslo Kootenaian*, 1903-06-04.

Chapter 4: The Race for Republic

1. An interesting challenge to this law came in 1971 when the provincially chartered Kootenay & Elk Railway sought to avoid federal jurisdiction while still connecting with the Great Northern Railway near Crows Nest Pass by proposing to leave a half-inch gap between its own rails and those of the GN at the international boundary. The challenge was rejected.

2. The author noted one legal document relating to the railway that actually referred to the corporation as the "Hot Air Railroad."

3. The Kettle Valley Lines had three locomotives. Engine 1 was a second-hand 4-4-0 delivered in October 1901. Engines 2 and 3 were twin 4-6-0s delivered in February 1902. The author was unable to determine any other information about these locomotives.

4. *Vancouver Province*, 1902-02-21.

5. *Vancouver Province*, 1902-10-29.

6. Despite many years of effort, the KRVR was never able to obtain a diamond crossing across the CPR at Cuprum. A wye on the north side of the CPR tracks and a double semaphore were added at Cuprum to enable trains from Republic to reach downtown Grand Forks, but in so doing they were forced to run over a portion of the CPR. This procedure continued until the KRVR track into downtown was abandoned.

7. The KRVR station was the first railway station built within the City of Grand Forks. When the CPR built through the area in 1899 it had not entered the city because it could not secure right-of-way on terms the corporation considered satisfactory. Instead, the CPR bypassed Grand Forks by keeping its line on the south side of the Kettle River and establishing a station at Columbia, a mile west of Grand Forks. After the KRVR line through Grand Forks was abandoned, the Columbia station was renamed Grand Forks.

8. A ninth name was added in 1911 when the Kettle River Valley Railway was legally renamed the Kettle Valley Railway during the period of construction westward from Midway. In time the entire rail line across southern British Columbia, including the continuation of the railway into Alberta east to Medicine Hat, became popularly known as the Kettle Valley Railway or the Kettle Valley Line. Numerous sources, including official government documents and maps, have identified the Kootenay and Alberta rail lines as such. It should be recognized that legally the Kettle Valley Railway was only that section of trackage from Midway west to Hope, including branch lines, and the limited trackage on the Canadian side of the international boundary near Grand Forks. Similarly the Kettle Valley Lines had a distinct corporate definition quite different from the generally conceived notion of the Kettle Valley Line.

Chapter 5: Makeshift & Visionary

1. Robert Wood was not the first to suggest connecting Midway with Vernon. Both the CPR and an American syndicate had examined the possibilities of building between the two communities. In 1898 the American syndicate announced it would apply for a charter, but withdrew the request before the government could discuss the application.

2. British Columbia Statutes 1902, Chapter 45.

3. The M&V grading near Vernon remained as three separate cuts in the rocky

bench land at the northwest end of Kalamalka Lake, midway up the hillside between the CN tracks and Highway 97. The best location to see the grade is from the A.E. Ashcroft memorial at the viewpoint on Highway 97 just south of Vernon. Likely the grade will not last long, owing to the steady encroachment of housing development into the area.

4.   *Boundary Creek Times*, 1905-10-27.

5.   Details of the M&V grade at Midway are given in the notes to Chapter 9.

Chapter 6: Steel Trail to Nicola

1.   The CPR Annual Report for 1893 states the company had leased the Nicola Valley Railway, but there is no statutory record of such a lease being granted. This report is the only evidence to suggest the CPR was behind the Nicola Valley Railway.

2.   The CPR lease of the NK&S took effect November 16, 1905.

3.   *Vancouver Province*, 1905-09-18.

4.   The contract was let to the firm of Loss, Macdonell & Company, which subcontracted most of the work. A number of newspapers at the time incorrectly reported the contract had been awarded to the Atlantic Construction Company.

5.   *Nicola Herald*, 1905-10-12.

6.   A short siding had been built at Spences Bridge in September 1905 to store cars of supplies that were being unloaded, and this trackage was utilized as the first part of the rail line to Nicola. However, it was not until January 1906 that full-scale tracklaying began. CPR locomotive 25 had been regularly assigned to the *Sockeye Limited* passenger train on the CPR's Vancouver & Lulu Island Railway line between Vancouver and Steveston but was rendered surplus when the line was leased to the British Columbia Electric Railway and electrified for interurban use. Engine 25 became engine 89 under the CPR 1912 Series III numbering scheme with which rail historians are generally most familiar.

7.   Stations and passing tracks on the Nicola Valley line were at Clapperton, Dot, Canford, Coyle, Coutlee, Merritt and Nicola. An additional passenger flagstop was established at Agate, midway between Clapperton and Dot. Clapperton was named after John Clapperton (1835-1913), who filed the first pre-emption in the Nicola Valley. CPR files record Agate as being named after E.T. Agate, district engineer for the CPR at the time, but the local creek had been named Agate Creek prior to the railway's arrival. Likely the CPR chose to honour one of its officials with a name already known locally. Dot was named after Dalton "Dot" Pemberthy Marpole (1880-1908), son of CPR official Richard Marpole. "Dot" owned a ranch at the station site and died there in a tragic fire early in 1908. Canford assumed the same name given the

location some years before by local resident Theophilus Hardiman after his birthplace at Canford Manor in Bournemouth, England. The station at Lower Nicola was named Coyle, after Edward James Coyle (1870-1949), the CPR's assistant passenger agent at Vancouver at the time, to avoid confusion with Nicola (sometimes called Upper Nicola) at the end of the line. Coutlee was named after Alexander Coutlee (ca.1826-1901), a local rancher. His son, Alexander Coutlee (1862-1938), owned and operated the hotel at the time of the railway's arrival. Merritt was named after William Hamilton Merritt (1855-1918), one of the NK&S promoters. Merritt's grandfather and cousin also had the same name; often they have been confused in documents and publications.

8.   Regular service on the Nicola Branch had been scheduled to begin April 1, 1907 but a heavy rainstorm caused slides and washouts that delayed the first train until April 3.

9.   Merritt's first station building remained in service until 1912, when replaced by a new station that served the community until its closure in 1988. In 1995 the station was relocated to Canford where attempts have been made to preserve it. As of 2002, the freight shed originally behind the station remained on site. One old railroader informed the author the cut stone foundations of this structure were salvaged from the first station.

10. *Nicola Herald*, 1908-06-25.

11. The roundhouse at Nicola was destroyed by fire on June 6, 1912 and was never rebuilt. The station was closed January 2, 1926 and demolished in 1945. Rails on the "Nicola Spur" between Merritt and Nicola were pulled up in 1980, 11 years before rails on the line between Spences Bridge and Penticton were removed.

Chapter 7: The Battle of Midway—and Elsewhere

1.   Dominion Statutes 1905, Chapter 172.

2.   *Victoria Colonist*, 1905-01-15.

3.   *Vancouver Province*, 1905-09-29.

4.   *Vancouver Province*, 1905-09-29.

5.   *Victoria Colonist*, 1905-11-02.

6.   *Vancouver Province*, 1905-11-18.

7.   *Vancouver Province*, 1905-11-18.

8.   As quoted in Boundary Historical Society, *Report No. 1*, page 24.

9.   For years GN train crews referred to the nearby spur on the VV&E line as "Hooligan Siding."

10. *The Canadian Annual Review of Public Affairs*, 1907, page 153.

11. The proposed VV&E tunnel was reported by the press to be seven and a half miles in length, with a maximum elevation of 2,915 feet and grades of 1.0%

against westbound traffic leading up to the tunnel and 2.0% against east-bound traffic. The proposed tunnel was under Railroad Pass, more or less along the route of one of the Dewdney surveys in 1901. It is difficult to determine how serious Hill was about building the tunnel in the near future. Hill was a firm believer in well-constructed railways and had considerable engineering study of the tunnel proposal done, but he was always prepared to spend much more than other railway managers in preparatory analysis of possible projects, so this fact alone provides little evidence. Hill was aware Shaughnessy was coming to British Columbia to talk with McBride in September 1909 so his announcement earlier that same month might have been made in hope of convincing McBride not to write off the VV&E as a potential player in building a railway across the Hope Mountains. The fact Hill kept surveyors at work on the original line even as he publicly talked about the tunnel and then "postponed" the proposal shortly after McBride won the November 1909 provincial election is strongly suggestive the tunnel had more political purpose than practical probability. R.G. Harvey, in his book *Carving the Western Path* (Heritage House Publishing, 1998) offers the opinion this was the proper route for a railway across the Hope Mountains, not the Coquihalla Pass route built by the KVR. While the history of rail-roading in southern British Columbia might well have been very different had the tunnel been built, any honest critique of early decision makers has to be tempered with knowledge of the realities of their times. The longest rail-way tunnel in Canada in 1909 was just over 3,000 feet long, less than 10% the length of the tunnel Hill was suggesting, and tunnel-driving methods, while advanced from earlier techniques, were still only capable of advancing 10 to 15 feet per day. Moreover, the tunnel would have had to be electrified at further expense. Shaughnessy scoffed at the tunnel proposal, saying that all the mining trade of southern British Columbia could not justify its cost. The author offers his own opinion on alternatives in Chapter 15.

12. The station built by the VV&E at Princeton was turned over to the KVR in 1921.

13. The Abbotsford-Hope section was contracted to Pat Welch of Spokane on January 13, 1910. The Princeton-Tulameen contract was let to J.W. Stewart & Company the following day.

Chapter 8: Disciples of Destiny

1. Neither Crown Trust (the successor of Trusts & Guarantee Company) nor the CPR has any record of the meeting between Shaughnessy and Warren aboard the *Empress of Britain* in April 1908. The author learned of this meeting and the discussions that took place from a personal interview in 1970 with Charles Gordon, who as a young man accompanied Shaughnessy on

this trip as his private secretary. Despite the absence of formal records, the fact both men were aboard the ship during the voyage is strong evidence to support Gordon's statement that this was when the introductory meeting between Shaughnessy and Warren took place.

2. Richard Arthur Henderson (1877-1917). Henderson Creek, a tributary to Boundary Creek near Greenwood, is named after this man. He was killed in military service during World War I.

3. *Victoria Colonist*, 1908-10-02.

4. Remains of the brigade trail were plainly visible on the south side of the Coquihalla River at mile 27.2 of the Coquihalla Subdivision rail line, between Iago and Romeo, until 1980, when a logging company thoughtlessly destroyed the trail in the process of creating a logging road.

5. Sandford Fleming, *Report on Surveys and Preliminary Operations of the Canadian Pacific Railway up to 1877* (Ottawa, MacLean, Rogers & Co. 1877), page 21.

6. *Victoria Colonist*, 1909-09-21.

7. *Vancouver Province*, 1910-03-02.

8. John G. Sullivan, former chief engineer of the CPR, in a letter to Andrew McCulloch dated 1937-03-02, in which Sullivan relates his memories of earlier days.

9. Okanagan Historical Society, *13th Report*, 1949, page 71.

10. Andrew McCulloch Diary, 1890-04-14. McCulloch's younger daughter, Ruth, preserved the diaries. She in turn willed them to the author prior to her death in 1981.

11. Tom Crump, a CPR official based at Field in 1905 and father of a later CPR president, repeatedly insisted it was Andrew McCulloch who conceived the Spiral Tunnels, not John Schwitzer, the man traditionally credited. When asked about the matter some 30 years later, McCulloch declined to either confirm or deny Crump's assertion, saying only that large projects invariably involve the contributions of many people. This response was hardly surprising from McCulloch, who was highly modest about all of his life's accomplishments. Unfortunately, Schwitzer died shortly after the Spiral Tunnels project was completed and his views on the controversy are unknown, if he was aware of the controversy at all.

12. By coincidence the Andrew McCulloch of the Kettle Valley Railway was not the only Andrew McCulloch to make a significant contribution to southern British Columbia history. Andrew Lake McCulloch (1865-1940) was a pioneer hydraulic engineer who designed and built many of the waterworks systems within southern interior communities. Although the two men were unrelated, they had met on several occasions and were friends.

Chapter 9: Bridging the Gap

1. John W. Dafoe, *Clifford Sifton in Relations to his Times* (Toronto, MacMillan Company of Canada, 1931), page 263.

2. The M&V grade began about 1.5 miles west of the CPR station at Midway and continued 9.5 miles to a point near Rock Creek, with the exception of a short section of right-of-way that had not yet been acquired when work on the railway stopped in 1905. In October 1905, the CPR extended its trackage for 2.5 miles west of Midway station, thus creating a parallel grade to the south of the M&V grade for about one mile. When the KVR commenced work in 1910, it merely graded a short section of roadbed to connect the end of the CPR track with the M&V grade and then used the existing M&V grade westward. For many years the mile of original M&V grade could be seen 100 feet north of the abandoned CPR grade, westward from the entrance roadway to the Pope & Talbot sawmill, but more recently most of the grade has been destroyed.

3. Tuzo Creek, a tributary to the West Fork of the Kettle River, was named after this man. In the first edition of *McCulloch's Wonder* the author stated this creek was named as a war memorial to Tuzo, one of the first KVR employees to enlist in World War I. The author has since learned the name was assigned to the creek before 1914.

4. For a short time the KVR had an office in Vancouver in the Carter-Cotton Building. It was closed when the KVR's permanent headquarters were opened in Penticton.

5. Edmund Ernest Coley (1864-1946). Coley Creek near Brookmere was named in recognition of Coley's work with the KVR.

6. In 1938 McCulloch wrote an article titled "Railway Development in Southern British Columbia from 1890 On." This article was based on McCulloch's memories of KVR construction and his diary notes, and has since been reproduced in a number of publications, most notably the Boundary Historical Report of 1964. In his article McCulloch records that the first contract was awarded July 5, not June 30 as noted in this book. The July date was actually the date McCulloch received word the contract had been awarded by Warren six days earlier.

7. The company principals were James Alexander Macdonell (1861-1918) and Casimir Stanislaus Gzowski III (1876-1940). Macdonell had also been a principal of Loss, Macdonell & Company, which had contracted construction of the Nicola Branch between 1905 and 1907. Gzowski's grandfather, of the same name, had been a major canal builder in eastern Canada and was one of the founders of what is now the Engineering Institute of Canada. The work on this section was further subcontracted to other companies and individuals.

8. During July and August of 1909 a small amount of clearing work was done to prepare the M&V roadbed. Strictly speaking, this was the first work done by the KVR on the Midway-Merritt line.

9. *Merritt Herald*, 1910-07-22. The labourers were mostly Scandinavians (Swedes, Norwegians, Danes), central Europeans (Italians, Bulgarians) and Slavs. There were few English, Canadian or Americans labourers, although Scottish and Italian stonemasons were used in the more skilled work of constructing retaining walls and bridge foundations. There were virtually no Chinese or Japanese labourers because of the Asiatic exclusion laws in effect at the time. Early railway labourers in the United States were called "navvies" and post-1960 publications about Canadian railway construction frequently use this term in reference to Canadian railway labourers. However, the author found the term navvy rarely used in original documents related to the railway construction of that era. The term "labourer/laborer" was more common.

10. The railway yard on Fairview Road was originally named South Penticton to distinguish it from Penticton station on the lakeshore of Okanagan Lake. As the community of Penticton expanded, the distinction between the two locations became less apparent. In 1941, when the lakeshore station was closed, the yard and new station were renamed Penticton.

11. Andrew McCulloch Diary, 1910-12-14.

12. Early in November 1910 R.J. Mancantelli, the local secretary for the KVR, drove down a spike in Merritt yard, which officially represented the start of track work. However, no other rail work was done until the first rail was laid on December 17, 1910.

13. CPR locomotive 496 retained its same number in the general CPR Series III renumbering that started in 1912. Since the Series III numbering scheme, which continued until the end of steam in 1960, is the numbering scheme most students of CPR motive power are familiar with, the author has noted the number changes of any locomotives mentioned.

14. William Anstie Gourlay (1882-1937).

15. CPR 4-4-0 locomotive 149 was renumbered 101 in October 1913.

16. CPR 2-8-0 locomotive 1284 was renumbered 3034 in September 1912.

17. The *Merritt Herald* issue of 1911-06-16 reported the KVR was operating two locomotives at Merritt. CPR records show no CPR engine other than 1284 assigned to the KVR at that time and the author was unable to find any other reports of a second locomotive.

18. CPR 2-8-0 locomotive 1330 was renumbered 3130 in September 1912. It was in service on the KVR from August to November 1911 only.

19. The station name was later shortened to Glenwalker. The man for whom it was named was probably Edward George Walker but the author could not determine any additional information about him.

20. Delbert "Dell" King (1870-1953).
21. Andrew McCulloch Diary, 1911-11-29.
22. *Vancouver Province*, 1912-03-04.
23. The author was unable to determine the identity of this locomotive but it was likely the Kettle Valley Lines 2. The volume of traffic on the Grand Forks-Republic line certainly did not justify retaining two locomotives at Grand Forks.
24. Passing tracks on the Midway-Carmi section were constructed at Rock Creek, Zamora, Rhone, Taurus, Beaverdell and Carmi. Flag stops were also established at Kettle Valley, Westbridge and Sawyer (mile 48.8). Rock Creek was named after the local community of that name. Zamora and Rhone were named after the Spanish province and French river respectively. The area around Rhone had been unofficially called Frenchtown, which likely had some influence on the naming. Taurus was originally named Bull Creek but it was thought confusion might arise with Bull River on the CPR Windermere Subdivision near Fort Steele so an appropriate alternate name—the astrological sign of the bull—was adopted. Beaverdell and Carmi had both been named prior to the KVR's arrival. Beaverdell was a combination of two existing hamlets, Beaverton and Randell, and Carmi the Carmi mining claim, staked by prospector James Dale, who named it for his hometown of Carmi, Illinois. In later years a wye was built at mile 34.4 for turning snowplows used eastward from Penticton to the point in the Kettle Valley where snow levels usually eased. The wye location was named Dellwye, a combination of Beaverdell and wye.
25. *Summerland Review*, 1911-06-03.
26. The CPR bridge over Stoney Creek near Rogers Pass and the bridge over Deep Creek on the BCR north of Williams Lake are both somewhat higher than Trout Creek Bridge.
27. In earlier editions of *McCulloch's Wonder* the author reported the contract was let to L.M. Rice & Company. This error resulted from a document listing G.A. Carlson & Company as a subcontractor on the work when in fact it was the main contractor.
28. A CPR locomotive was in use at Merritt for a short time starting in May 1912, but the author was not able to determine its identity.
29. CPR 4-4-0 locomotive 131 was renumbered 84 in April 1913.
30. The locomotives received in July 1912 were numbered KVR 1, 2, 3 and 4. Locomotives 1 and 2 were twin Alco 4-6-0s (serial numbers 29786 and 29787) built in June 1904 for the Newton & Northwestern Railway. Locomotive 3 was a 2-6-0. Locomotive 4 was a 4-6-0 built by the Schenectady Locomotive Works sometime in the 1880s or 1890s. The author was unable to determine any other information. It appears that initially locomotives 1

and 2 went to Merritt and 3 and 4 went to Midway.

31. The route change was actually made shortly after the contracts had been awarded. Although contractor Grant Smith & Company had not yet begun work and the unit prices in the contract were not affected by the route change, Grant Smith & Company later sued the KVR for $600,000 for losses allegedly sustained on the project. The suit was settled out of court for $235,000 in 1917.

32. Despite the official announcement of the route change, McCulloch continued to assign surveyors to the route of Carry's preliminary survey and no construction contracts were awarded for well over a year. This is evidence the KVR was not resolutely committed to the new route. Probably the KVR was willing to commit itself only if it could use the VV&E tracks west of Princeton. If the KVR could not use the VV&E it would likely have stayed with the original route rather than build a second—and very expensive— railway line through the rugged Tulameen River canyon. The announcement may have been solely to test if a compromise with Hill was possible.

Chapter 10: Death Duel at Coquihalla Pass

1. *Phoenix Pioneer*, 1910-10-01.
2. *Similkameen Star*, 1910-08-03.
3. *Similkameen Star*, 1910-11-23.
4. James Henry Kennedy (1852-1927).
5. The entire VV&E-W&GN route from the Columbia River to the coast had a maximum grade of 1.25% against westbound traffic, a remarkably low grade considering the difficult terrain. The CPR-KVR route from the Columbia River westbound had some 65 miles of ascending grade exceeding this amount.
6. Sumas Lake no longer exists, the lakebed having been reclaimed as farmland. The remains of the abandoned VV&E roadbed along the slope of Sumas Mountain are still plainly visible in several places.
7. The GN also sold to the Canadian Northern Pacific part of its New Westminster Southern Railway from the New Westminster Bridge to a point east of Port Mann, as the GN had built a replacement line through Delta and along Semiahmoo Bay, which opened in March 1909. The original informal agreement was not formalized until November 6, 1915. A copy appears in Dominion Statutes 1917, Chapter 59.
8. The BRC would not allow the rail line between Princeton and Coalmont to be opened for regular service until a telegraph line had been built, and regular operations did not begin until May 1, 1912.
9. There is no evidence the CPR ever seriously considered the KVR as a permanent alternative to its original mainline, as the route was both longer and had

more adverse grades. In 1912 the CPR investigated constructing a railway from Grand Forks south to the Spokane International to bypass the heavy grades west of Robson and the gap in trackage along Kootenay Lake, but the company declined this route. Electrification of the railway was quite seriously considered for a time but this idea was dropped during the hard times of World War 1.

10. G.A. Mountain in a letter to the BRC Chief Commissioner, 1912-03-06. Canadian Transport Commission files, Ottawa.

11. *Similkameen Star*, 1912-02-07.

12. A.T. Kerr in a letter to G.A. Mountain, 1912-11-20. Canadian Transport Commission files, Ottawa.

13. *Similkameen Star*, 1912-07-24.

14. *Similkameen Star*, 1913-04-18.

15. The agreement between Warren and Gilman was only informal and it was revised several times before it was formally signed on November 20, 1913. A copy appears in Dominion Statutes 1914, Chapter 92.

16. *Vancouver Province*, 1913-08-07.

17. In actuality only 12 tunnels were constructed. Tunnel 4, planned at mile 21.4, was started but was made into an open cut instead. With Tunnel 4 eliminated, Tunnels 5 through 9 were renumbered 4 through 8 respectively. Tunnels 10 through 13, already having been started when the original Tunnel 4 was cancelled, were not renumbered. Thus there was no Tunnel 9 on the Coquihalla railway.

18. Vaughan, page 348.

19. Vaughan, page 347.

20. O.D. Skelton, *The Life and Letters of Sir Wilfrid Laurier* (Toronto, McClelland & Stewart, 1965), page 138.

Chapter 11: The Dream Fulfilled

1. The locomotive delivered to Penticton on December 20, 1912 was KVR 1, transferred from Merritt.

2. The locomotive delivered to Penticton on March 27, 1913 was probably KVR 2.

3. The CPR lakeboat *Kaleden* was designated exclusively for the purpose of hauling explosives from Okanagan Landing.

4. Ted Logie, *Ted Tells Tales: True Stories from our Okanagan Pioneers* (Penticton, Penticton Herald Press, 1967), page 61.

5. Many railway construction workers disparagingly said the initials IWW really meant "I Won't Work."

6. G.R. Stevens, *Canadian National Railways* (Vancouver, Clarke, Irwin & Co., 1962), Volume 2, page 63.

7. Work trains had travelled over the bridge earlier in the week.

8. Records show only four CPR locomotives delivered to the KVR in 1913: 3000, 3120, 3121 and 3122. Two more locomotives, 3111 and 3115, were delivered in early 1914. All were 2-8-0s.

9. On the Penticton-Osprey Lake section, passing tracks were built at Winslow, West Summerland, Faulder, Kirton, Thirsk and Osprey Lake. Winslow was named after Roy Maywood Winslow, of the Provincial Department of Agriculture, who was then primarily responsible for the establishment of the Summerland Experimental Farm. Faulder was named after Evelyn Robert Faulder (1872-1940), an immigrant who settled there in 1891. Kirton was an aberrant name derived from the first part of the name of James Kirkpatrick, the first KVR agent at Penticton and later reeve of that community, and the last part of the name Penticton. Thirsk was named after the Thirsk district in Great Britain. Osprey Lake was named after the lake of the same name although the station was actually about a mile east of Osprey Lake. Flag stops were later added at Crump (mile 20.2) and Demuth (mile 27.6). Crump was named after Thomas Huntley Crump (1871-1964), KVR superintendent from 1925 to 1935 and the father of Norris Crump, a later CPR president. Demuth was named after John Frederick Demuth (1861-1932), KVR motive power superintendent. Water tanks were constructed at mile 20.9 (Twenty Mile Tank), mile 29.5 (Thirty Mile Tank) and Osprey Lake. A wye was built at Kirton for turning helper engines at the point where the 2.2% ruling grade reduced to 1.0%. A wye was also built at Osprey Lake for use during construction but this was removed not long after the railway opened in 1915.

10. One of the locomotives was CPR 2-8-0 3000. The author could not determine the identity of the other locomotive but it would have been one of the three noted in note 8.

11. John "Jack" Crosby was fatally injured in the derailment of Train 11, engine 3206, just east of Beaverdell on November 26, 1924.

12. This train service ran once per week between Grand Forks and Carmi under train orders of the Spokane & British Columbia Railway. Presumably this indicated the service was being run with Kettle Valley Lines locomotives, although neither S&BC nor KVL had formal trackage rights to operate over the CPR between Grand Forks and Midway, nor for that matter did the S&BC even have any legal existence in Canada.

13. Passing tracks on the Carmi-Hydraulic Lake section were built at Lakevale, Cookson and McCulloch. Lakevale was originally named Arlington Lakes because of its proximity to the lake of that name but confusion resulted between it and Arlington Station on the E&N so the name was changed to Lakevale. Cookson was named after Wilfred Cookson (1861-1944), a pioneer who owned a ranch on nearby Kallis Creek. McCulloch was renamed from

Hydraulic Lake after the KVR chief engineer. Water tanks were built at Carmi, Lakevale and McCulloch. A coal tower was built at Carmi, although not until some years after completion of the railway. A flagstop and short siding at mile 54.2 was named Lois, probably after the daughter of a tracklaying foreman.

14. The lease agreement concerned only the Kettle Valley Railway, not the Kettle Valley Lines or the Spokane & British Columbia Railway. Thus the CPR never controlled the American portion of the Kettle Valley Lines system.

15. In 1921 the KVR bridge at Grand Forks was damaged by high water and the CPR declined to repair the damage. Instead it commenced operating passenger trains into the Grand Forks "City Station" from the west end only, eastbound trains heading in and westbound trains backing in. This awkward procedure continued until 1952, when the CPR again reverted to using its original station at Columbia, which it then renamed Grand Forks.

16. A copy of this agreement appears in Dominion Statutes 1916, Chapter 45.

17. For a time, the railway operated a demonstration farm called the Kettle Valley Railway Farm on a piece of expropriated property on Westminster Avenue to encourage diversification of the Okanagan agricultural industry. The farm was sold when the research station at Winslow took over the agricultural research function.

18. Passing tracks on the Hydraulic Lake-Penticton section were built at Myra, Ruth, Lorna, Chute Lake, Adra, Glen Fir and Arawana. Myra, the first of the three "daughter stations," was named after Myra Newman, the daughter of tracklaying foreman J.L. Newman. Ruth was originally named Kelowna Siding because of its proximity to Kelowna, but confusion in waybills resulted in the name quickly being changed. The new name of Ruth was chosen after Ruth Eloise McCulloch (1910-1981), the younger daughter of Andrew McCulloch. Lorna was named after Lorna Edith Warren (1906-1934), youngest daughter of J.J. Warren. Chute Lake was named after the lake of that name, which in turn had been named for the creek resembling a chute or waterfall in its rapid drop to Okanagan Lake. Adra was probably named after the seaport town in Spain of that name, but the reason for the choice is not known; possibly it was named after another daughter of a KVR employee. Glen Fir, named after the groves of fir trees in the area, was later shortened to the single word name Glenfir. Arawana was originally named Naramata Siding because of its proximity to Naramata but confusion in waybills between boat and rail service resulted in the siding being renamed Arawana. There is some evidence the name was chosen after a popular song of the period, Aeeah Wannah; alternately it may have simply been a rearranging of the letters of the name Naramata with a "w" added for Warren or the "m" in Naramata turned upside down. Often a station being renamed received a new

name from the rearranged letters of the original name, such as Sullivan station on the CNR near Kamloops being renamed Vinsulla. Water tanks were built at mile 86.8 in Myra Canyon, mile 96.7 near Lorna, Chute Lake, Adra and Arawana. Wyes for turning helper engines and snowplows were built at McCulloch and Chute Lake.

19. Louis Henry "Harry" Brooks (1857-1916). Following his death at Coalmont in July 1916, the body of Harry Brooks was brought by train from Coalmont and buried on top of the knoll above the water tower in Brookmere. The citizens of Brookmere still tend his grave.

20. Passing tracks on the VV&E between Tulameen and Brookmere were constructed at Manning, Canyon and Koyl. Manning was named by the VV&E after a local pioneer, William Manning. The KVR first chose to name this station Manion, after another local pioneer, Michael Manion, but later adopted the VV&E's chosen name. Canyon was named by the VV&E after Canyon House, the name given the stage stop at the base of the canyon on Otter Creek on the original road between Merritt and Princeton. The KVR called this station Roberts, after Alonzo Buragard Roberts (1860-1955), a local homesteader. Both railways renamed the station Thalia. One record states the name was chosen after the daughter of a GN official, but perhaps it was named after the Greek goddess of poetry because of McCulloch's love of poetry. Koyl was also quickly renamed when confusion between it and Coyle station below Merritt was encountered. The new name chosen was Spearing, after Gustavus Spearing, a trapper in the Otter Valley. A flagstop was also established between Manning and Thalia named Myren, after Gahr Pederson Myren (1858-1932), another early settler in the area.

21. *Similkameen Star*, 1915-04-23.

22. Passing tracks on the Osprey Lake-Princeton section were built at Jellicoe, Erris, Jura and Belfort. Jellicoe station was originally named Usk but it was discovered the GTP had already used this name for a station near Terrace and the government ordered the KVR to rename its station. The new name chosen was Jellicoe after John Jellicoe, the British admiral who distinguished himself at the Battle of Jutland in June 1916. Erris was named after the mountain of the same name in Ireland. Belfort was named after the famous French garrison in the Jura Mountains that stubbornly resisted the German invasion of 1870. Both Belfort and Jura seemed appropriate names for patriotic-conscious Canada at the time. Water tanks were built at mile 50.2 (Fifty Mile Tank) and at Jura. A wye was built at Jura for turning helper engines at the point where the 2.2% grade slackened to 1.0%.

23. *Penticton Herald*, 1915-06-03.

24. The four KVR locomotives were relegated to use in construction of the Coquihalla Pass line and work train service until about 1917, when it is

believed they were scrapped. The 3100 was scrapped after a spectacular accident in Merritt on June 22, 1916. A special silk train for eastern Canada, headed by locomotive 522, had been diverted over the KVR from Spences Bridge as a result of a washout on the mainline near Field. A track crew at Merritt, unaware of the special train, opened the switch to the siding where the 3100 waited, and the 522 ran into the 3100 at considerable speed. This was the only silk train known to have operated over the KVR and one of the few such trains in Canada ever involved in an accident.

25. N. Thompson and J.H. Edgar, *Canadian Railway Development from the Earliest Times* (Toronto, Macmillan Company of Canada, 1933), page 313.

26. The name Quintette Tunnels was adopted even though there were actually only four tunnels because the tunnel at Mile 49.65 was "daylighted" on a portion of its north side, creating the illusion of a fifth tunnel.

27. Thompson and Edgar, page 313.

28. The snowfall record set in the winter of 1915-16 remained intact for all the years the railway operated through Coquihalla Pass.

29. Skelton, page 114.

30. Board of Railway Commissioners records show the GN had applied to build its roundhouse and turntable at Hope on a site on the south side of the CN tracks just east of what is now Third Avenue. Several old railroaders with whom the author spoke stated the GN roundhouse was at the end of the wye about 1,000 feet to the east. Physical evidence suggests the latter was correct.

31. The original station at Brookmere was destroyed by fire January 30, 1917 and was replaced by a new station that remained in service until 1966. The roundhouse at Brookmere was enlarged to four stalls during the busy times of World War II but was destroyed on March 21, 1949 when locomotive 907 blew its boiler inside the roundhouse. A replacement four-stall roundhouse was built, which survived until 1970 when it was sold to a local resident who disassembled it over the next two years for salvage of the heavy timbers.

32. The GN had discontinued its twice-weekly mixed train between Princeton and Coalmont when the KVR inaugurated service over the line in May 1915 and only a limited numbers of GN freight trains operated west of Princeton after that time, mostly to pick up coal from Coalmont or ice from Otter Lake. There is no record of any GN trains operating west of Tulameen after September 1916. The GN roundhouse at Hope was destroyed by fire not long after being built. The turntable at Hope was removed in 1919 when GN ceased operating the tri-weekly mixed train it had inaugurated between Abbotsford and Hope.

33. "The Loop" was renamed Mons Junction in 1915 after the celebrated World War I battlesite, but it retained this name only briefly. The PGE had already named one of its stations Mons and the KVR renamed the station Brodie

after Harry Walter Brodie (1874-1955), the CPR general passenger agent at Vancouver at the time. The junction with the CPR mainline west of Hope was originally named Petain after the French Army hero of World War I, but it was renamed Odlum in September 1940 when Petain sided with the pro-Nazi Vichy government in France. Odlum was named after Victor Wentworth Odlum (1880-1971), commander of Canada's overseas forces at the time. Water tanks were built at Juliet, Coquihalla, Iago and Jessica. Later, a water tower was built at Lear to replace the one at Jessica. A coal tower was also later built at Iago. Wyes were built at Coquihalla and Portia. The Portia wye was used primarily for turning snowplows operating between there and Coquihalla, where snow conditions were most severe.

34. The most commonly repeated story is that McCulloch was influenced into naming the stations after Shakespearian characters by his daughter, who was studying Shakespeare at university. McCulloch's daughter Ruth was only six years old at the time, much too young to attend university or have such a commanding influence on her father.

35. *Victoria Colonist*, 1916-09-17.

36. The author was unable to find any documents recording the total cost of the KVR's construction, but based on partial figures available, it was probably about $20 million in the dollars of the days. There is no record of what the project was originally estimated to cost, if any estimate was even done. The author was able to verify the deaths of 39 workers killed in accidents during the railway's construction: 3 on the Nicola Branch, 17 on the Merritt-Midway line, 1 on the VV&E between Princeton and Brookmere later sold to the CPR, and 18 on the Coquihalla line. An additional 3 were killed during construction of the Copper Mountain branch. These figures do not include those who died of heart attacks, illness or other medical causes while on construction work. Since many records are incomplete, the actual number of people killed during construction is undoubtedly greater.

Chapter 12: Steel Rails and Iron Men

1. The early operational organizational structure of the KVR is difficult to determine with certainty. When the railway opened, O.E. Fisher was officially superintendent but evidence suggests he was rarely in Penticton and it is clear Warren passed many of the operational responsibilities onto McCulloch, who he had come to trust. In July 1917 J.W. Mulhern became superintendent and for a time McCulloch was able to concentrate on the engineering of the Copper Mountain line. In December 1918 McCulloch officially became superintendent. In February 1919 he became general superintendent but also retained his position as chief engineer.

2. Augusto Taylor Hayden died in Merritt hospital November 8 from injuries

sustained in the rockslide. The accident location at mile 21.4 Coquihalla Subdivision became known as "Hayden's Cut."

3. Midway, although technically a CPR divisional point, was never granted the customary status of such a designation. It never had either roundhouse or coal chute and crews were not based there. The CPR had a roundhouse at Grand Forks, which it shared with KVL engines operating on the North Fork line or to Republic, and this served the needs for engines operating on the Boundary Subdivision between Nelson and Midway. Crews from Nelson stopped at Grand Forks and crews based at Grand Forks made a quick run to Midway and back. Coal chutes for locomotives were provided at Grand Forks and Carmi, not Midway. If locomotives needed coal at Midway the coal had to be shovelled into the tender by hand. Only in later years, following absorption of the KVR into the CPR, did train crews run straight through from Nelson to Midway.

4. The GN surveyed a line to Copper Mountain in 1905, but its survey followed Wolfe Creek, not the Similkameen River as did the KVR.

5. A water tower and turntable were built at Copper Mountain. A one-stall train shed and turntable were built at Allenby. Allenby was named after the British general who had recaptured Palestine from the Germans and Turks during World War I.

6. Not all the Republic line trackage was removed. The track from Cuprum to the crossing with the GN was left in place and a junction track constructed so the CPR and GN could interchange freight cars. Ironically, the first piece of track on the KVR outlasted the track on all of the rest of the KVR with the exception of a few miles in Summerland saved for a heritage railway.

7. *Princeton Star*, 1919-08-01.

8. *Princeton Star*, 1919-12-05.

9. The United Empire Colliery, Princeton Coal & Land Company, Tulameen Collieries, Pleasant Valley Mining Company and the Princeton-Tulameen Coal Company all had rail spurs. An excellent history of the Princeton coal mines can be found in Geological Survey of Canada, Memoir 243.

10. Passing tracks on the original line to Oliver were at Okanagan Falls, McIntyre, Oliver and Haynes. Okanagan Falls was named after the falls at the outlet of Skaha Lake, later destroyed as a result of flood control measures. McIntyre was named after Peter McIntyre (1835-1925), who settled at the base of the bluff there in 1886. Oliver was named after John Oliver (1856-1927), premier of the province from 1918 to 1927. Haynes, then the end of track, was named after John Carmichael Haynes (1829-1888), an early county court judge of the region. A wye was built at Haynes.

11. Andrew McCulloch Diary, 1925-06-16.

12. Engine 3401 crashed slightly away from the rest of the wreckage and thus

escaped being destroyed in the fire. It was returned to service after undergoing extensive repairs.

13. The author is reasonably convinced youths Ralph Racklyeft and Bert Walton died in the wreck. The death of any others is conjecture, although numerous possible names have been suggested. Unfortunately, it was quite common at that time for people to go missing and never be heard from again. Newspapers frequently contained heart-wrenching pleas from people seeking information about missing loved ones.

14. In tribute to the four dead railroaders, Francis Whitehouse of Summerland wrote a poem titled "The Coquihalla Wreck" published in 1932 by Ryerson Press. Interestingly, on the Labour Day weekend in 1989, 63 years almost to the day of the 1926 runaway, a transport truck on the new Coquihalla Highway lost its air brakes west of Coquihalla, ran out of control for some 10 miles and crashed in a flaming heap on almost the same spot as the train runaway.

15. *Merritt Herald*, 1930-04-04.

16. *Penticton Herald*, 1939-02-02.

Chapter 13: Coming of Age

1. There was one passing track on the Skaha Lake line, Kaleden.

2. *Penticton Herald*, 1933-03-16. The desk presented McCulloch is now in the Penticton Museum.

3. Warren, in a letter to McCulloch, 1937-02-02.

4. Andrew McCulloch was buried in Penticton cemetery, overlooking the railway he built. A memorial to him was erected in Penticton's Gyro Park in 1959 and another at Midway in 1988.

5. CPR 5134 and 5172 were assigned to the Kettle Valley Division in 1932. N2 class 2-8-0 locomotives in the 3600 series were also introduced and replaced many of the older 3200s and 3400s.

6. The GN tried repeatedly, beginning as early as 1919, to interest the CPR in acquiring the GN's Princeton-Grand Forks line as an alternative to the KVR. The line was about 80 miles shorter and offered superior grades than the KVR. The CPR seriously considered the offers and likely would have accepted them if it had believed it could use the GN line to replace the KVR. The CPR feared it would be unable to get political approval to abandon the KVR and concluded that the operational savings of routing through traffic over the GN line, while significant, would not be enough to support the cost of maintaining two lines.

7. The GN abandoned trackage on the Cloverdale-Sumas and Kilgard-Cannor (now Arnold, just west of Chilliwack) section. The Abbotsford-Kilgard section was sold to Clayburn Brick Company, which operated it privately for a

number of years to connect its brick plant at Kilgard with the CPR at Abbotsford.

8. The KVR had extended the North Fork line about a mile in 1919 to serve the Rock Candy fluorite mine, but the mine did not provide enough traffic to prevent the line's abandonment.

9. The line between Hedley and Keremeos was abandoned in 1955 following closure of the Nickel Plate Mine at Hedley. Service on the line between Oroville and Keremeos was suspended in the spring of 1972 when a bridge washed out and was never restored. The line was later officially abandoned although some of the rails are still in place.

10. Confidential CPR documents indicate the annual payment from the GN was the principal reason the company did not abandon the Coquihalla Subdivision in the 1930s. Another concern was the need to maintain the telegraph and telephone lines through Coquihalla Pass. As well as its own telegraph system, the CPR had allowed the wires of the Trans-Canada telephone system to be strung on its telegraph poles through Coquihalla Pass and would undoubtedly have faced a loss of telephone revenue if the line were not maintained.

11. Just before the train was rescued, efforts were being made in Vancouver to organize the first planned aerial food drop in provincial history. A plane was to fly from Vancouver airport to Brookmere and drop food for the town and passenger train but was cancelled at the last moment.

12. *Penticton Herald*, 1939-03-16.

13. Passing tracks on the Osoyoos extension were located at Ellis and Osoyoos. Ellis was named after Thomas Ellis (1844-1918), a local rancher who earned the nickname "Cattle King of the Okanagan." Osoyoos was named prior to the railway's arrival. A station, wye and coal tower were built at Osoyoos. An extension of the line to connect with the GN at Oroville, four miles away, was suggested, but never constructed.

14. The tunnel was officially called the Tulameen Diversion Tunnel but was more popularly known as Parr Tunnel. A short spur of the original track near the tunnel site was left in place as a spur and was given the name Parr, after Eric H. Parr, an engineer with Wood, Parr & McClay, the contracting firm that subcontracted the tunnel construction from Highway Construction Company.

15. The CPR had assigned 2-10-0s 5761 and 5788 to Penticton for helper service in early 1939, possibly as a test, but left them there when the sudden flood of war traffic hit the railway.

16. The first diesel operated on the Copper Mountain Subdivision on July 5, 1953 and on the Merritt Subdivision on August 18, 1953.

17. The run by 5212, while recorded by several newspapers at the time as the last

run of a steam locomotive on the KVR, was not in actuality the last such run. Several railroaders informed the author that steam locomotives handled Trains 11 or 12 between Vancouver and Brookmere on a few occasions during the fall of 1954 when the assigned diesels were not available. Moreover, CPR dispatch records show that on March 8, 1956 the KVR suffered a bad slide at Portia and CPR 2390, a steam locomotive from the Coquitlam pool, was used for several days on a work train between Hope and the slide. Steam locomotives also operated over the KVR in 1973 for filming of the CBC historical production *The National Dream* and when the provincial museum train travelled from Spences Bridge to Penticton and Osoyoos in 1977 and from Nelson to Midway in 1978.

18. When the CPR introduced its new deluxe passenger train *The Canadian* in April 1955, it was numbered Trains 1 and 2 between Montreal and Vancouver. The Toronto-Sudbury section of *The Canadian* was given numbers 11 and 12, formerly assigned to the KVR trains. KVR trains at that time became Trains 67 and 68. In October 1957 they became Trains 45 and 46.

19. The last day of daily passenger service in both directions on the Carmi Subdivision was Monday February 3, 1958. On Tuesday only Train 45 operated. On Wednesday, February 5, 1958, the date given by the Board of Transport Commissioners as the effective date of the curtailment, no trains were operated.

20. In August 1954 the CPR brought two Budd Cars over the KVR for publicity purposes and they were displayed for several hours at Penticton on their way to Vancouver. Budd Cars did not appear on the KVR again until February 7, 1958 when car 9022 ran from Midway through to Vancouver as a test. On March 3, 1958, CPR 9197 made the first passenger run with Train 45 from Vancouver to Penticton.

21. Board of Transport Commissioners for Canada, *Judgments, Orders, Regulations and Rulings*, Volume 49, page 597.

22. On May 11, 1959 a major portion of Tunnel 4 at mile 22.5 Coquihalla Subdivision collapsed and the railway decided to build a diversion around the tunnel site. The diversion was completed June 22. The new line remained in service only until November, when the entire Coquihalla line was rendered out of commission.

Chapter 14: Curtain Call for Coquihalla

1. Work Extra 8606 leaving Brookmere at 1300 on November 23 and arriving at Hope on November 28 was the last train to traverse the entire length of the Coquihalla rail line. One might argue that because the train had operated over so many temporary detours en route the preceding train really earned the honours of being the last train over the line. Extra 4079 East, engines

4079, 8725, 8714 and 4064, on November 23, 1959 was the last freight train to travel the entire length of the line before disruption. Westbound Train 45, Budd Car 9197, on the evening of November 22 was the last passenger train over the line.

2. The author was able to verify the deaths of 27 people involved with the operation of the Coquihalla rail line. This figure does not include an additional 18 people killed during the line's construction, two operating employees who died of heart attacks while on duty or five transients known to have been killed in falls from trains. The figure also does not include a significant number of people who died in Coquihalla Pass but whose cause of death was not recorded. Some of these may also have been railway employees at work when killed. The final death occurred July 6, 1962 during dismantlement of the line.

3. Tragically, almost all the washouts on the Coquihalla line occurred at trestle sites that had been filled in during the early 1950s as part of line "improvements." Many veterans of the Coquihalla line advised the author they were horrified at the small size of culverts being installed where trestles were to be filled, as the tributary creeks of the Coquihalla were well known to locals to have enormous variations in flow volumes.

4. *Similkameen Spotlight*, 1961-02-22

5. In 1961 track at the Hope end of the line was left in place from just west of the Othello Road crossing, about a half-mile east of the interchange with the CNR at Hope, through to the junction with the mainline at Odlum. This trackage was left in place so that CPR or CNR passenger trains could be diverted onto alternate tracks whenever the Fraser Canyon section of either railway was blocked. In the spring of 1963 the CPR bridge over the Coquihalla River just above the interchange was damaged by high water and the CPR declined to repair the damage. The very short length of track between the interchange and the bridge meant only short trains could be handled, which effectively spelled the end to any interchange movements between the two railways over the Hope Bridge. The CPR continued to operate trains into Hope from the mainline at Odlum for a time thereafter to serve a bulk oil plant, but in 1970 trackage was removed from Hope to the west end of the Hope Bridge. Shortly afterwards, the track between the bridge and Odlum was removed and Odlum ceased to be a station on the CPR system.

6. This date was provided to the author from the work log of Cliff Inkster, who was present at the event. Alex Price, the Divisional Engineer at the time, informed the author the event occurred several days before that date. Joe Smuin, who has also written extensively about the KVR, stated he believed the event occurred October 25. The author cannot verify which report is correct.

7. The following plate girder spans bridges were removed at the time of abandonment: mile 21.7 (Tack Creek 5 spans), 25.8 (Slide Creek 2 approach spans), 32.0 (3 spans), 33.9 (Boston Bar Creek 1 span), 37.1 (Twenty Mile Creek 2 spans), 38.5 (1 span) and 49.6 (Coquihalla River 1 span). All other bridges were left in place. The truss span at mile 53.4 (Coquihalla River near Hope) was removed in 1965 or 1966 and possibly reused on the crossing of the Elk River on the Kaiser Coal spur at Sparwood in 1970. The CPR seriously investigated dismantling the main 320-foot span at mile 25.8 (Slide Creek) and reassembling it at mile 31.8 of the Mountain Subdivision where a replacement for a bridge over the Kicking Horse River was needed. The plan was not adopted and Canadian Forces personnel blew up the bridge in a demolition exercise on April 30, 1981, with the steel being subsequently salvaged for scrap. The deck truss bridge over the Coldwater River at mile 4.1 (Brodie) was disassembled for scrap over a four-day period between September 8 and 11, 2000 when it became apparent the west abutment of the bridge was in danger of collapse. The bridges at mile 10.2 (July Creek) and mile 16.4 (Coldwater River) remain in place and are used for local roads accessing the Coquihalla Highway. The bridge at mile 49.7 (Coquihalla River) serves as a footbridge in the Coquihalla Canyon Provincial Park. The bridge over the Fraser River at mile 54.7 serves as a roadway bridge for Highway 1. The bridge at mile 36.8 (Ladner Creek) remains abandoned in place and is visible from the new highway bridge downstream.

8. Two of the Shakespearian stationboards were publicly preserved, the Lear stationboard in the Penticton Museum and the Jessica station board in the Hope Museum, the latter donated by the author who was given it by a Jessica resident. The author is aware of two other stationboards in private collections.

9. The last advertised run of Train 46 on the Princeton Subdivision was on January 16, 1964 when Budd Car 9022 ran from Spences Bridge to Penticton. The train arrived at Penticton approximately six hours late because there had been a heavy snowstorm during the night and the train waited at Merritt until the line was plowed. It arrived in Penticton with about 100 passengers, almost all having boarded at West Summerland to be on the "last run" to Penticton. That same day Train 45, Budd Car 9100 ran from Nelson to Penticton. After arrival at Penticton it continued on to Spences Bridge, operating as Train 45. The following morning, January 17, on time and with only one fare-paying passenger on board, Budd Car 9100 ran as Train 46 from Spences Bridge to Penticton. At Penticton, 9100 was joined by 9022 and the two cars ran through to Nelson, where the run of Train 46 terminated. The Boundary Historical Society has printed several detailed accounts of the last run. On the Victoria Day weekends in 1983 and 1984 the British Columbia

Chapter of the National Railway Historical Society operated a passenger excursion train called *The Okanagan Express* from Vancouver to Penticton and return.

Chapter 15: Gone But Not Forgotten

1. The crew changeover and official closure of the Brookmere station occurred August 1, 1966. The station was later sold to a private individual. It was relocated to the site of the former roundhouse in late 1979 but was destroyed in a fire on February 12, 1986. The former GN station at Coalmont was destroyed in a fire on May 13, 1957. The former GN station at Tulameen was relocated onto private property nearby in July 1961 and as of 2002 remained in good condition. The former GN station at Princeton closed in 1975 and after many years standing vacant was converted into a restaurant. The former GN sectionhouse at Manning also survives.

2. The last regular freight train to operate over the entire Carmi Subdivision was on May 19, 1973, when engine 8724 made a trip from Penticton to Midway and return. During June 1973 former CPR steam locomotive 136 was operated in Myra Canyon for filming of the CBC historical production *The National Dream*. On June 25, diesel 8509, pulling the 136 and other equipment used in the filming, ran from Penticton through to Midway and on to Nelson, the final train to operate between Penticton and Beaverdell. Freight trains occasionally operated between Midway and Beaverdell until 1976. Trackage from a point about two miles west of Midway to Lalonde Creek at mile 67.9 near Cookson, where a washout occurred in early 1979, was removed in 1979. The remainder of the trackage between that point and Penticton was removed in 1980. The bridge over the West Fork of the Kettle River at mile 26.9 near Rhone was salvaged and relocated downstream four miles for use as a road bridge. The bridge over Wilkinson Creek at mile 50.4 was relocated to Beaverdell, also for use as a road bridge. Other bridges on the line were left in place.

3. During the salvage work in 1991 only ties and rails were removed. All bridges on the Princeton Subdivision were left in place at the time, but some of the bridges were subsequently removed. The plate girder spans over Trout Creek at mile 23.4 near Kirton and mile 37.0 near Osprey Lake, and over the Tulameen River at Mile 69.9 just east of Princeton, were removed in September 1995 and some of the spans used for a new bridge over the Coquitlam River as part of the West Coast Express commuter rail project. The plate girder span over Voght Creek and the Coldwater Road at mile 120.3 at Kingsvale was removed March 24, 1999 to improve clearance for road traffic; the bridge now sits in the public works yard a short distance away. The former sectionhouse at nearby Kingsvale, converted into a private residence, burned down on December 18, 1998.

4. John G. Sullivan in a letter to McCulloch, 1937-03-02. R.G. Harvey in his book *Carving the Western Path* (Heritage House Publishing, 1998) refers to this quote from earlier editions of *McCulloch's Wonder* and opines that Sullivan ". . . must have been an accountant, as only an accountant would have written to the revered Andrew McCulloch in that manner." Such a statement is unfair to both men. Sullivan was in fact a former CPR chief engineer who had been a work associate and close friend of McCulloch for more than 40 years when the letter passed hands. McCulloch, whatever other shortcomings he may have had, certainly cannot be fairly accused of ever having an inflated or sentimental view of the KVR. From the day he was assigned the task of building the railway in 1910 until his death, McCulloch was sceptical of the wisdom of the railway's construction and he was exceedingly modest about his contributions to the railway, as he was with all his other achievements in life. Harvey also accuses McCulloch of building the railway over the wrong route between Penticton and Princeton and through the Coquihalla. This thesis ignores numerous serious engineering, economic, traffic and operating considerations facing the railway builders of 1910. Moreover, Harvey ignores the well-documented fact the routing in both cases was decided by Thomas Shaughnessy, not McCulloch. Ultimate responsibility for the wisdom or folly of building the Kettle Valley Railway remains with Shaughnessy.

Index